Within My Heart

Within My Heart

The Enlightenment Epistemic Reversal and the Subjective Justification of Religious Belief

Michael A. Van Horn

FOREWORD BY
Paul Badham

☙PICKWICK *Publications* · Eugene, Oregon

WITHIN MY HEART
The Enlightenment Epistemic Reversal
and the Subjective Justification of Religious Belief

Copyright © 2017 Michael A. Van Horn. All rights reserved. Except for brief quotations in critical publications or reviews, no part of this book may be reproduced in any manner without prior written permission from the publisher. Write: Permissions, Wipf and Stock Publishers, 199 W. 8th Ave., Suite 3, Eugene, OR 97401.

Pickwick Publications
An Imprint of Wipf and Stock Publishers
199 W. 8th Ave., Suite 3
Eugene, OR 97401

www.wipfandstock.com

PAPERBACK ISBN: 978-1-61097-995-5
HARDCOVER ISBN: 978-1-4982-8868-2
EBOOK ISBN: 978-1-5326-1372-2

Cataloguing-in-Publication data:

Names: Van Horn, Michael A. | foreword by Badham, Paul

Title: Within my heart : the Enlightenment epistemic reversal and the subjective justification of religious belief / Michael A. Van Horn, with a foreword by Paul Badham.

Description: Eugene, OR: Pickwick Publications, 2017 | **Includes bibliographical references.**

Identifiers: ISBN 978-1-61097-995-5 (paperback) | ISBN 978-1-4982-8868-2 (hardcover) | ISBN 978-1-5326-1372-2 (ebook)

Subjects: LSCH: Philosophy and religion | Enlightenment | Kant, Immanuel, 1724–1804—Religion | Schleiermacher, Friedrich, 1768–1834 | Kierkegaard, Søren, 1813–1855 | Evangelicalism—History | Faith and reason | Knowledge, Theory of (Religion)

Classification: BL51 V16 2017 (print) | BL51 (ebook)

Manufactured in the U.S.A.   03/01/17

I dedicate this book to my Father Verlin Van Horn.

"Guard for me my feet upon the gentle earth of Wales."
—*an ancient Celtic monk's prayer*

Contents

Foreword by Paul Badham | ix

Acknowledgements | xi

Introduction   Religious Experience in Modernity: Faith Itself as the "Unknown God" | 1

1 *Fides Qua Creditur*: The Enlightenment Mind and the Theology of the Heart | 20

2 Within the Bounds of Reason Alone: The Subjective Justification of Religious Belief in the Thought of Immanuel Kant | 46

3 Schleiermacher's "Higher Order Pietism": Subjectivity and Protestant Liberal Thought | 77

4 Søren Kierkegaard and the Paradox of Faith: Subjectivity in Christian Existentialism | 109

5 Subjectivity and Religious Belief in Anglo-American Revivalism: Jonathan Edwards and John Wesley | 141

6 Subjectivity and Religious Belief in Anglo-American Revivalism: George Whitefield and Charles G. Finney | 168

Conclusion | 193

Bibliography | 197

Foreword

THIS BOOK MAKES A major contribution to our understanding of the real foundations on which Protestant Christianity has built in recent years. Dr. Van Horn shows that ever since the eighteenth century all branches of Protestant Christianity have in practice emphasized the importance of inner experience as the real foundation of living faith. This foundation has always been recognized as true in Liberal Protestantism. The reason this book is so valuable is that Dr. Van Horn shows that this is also true of the classic Evangelical tradition. Although it is common in the Evangelical tradition to claim with the Reformers that faith is based on acceptance of the infallible word of God, this actually plays surprisingly little part in their foundational thinking.

Dr. Van Horn documents in detail how eighteenth-century evangelists like Jonathan Edwards, John Wesley, and George Whitefield constantly appealed to human feelings. What really mattered to them was not intellectual belief in the authority of scripture, but rather that those who heard them preach should be "slain in the spirit" or "born again." What an evangelist most wanted to share with his hearers was the blessed assurance of salvation, of feeling their "heart strangely warmed," of experiencing the "amazing grace" that led to salvation. These are the things that really mattered to them.

The book goes on to show that the same is true of the leaders of the American and Welsh revivals of the nineteenth century. Most revivalist preaching was a direct appeal to human emotions seeking to trigger a conversion experience that would change the direction of their hearer's lives.

FOREWORD

When those lives are changed by the experience it is that experience which is celebrated in the hymns and choruses through which their faith is expressed. Dr. Van Horn gives many examples of this book, including the one from which his book takes its title. The true believer characteristically affirms faith in the risen Christ not by an appeal to Scripture but by an appeal to *inner experience:* "You ask me how I know He lives. He lives within my heart."

The Reverend Dr. Paul Badham

Emeritus Professor of Theology,
University of Wales, Trinity Saint David
United Kingdom.

Acknowledgements

THIS BOOK IS BASED on my doctoral thesis. That path would never have been chosen had it not been for those professors and scholars who found ways to encourage me and nurture the gift of scholarship. Among those are Stephen R. Spencer, the late James M. Grier, the late Carl B. Hoch, David L. Turner, the late Albert "Joe" Crawford, Nicholas Wolterstorff, George Marsden, Mary Stewart Van Leeuwen, the late Gordon Spykman, Todd Johnson, J. Richard Middleton, and many others. Likewise, the input of Professors Paul Badham, Ian Markham, and J. I. Daniels proved extremely useful.

Sincere thanks to those friends who bolstered me to careful studies by their high intellectual standards and amused me by their good sense of humor. Thanks especially to Todd Cioffi who had enough anxiety for both of us, yet provided constant motivation to complete a doctoral program. Much credit goes to the good people of Trinity Church of Livonia for bearing with a pastor who was also a student and a college professor. Their encouragement and understanding throughout a long academic process made both ongoing thesis work and occasional academic pilgrimages to Wales less burdensome, and even something of a joy. Thanks for manuscript preparation go to Abigail Austin, Paul Koptak, and Stephen Spencer of North Park Theological Seminary and Jeremy Mann and Daniel Treier of Wheaton College.

Special gratitude goes to my father, Verlin L. Van Horn. His many years of self-sacrifice and generosity have provided a true image of the unfailing love of God. His strong work ethic and his deep devotion for family have been a constant encouragement to me. Without his gracious support and faithfulness, the pursuit of this degree would have been impossible. Thank you, Dad.

Above all, I offer my thanks to God, whose constant nurture and love for His creatures continues to be a source of surprise and delight to me. Signs of Providential care during my studies with the University of Wales have been simultaneously heartening and humbling.

Soli Deo Gloria

INTRODUCTION

Religious Experience in Modernity

Faith Itself as the "Unknown God"

> "Our government makes no sense unless it is founded in a deeply felt religious faith—and I don't care what it is."[1]
>
> –Dwight D. Eisenhower,
> 34th President of the United States

THIS PROJECT BEGAN FROM a curiosity about the character and understanding of the modern faith experience—particularly as it has been formed within the Anglo-American, Evangelical Protestant tradition. Religious faith has always played a significant role in American life, culture, politics, education, etc. Who can forget G. K. Chesterton's succinct description of America as a "nation with the soul of a church"?[2] Contrary to the more pessimistic predictions of Enlightenment and post-Enlightenment thinkers

---

1. "Text of Eisenhower Speech," *The New York Times,* December 23, 1952, 16, cols. 3–6.

2. Chesterton, *What I Saw in America,* 45. Chesterton also writes that America is "the only nation of the world founded on a creed." Ibid., 41. Likewise, in his *Illustrated London News* column, Chesterton opined that "the historic glory of America lies in the fact that it is the one nation that was founded like a church" (January 8, 1921) and elsewhere, "There is really something about the Declaration of Independence that is almost like the stone tablets of the Ten Commandments" (March 23, 1918). Both *Illustrated London News* column citations are found in *The More Quotable Chesterton,* 24–25.

about the demise of theism, religious faith has neither abated nor vanished under the pressure of modern science and reason. In fact, quite the opposite is true. Evangelicalism, in particular, has been a vibrant and thriving movement in the modern era. Even in the age which spawned Enlightenment secularism, religion appears to be alive and well. Indeed, the modern age seems to have spawned certain unique catalysts for the popular subjective understanding of faith experience. While it is true that religious faith has nearly always had a subjective component, the modern era is distinguished for bringing this element to the foreground.

The purpose of this book is to trace the "subjectivism" of faith in the modern understanding, particularly its highly individual and personal expressions found in the influential movement of Anglo-American Evangelical revivalism. The book's premise is that the shape of the post-Enlightenment world has created a distinct need for this "affective-experiential" approach to faith. Subjectivity has become a cardinal ingredient in the modern vocabulary of faith. Indeed, the "affective-experiential" dimension of faith has become more than incidental; in modernity it has taken on an unmistakable apologetic character. For many moderns, "the argument from morality to religion and from the subjective experience of the soul to the reality of God was no less legitimate than the traditional argument for the existence of God."[3]

This subjective shift has been generally traced in the Enlightenment religion of Kant and the modernist theological tradition spawned by Schleiermacher. I maintain that this same modern "affectional transposition"[4] of faith is correspondingly evident in the development of Protestant Evangelicalism in North America and its symbiotic counterparts in Great Britain. In this respect, contrary to the typical self-understanding, Evangelicalism is a distinctly modern religious movement.

Modern Americans take matters of faith quite seriously. Yet it is the distinct character of that "faith" that is particularly telling. In spite of the fact that organized religion has been constitutionally disestablished in the American system, many Americans still see it as integral to their political identity. It is possible because faith has increasingly been relegated to the private (and later individual) sphere. This is seemingly why Americans are

---

3. Pelikan, *Christian Doctrine and Modern Culture*, 119.

4. Ibid., 118, 119. Pelikan refers to "the theology of the heart" and the "affectional transposition of doctrine" which characterizes the religious trends resulting from the Enlightenment.

so comfortable making reference to such a vaguely a-historical and virtually content-less concepts as "Judeo-Christian values," or "America as a Christian nation," or "a country founded on God," as a basis for public policy or moral law. Although the language makes reference to historic entities of Judaism or the Christian church, the values to which they refer are usually neither specifically "Jewish" nor "Christian," much less simultaneously both![5] For, rather than referencing the Scriptures or historic traditions of these religious communities, the concept of "Judeo-Christian values" tends to mean little more than the subjective moral sensibilities and general religious values which ought to be held by every person with common sense.

What is implied is that the moral principles reflected in these two great faiths are not so much grounded in any specific historic revelation, but are common to every human being. Thus, the recitation of prayer in a state-operated school or the posting of the biblical Decalogue in a municipal courthouse is often not deemed in violation of the principle of "separation of church and state" because no specific, objective religion is perceived as being cited or endorsed—but merely the vague religious sentiment which is presumably available to all. "In this reversal the Christian and Jewish faiths tend to be prized because they help promote ideals and standards that all Americans are expected to share on a deeper level than merely 'official religion.'"[6] And yet, in this religious sentiment, "'first allegiance' is 'reserved . . . to the kingdom of the spirit' . . . and not any commitment to the doctrines or traditions of the historic faiths."[7] The values or religion to which they refer are not seen primarily as an historic or special revelatory phenomenon (despite the liberal use of language such as "Judeo-Christian," or "Jehovah," or even "Jesus"), or of referring to a particular ecclesial community or institution, but simply a matter of the heart.

"Faith" has come to be understood largely as an introspective attitude or subjective expression of the individual, often without an object

---

5. Paul Tillich speaks of the common ground of Judaism and Christianity as sharing an "identity of structure at all points and identity of content in most." "Is There a Judeo-Christian Tradition?" 106–9. This is granted as a technical point in the ecumenical study of these two faiths. However, I still contend for the meaninglessness of the notion of "Judeo-Christian values" for the typical, non-theologically trained American citizen. See also Will Herberg, "Judaism and Christianity," *Journal of Bible and Religion*, 67–78. Herberg notes elsewhere that a "well-known religious newsletter carries the following injunction in a box on its first page. 'Boost the best in American Life: Support Your Churches and Synagogues.'" Herberg, *Protestant—Catholic—Jew*, 274.

6. Herberg, *Protestant—Catholic—Jew*, 96.

7. Ibid., 98.

other than the self. As American theologian Reinhold Niebuhr puts it, "The 'unknown God' of Americans seems to be faith itself."[8] The classic expression of anthropocentric American faith, according to Will Herberg, is epitomized in American churchman Daniel Poling's formula: "I began saying in the morning two words, '*I believe*'—those two words with nothing added."[9] "What Americans come to believe in, when they are religious," comments Herberg, "is religion itself" for "what they seem to regard as really redemptive is primarily . . . the 'positive' attitude of believing."[10] In this vein, religious faith often becomes easily reduced to technique with a pragmatic goal, as the Rev. Irving E. Howard illustrates in this frank homiletical nugget: "Jesus recommended faith as a technique for getting results . . . ."[11] Those "results" might well be the singular experience of personal peace and assurance of salvation, or even tangible things like financial success and physical wholeness,[12] but the common factor seems to be that faith is

8. Niebuhr, "Religiosity and the Christian Faith," 1.

9. Poling, "A Running Start for Every Day," 165.

10. Herberg, *Protestant—Catholic—Jew*, 265. Herberg offers Protestant, Catholic, and Jewish examples of this "cult of faith." Among those named are the enormously popular Reformed minister, the Reverend Dr. Norman Vincent Peale, who wrote in his best-seller *The Power of Positive Thinking*, 154, "How do you practice faith? First thing every morning, before you arise, say out loud, 'I believe,' three times." Herberg also cites exemplary titles of Peale's syndicated column in the New York Herald Tribune: "Have Faith in Faith," "Believe You Can and You Can," "Your Faith Makes Miracles." A Jewish representative of the same ilk is found in Rabbi Louis Binstock, who writes in *The Power of Faith*, 4, "You, like everyone else, have access to a great storehouse of dynamic power on which you can draw . . . . That storehouse is *Faith*. Not religion. Not your immortal soul. Not this House of Worship. Not God. But—FAITH." Herberg, *Protestant—Catholic—Jew*, 278.

11. Howard, "Random Reflections," 2.

12. The so-called "health and wealth gospel" has become the hallmark of American "televangelism," a highly polished, technologically savvy, entertainment-style version of the old evangelical revival tent meeting. In this version of evangelism, a kind of "over-realized eschatology" (to borrow Oscar Cullmann's phrase) offers, not only salvation in the hereafter, but the prospect of physical wholeness and financial well-being in the present as a sign of the kingdom of God. Contemporary revivalist Evangelicals, who had once been identified as the disenfranchised and poor of society (see H. Richard Niebuhr, *The Social Sources of Denominationalism*, 151–52) were finding it necessary to account for their increasing status and wealth in the contemporary era. While the original offer of "assurance of salvation" and the guarantee of heavenly existence in the hereafter was appealing to the culturally marginalized, the "health and wealth" here-and-now message gave them the theological language to describe their new-found experience of prosperity without losing the original hope of eternal life. All the better to have temporal happiness and success now *and* eternal bliss in the afterlife, as well! Cultural critic Neil Postman devotes an entire chapter in *Amusing Ourselves to Death* (a less-than-optimistic

viewed as the key to the door that unlocks the way to individual fulfillment and happiness. The test of faith is largely subjective and pragmatic. H. Richard Niebuhr succinctly describes this "cult of faith" as a "man-centered, this-worldly, lift-yourself-by-your-own-bootstraps doctrine."[13]

This "new" version of religious belief is unique to Christendom in that it is no longer seen as integrally connected to faith communities, orthodox confession, or historic traditions, as it once was. In fact, the tendency is to see this faith as, if not independent of, at least prior to and above, the established, organized faith communities. Religion has become simply a private matter. Some 80 percent of Americans tabulated in the 1978 Gallup poll thought that "an individual should arrive at his or her own religious beliefs independent of any churches or synagogues."[14] Thus, the following statement has become something of a mantra—a credo, if you will, of the creedless Evangelical: "It is not the religion or the church you go to that's going to save you, but in your own personal relationship you have with him through his son Jesus Christ. You ask him to come into your heart and make himself more real in your life and he will, if you are sincere."[15] As Bellah and his colleagues note, this can be "without any church at all."[16] In this perspective, a high premium is placed on the act or experience of faith, but often very little can be said about the actual objective content or focus of faith. In this individualist form of religion the visible community of believers is often seen as incidental, or even detrimental, to actual faith.

Indeed, the concept of "faith" itself, which has always been a cornerstone of Protestant experience, in modern thinking is driven through

---

assessment of the impact of the medium of television on modern life and culture) to the phenomenon of "the electronic church." Postman says that "the [television] preachers are forthright about how they control the content of their preaching to maximize their ratings. You shall wait a very long time indeed if you wish to hear an electronic preacher refer to the difficulties a rich man will have in gaining access to heaven." Postman, *Amusing Ourselves to Death*, 121. Postman also cites the executive director of the National Religious Broadcasters Association as he "sums up what he calls the unwritten law of all television preachers: 'You can get your share of the audience only by offering people something they want'" (Postman, *Amusing Ourselves to Death*, 121, quoting from Abelman and Neuendorf, "Religion in Broadcasting," 2). All of this confirms the American "predisposition to believe that prosperity is the true aim of religion." Postman, *Amusing Ourselves to Death*, 114.

13. Niebuhr, *The Social Sources of Denominationalism*, 104.
14. Hoge, *Converts, Dropouts, Returnees*, 167.
15. Fee et al., *Young Catholics*, 242.
16. Bellah et al., *Habits of the Heart*, 234.

a remarkably complex cultural grid of individualism and subjectivism. The by-product would be virtually unrecognizable to most of traditional European Christendom in the almost complete disregard for creed, sacrament, and ecclesiastical community. However, this modern formation of faith would be more than recognizable to those believers who have been influenced by Evangelical-revivalist phenomena. In marked contrast to traditional orthodox views of faith as explicit trust in a particular God (of Scripture), modern faith has often become transformed into an individual, human-centered, internal disposition. In the end, it seems that such faith has become largely "self-referential." As such, the act of believing is often more important than the thing (or person) which is believed, and faith has become little more than a synonym for "peace of mind" or "positive thinking."[17] Herberg concludes that there is little "concern about what the religion or the faith is all about, since it is not the content of the belief but the attitude of believing that is felt to be operative."[18] In the end, this approach to faith can be reduced to a religious version of narcissism. Faith can gradually become emptied of content. Sentiments like "Keep the faith," which once implied that one should sustain a firm trust in the God who has been faithful in covenant, can now mean little more than, "have self-confidence" or "believe in yourself!" Thus faith has become "emphatically inner-directed," personal and individualistic to the point of being largely content-less. Two illustrations from contemporary cinema will serve this point.

The highly controversial film *Dogma* is a post-modern attempt to communicate faith in terms that would be meaningful to contemporary "cultured despisers" of religion.[19] The film is clearly not anti-religion; still it is decidedly opposed to "organized," institutional religion. In a pivotal scene, an angelic messenger of God is explaining to a potential modern messianic character the nature of true faith: Which religion is the right one? "It's not about who's right or wrong, it doesn't matter *what* you have faith in, just that you *have faith* . . . ." What is most important is that "your heart's

---

17. See Schneider and Dornbusch, *Popular Religion*, for a helpful study of the "peace of mind" and "positive thinking" views of faith.

18. Herberg, *Protestant–Catholic–Jew*, 282.

19. Kevin Smith, director/producer, *Dogma*. Throughout the film, reoccurring themes are the unreliability of the church (which has made mistakes, a motif reminiscent of Luther's criticism before the Diet at Worms) and the untrustworthy character of the Bible (which, it is charged, has misrepresented the true message of Jesus and encouraged slavery, racism, and patriarchal suppression of women, to name a few).

in the right place,"[20] then your head should follow accordingly. If religious faith comes from outside the self (say, from the Bible or the church), then it is untrustworthy. But if it is from the heart, then it is viable. As with much of modernity, there is no place for dogma in the religion of *Dogma;* the starting point of faith (and, perhaps, the focal point) is the heart.

Likewise, in the American film *Leap of Faith* an Elmer Gantry-like travelling revival preacher is charged with being a fraud.[21] He is accused of fabricating miracles and rousing pious enthusiasm at his tent revival meetings in order to swindle money from credulous townsfolk in a small, drought-stricken, farming town in the American South. The self-styled evangelist, Jonas Nightengale, does not even bother to mask his deception. When charged with being a con-man, The Reverend Nightengale replies, "Maybe I am and maybe I'm not, but if I get the job done, what difference does it make?"[22] So what if the revival meeting was full of theatrics and the miracles are pure chicanery? "I give my people a good show . . ." he argued, filled "with worthwhile sentiments . . . ."[23] He concluded, "Never underestimate the power of belief . . . [because] with belief you have everything . . . without it, you have nothing.[24] Nevertheless, the fraudulent preacher is clear: "you have to create your own faith" because "nobody up there's gonna do it for you."[25] The evangelist saw his task in wholly pragmatic terms: to evoke the experience of pious faith was a good end in itself, whether that faith's object was mere illusion or not.

20. Ibid.

21. Michael Manheim, Producer, *Leap of Faith*. The film's ironic twist comes when, in contrast to the multiple staged "healings," a young crippled boy is actually healed at the revival meeting. Rev. Nightengale angrily believes that he has been out-conned by God himself and therefore quits the business of preaching! As the former preacher hitchhikes out of town, a downpour begins, providing much-needed moisture for the failing crops. The rain comes as if to suggest, in spite of the machinations of the false prophet, God has the final laugh. Sinclair Lewis's novel *Elmer Gantry*, set in Kansas City, pictures the career of a self-styled Protestant minister, a charlatan who shrouds his carnality and greed behind a semblance of evangelical piety and enthusiasm. The novel presents a portrait of religious revivalism in the Mid-Western United States in the early part of the twentieth century. Gantry has become the classic literary paradigm of the hypocritical clergyman who confuses commercial success with salvation.

22. Manheim, *Leap of Faith*.

23. Ibid.

24. Ibid.

25. Ibid.

The publication of *Habits of the Heart* by Robert Bellah (head of a prominent University of California research team on dominant American religious values and beliefs) has underscored the "utilitarian individualism" that drives much of American life, and in particular American religion. The authors contend that, as a result of distinctly modern patterns of thought, religious faith in America has been largely privatized and etherealized. The authors of *Habits of the Heart* (a title taken from Alexis de Tocqueville's assessment of American religious individualism in the 1830s[26]) offer the transcript of an interview with a young nurse named Sheila Larson, which they believe to provide something of an abstract of the archetypical American view of religion: "It's just try to love *yourself* and be gentle with *yourself*." She adds: "I believe in God. I'm not a religious fanatic. I can't remember the last time I went to church. My *faith* has carried me a long way. It's Sheilaism. Just *my own* little voice" (my italics).[27] Bellah asks the intriguing question: "How did we get from the point where Anne Hutchinson, a seventeenth-century precursor of Sheila Larson's, could be run out of the Massachusetts Bay Colony to a situation where Anne Hutchinson is close to the norm?"[28] Bellah and his colleagues conclude that Americans have been "confined to a vocabulary of individualism" to the degree that in the realm of religion, faith is relegated to the "affections" and "religion took refuge in human subjectivity, in feeling and sentiment."[29]

James Davison Hunter notes this significant shift within modern Protestant Evangelical piety, a phenomenon he calls "psychological Christocentrism"[30] in which, while invoking the name of Jesus, Evangeli-

---

26. Tocqueville, *Democracy in America*, 287. This French social philosopher toured young America and offered an extensive and definitive assessment of the values of this experimental democracy. Tocqueville was one of the first to describe this phenomenon of "individualism" and sprinkled his admiration for America with various warnings about the potential dangers of this self-involved attitude: "Individualism is a calm and considered feeling which disposes each citizen to isolate himself from the mass of his fellows and withdraw into a circle of family and friends; with this little society formed to his taste, he gladly leaves the greater society to look after itself.... Such folk owe no man anything and hardly expect anything from anybody. They form the habit of thinking of themselves in isolation and imagine that their whole destiny is in their hands.... Each man is forever thrown back on himself alone, and there is danger that he may be shut up in the solitude of his own heart." 506–8.

27. Bellah, et al., *Habits of the Heart*, 221.

28. Ibid.

29. Ibid., 46.

30. Hunter, *American Evangelicalism*, 95; see 91–101.

cals actually focus their attention inward, on the health of their own souls. Hunter comments, "Subjectivism has displaced the traditional asceticism as the dominant attitude in theologically conservative Protestant culture. There is some variability, but in mainstream contemporary American Evangelicalism, an austere instrumentalism has been replaced by a malleable expressivity."[31]

This Evangelical perspective on faith is pervasive in American culture; it has had a prominent role in shaping American religious and cultural values, yet it is certainly not limited to America. American Evangelicals have become major players in the "import/export business" of religious faith. Perhaps one of the strongest transatlantic bonds in history has been sustained by the Evangelical communities of Britain and America. Therefore, it becomes difficult, if not impossible, to speak of American frontier revivalism without making reference to the commanding influence of such men as Charles Finney on the Evangelical renewals of Britain, nor is it imaginable to refer to the Great Awakenings of colonial America without assessing the impact of the "British invasion" of the Wesleys and Whitefield. Historian George Marsden notes that "despite forces from the Enlightenment . . . that have undermined Christianity's cultural impact, the churches actually gained influence during the succeeding era. . . . The great dynamo generating this remarkable American religious vigor was continuing revival."[32] Yet the revivalist movement in modern Evangelicalism did not exist simply in spite of the influences of the Enlightenment; it is the premise of this book that it existed, at least in part, *because* of it.

Jewish sociologist of religion Will Herberg often asked "why in secular mid-century America there was so much interest in religion."[33] Herberg puzzled over the phenomenon that "Americans think, feel, and act in terms quite obviously secularist at the very time that they exhibit every sign of widespread religious revival."[34] In the end, it occurred to Herberg that the reason this oxymoron could exist (actually, thrive) was that "both the religiousness and the secularism of the American people derive from very

---

31. Ibid.

32. Marsden, *Religion and American Culture*, 48. Marsden notes that "we can probably get a fair picture by noting that in 1860 there was church seating of 26 million for a population of 31 million. These figures suggest that if you had visited the United States on a Sunday in this era probably half the people would have been in church." Marsden adds whimsically, "virtually the whole United States was a Bible belt." Ibid., 50.

33. Martin Marty, "Introduction" in Herberg, *Protestant-Catholic-Jew*, ix.

34. Herberg, *Protestant-Catholic-Jew*, 3.

much the same sources,"[35] namely, the Enlightenment and its unlikely stepchild Evangelical revivalism.

The language may only be slightly hyperbolic when historian Perry Miller says that "the dominant theme in America from 1800 to 1860 is the invincible persistence of the revival technique."[36] William McLoughlin concurs: "The story of American Evangelicalism is the story of America itself in the years 1800–1900, for it was Evangelical religion which made Americans the most religious people in the world . . . ."[37] Miller concludes, "The revival fire . . . was the central mode of this culture's search for cultural identity."[38] Traditional forms of Christianity "gave way to a profound theological individualism, in which the individual was held to be sovereign and the deep stirrings of his religious emotions was understood to be the most authentic working of faith."[39]

Therefore, this study intends to look beyond Britain and America to the formative influence of European Pietism and its strange bed-fellow, Enlightenment epistemology, in shaping the distinctly modern subjective views of faith. "When science seemed to have dominated the explanatory schemas of the external world, morality and religion took refuge in human subjectivity, in feeling and sentiment."[40] Originally, this was "feeling and sentiment" about something, but gradually, for modern people, the "feeling and sentiment" became desirable as sufficient ends in themselves. Objective religious doctrinal claims divide and create conflict between persons; inward sentimentality and affective piety can, presumably, do no such thing. This would be the perfect religion for a pluralistic society: Not a "particular religion, but religion as such, religion-in-general."[41]

While the revivalist, or "Frontier tradition," as it is now being called, is the "dominant tradition in American Protestantism, it continues to expand rapidly, not only in familiar territory such as North America but also in almost every other part of the world—the Soviet Union, Central America, Asia, and Africa."[42] The spread of the Evangelical revivalist tradition around

---

35. Ibid.
36. Miller, *The Life of the Mind in America*, 7.
37. McLoughlin, *The American Evangelicals, 1800–1900*, 1.
38. Miller, *The Life of the Mind in America*, 6.
39. Herberg, *Protestant–Catholic–Jew*, 106
40. Bellah, et al., *Habits of the Heart*, 46
41. Herberg, *Protestant–Catholic–Jew*, 84.
42. White, *Protestant Worship*, 172.

the world has been characterized as "the Americanization of Protestant worship," even though "many of the consequences of this experience lay far in time and space from the woods and plains of the West."[43]

The Evangelical Morphology of Conversion

It is the premise of this book that Anglo-American Evangelicalism is derived from the same uniquely modern epistemological shift that characterizes such modern thinkers as Kant, Schleiermacher, and Kierkegaard.[44] The revivalist tradition of Britain and North America is typically seen as a fierce opponent to Enlightenment ideas rather than an adaptation of them. Indeed, the tradition itself consciously perpetuates a self-understanding that emphasizes its sole reliance upon biblical revelation and a return to the

---

43. Ibid.

44. The term "Evangelical" has many nuances. Martin Luther and the churches of the Reformation first claimed the term to emphasize their return to the elements of the gospel they thought had been neglected in the Roman Catholic tradition (i.e., *sola Scriptura, solo fide, sola gratia*, etc.). This use of the term is broad, but includes the Pietist tradition of Europe which has significant influence upon later revivalist thought. Within the Anglican tradition the term "Evangelical" is usually contrasted with "Anglo-Catholic," sometimes meaning merely "low church" as opposed to "high church," but usually implying a closer tie to the Reformation roots of that tradition (as conveyed in the *Thirty-Nine Articles* of the Church of England, 1571), and an emphasis upon personal conversion. A final understanding of "Evangelical" grows out of the legacy of eighteenth and nineteenth century revivals and religious awakenings associated with the ministries of such persons as John Wesley, George Whitefield, and Jonathan Edwards. This Anglo-American phenomenon had its roots in German Pietism and English Puritanism, and offered an "orthodox" and Scripture-based response to theological liberalism, while stressing the necessity for a personal conversion experience for each individual. It is this latter understanding of "Evangelical" that is being used within this book, knowing that the lines which separate it from the former types are hazy at best, and that much of what is true for revivalist Evangelicalism is also true of the other two types. See David Allan Hubbard, *What We Evangelicals Believe*, 7–16. George Marsden says, "'Evangelical' (from the Greek word for 'gospel') eventually became the common British and American name for the revival movements that swept back and forth across the English-speaking world and elsewhere during the eighteenth and nineteenth centuries. Central to the evangelical gospel was the proclamation of Christ's saving work through his death on the cross and the necessity of personally trusting him for eternal salvation. . . . The essential evangelical beliefs include (1) the Reformation doctrine of the final authority of the Bible, (2) the real historical character of God's saving work recorded in Scripture, (3) salvation to eternal life based on the redemptive work of Christ, (4) the importance of evangelism and missions, and (5) the importance of a spiritually transformed life." *Understanding Fundamentalism and Evangelicalism*, 2, 4–5.

"received tradition" in bold opposition to modern philosophy and culture. The theology and the subjective "morphology of conversion" which has become the defining characteristic of the Evangelical-revivalist tradition is often believed by its adherents to "come directly from Scripture, untainted by the traditions of men . . . untouched by history and culture."[45] And yet, in respect to this particular stress upon the "affective-experiential" or non-theoretical justification of religious faith, Anglo-American Evangelicalism is as distinctively modern as the modernists they claim to oppose.

Fyodor Dostoyevsky spoke, in the famous "Grand Inquisitor" section of *The Brothers Karamazov*, of "three powers" apart from which biblical Christianity would be bankrupt: "miracle, mystery and authority."[46] Some in the modern period would assume that these three powers had been sufficiently curtailed, or would soon be abolished by the force of the "age of reason." Instead, faith was resiliently recast in subjective form. "Miracle, mystery, and authority, whose validity as objective realities seemed to have reached a dead end, took on new life when they became, instead, ways of speaking about the subjective validity of inward experience."[47]

As an example of the subjective shape of the Evangelical morphology of conversion, take, for instance, the following account of a southern-American black revival service from the turn of the century:

> I was saved from sin when I was going on thirteen. But not really saved. It happened like this. There was a big revival at my Auntie Reed's church. Every night for weeks there had been much preaching, singing, praying, and shouting, and some very hardened sinners had been brought to Christ, and the membership of the church had grown by leaps and bounds. Then just before the revival ended, they held a special meeting for children, "to bring young lambs to the fold." My aunt spoke of it for days ahead. That night I was escorted to the front row and placed on the mourners' bench with all the other young sinners, who had not yet been brought to Jesus.
>
> My aunt told me that when you were saved you saw a light, and something happened to you inside! And Jesus came into your life! And God was with you from then on! She said you could see and hear and feel Jesus in your soul. I believed her. I had heard a great many old people say the same thing and it seemed to me they

---

45. Leonard, "Getting Saved in America," 112.
46. Dostoyevsky, *The Brothers Karamazov*, 297–319.
47. Pelikan, *Christian Doctrine and Modern Culture*, 119.

ought to know. So I sat there calmly in the hot, crowded church, waiting for Jesus to come to me.

The preacher preached a wonderful rhythmical sermon, all moans and shouts and lonely cries and dire pictures of hell, and then he sang a song about the ninety and nine safe in the fold, but one little lamb was left out in the cold. Then he said: "Won't you come? Won't you come to Jesus? Young lambs, won't you come?" And he held out his arms to all us young sinners there on the mourner's bench. And the little girls cried. And some of them jumped up and went to Jesus right away. But most of us just sat there.

A great many old people came and knelt around us and prayed, old women with jet-black faces and braided hair, old men with work-gnarled hands. And the church sang a song about the lower lights are burning, some poor sinners to be saved. And the whole building rocked with prayer and song.

Still I kept waiting to *see* Jesus.

Finally all the young people had gone to the altar and were saved, but one boy and me. He was a rounder's son named Westley. Westley and I were surrounded by sisters and deacons praying. It was very hot in the church, and getting late now. Finally Westley said to me in a whisper: "God damn! I'm tired o' sitting here. Let's get up and be saved." So he got up and was saved.

Then I was left all alone on the mourner's bench. My aunt came and knelt at my knees and cried, while prayers and songs swirled all around me in the little church. The whole congregation prayed for me alone, in a mighty wail of moans and voices. And I kept waiting serenely for Jesus, waiting, waiting—but he didn't come. I wanted to see him, but nothing happened to me. Nothing! I wanted something to happen to me but nothing happened.

I heard the songs and minister saying: "Why don't you come? Sister Reed, what is this child's name?"

"Langston," my aunt sobbed.

"Langston. Why don't you come? Why don't you come and be saved? Oh, Lamb of God! Why don't you come?"

Now it was really getting late. I began to be ashamed of myself, holding everything up so long. I began to wonder what God thought about Westley, who certainly hadn't seen Jesus either, but who was now sitting proudly on the platform, swinging his knickerbockered legs and grinning down at me, surrounded by deacons and old women on their knees praying. God had not struck Westley dead for taking his name in vain or for lying in the temple. So

I decided that maybe to save further trouble, I'd better lie, too, and say that Jesus had come, and get up and be saved.

So I got up.

Suddenly the whole room broke into a sea of shouting, as they saw me rise. Waves of rejoicing swept the place. Women leaped in the air. My aunt threw her arms around me. The minister took me by the hand and led me to the platform.

When things quieted down, in the hushed silence, punctuated by a few ecstatic "Amens," all the new young lambs were blessed in the name of God. Then joyous singing filled the room.

That night, for the last time in my life but one—for I was a big boy twelve years old—I cried, in bed alone, and couldn't stop. I buried my head under the quilts, but my aunt heard me. She woke up and told my uncle I was crying because the Holy Ghost had come into my life, and because I had seen Jesus. But I was really crying because I couldn't bear to tell her that I had lied, that I had deceived everybody in the church, that I hadn't seen Jesus, and that now I didn't believe there was a Jesus any more, since he didn't come to help me.[48]

This powerful anecdote is drawn from the autobiography of African-American poet Langston Hughes. The poignant narration may be full of peculiarities and unfamiliar language for those from outside the Evangelical Christian heritage, but for millions of persons within the Anglo-American revivalist tradition this sort of call to passionate, subjective religious experience would be common fare. Such an appeal for affective-experiential conversion transcends ethnicity, denominational boundaries, and, to some extent, time: for much of what Hughes describes might have taken place in a white Presbyterian congregation in New England in the 1850s, an African-American Methodist church in Kansas at the turn of the last century, or even in a blue-collar, British Baptist Church in the 1950s. Mainline, or more liturgical, Christians might wonder at the absence of sacrament or creed in this story of Christian "conversion," yet the appeal to experiential faith depicted in the vivid prose of Hughes portrays what may well be the mainspring of the modern Evangelical movement—the experiential bond that holds together such otherwise theologically and culturally diverse people, and places this movement squarely within the epistemology of the modern era.

---

48. Hughes, *The Big Sea: An Autobiography*, 18–21.

While the "mourner's bench" might be negotiable, and the ecstatic stylings of the preacher and enthusiastic congregational responses might come in a more moderate form, nevertheless, the highly subjective language of "something happening to you inside," and "Jesus coming into your life," and even "feeling Jesus in your soul" would become common parlance among Evangelical Christians from the time of the Great Awakenings to the present day. Although higher religious experience was often seen as limited to a mystic minority in the past, or confined to those with what Schleiermacher called "a talent for religion" or a natural endowment for "God-consciousness," the genius of the Evangelical Awakenings was the egalitarian sense that this experience was now available to all who would respond. The elusive and unknowable divine election of the Puritans and the protracted periods of "waiting on the Lord" gave way to a wholly democratic view of faith in the Awakenings, and finally to the "instant" conversions of modern Evangelicalism.

In some real respects, the revival meeting became the primary form of catechesis for Evangelical young people, while the "altar call" to conversion experience became the only (or, at least, primary) "sacrament" as the pre-eminence of baptism and Eucharist was circumvented by the subjective "born again" experience.

> Impatience with institutional forms, creeds, theologies, and liturgies constituted another aspect of this attitude, for these were all held to invade the rights of the sovereign individual and to inhibit the free flow of spirit. . . . Even more repugnant than theology, liturgy, and institutional order was any separation between clergy and laity. . . . In all these respects . . . frontier religion, the religion manifesting itself in the great evangelical denominations, was a true reflection of the frontier spirit with its individualism, emotionalism, pragmatism and impatience with forms and restraints.[49]

Whether liberal or Evangelical, modern Protestant perspectives on religion were shaped by a lively enthusiasm for the immediate coupled with a profound optimism about the future. Along with this attitude, however, came a disdain for the historical traditions and wisdom of the past. "It was commonly believed that the historical development of Christianity was not an accretion of valuable institutional forms and practices but a process of corruption and degeneration in which the purity of primitive Christianity

---

49. Herberg, *Protestant–Catholic–Jew*, 106.

had been lost."⁵⁰ This prevalent attitude set the agenda for much of modern Protestantism: "The goal of the devout . . . was not to preserve forms but to strike out anew in order to recapture this purity."⁵¹ In the case of Kant, Schleiermacher, and Kierkegaard, as well as for much of the Evangelical revivalist tradition, the original purity of faith was to be found in the "satisfaction of subjective needs and obligations."⁵²

Among the reasons for the new, modern attraction toward the subjective justification of religious belief, C. Stephen Evans suggests three: First, the subjective justification of faith was attractive due to the failure of the traditional theistic proofs of natural theology. Kant and Hume had seemingly dismantled the cosmological, teleological, and ontological arguments in their critical philosophies, thus creating a vacuum in the area of faith authentication and assurance. Second, the subjective justification of religious belief offered an unassailable sanctuary for faith during an era when scientific and historical inquiry were challenging the objective claims of faith and higher criticism assailed the authenticity of the Scriptures. Finally, the subjective justification of faith was attractive because the modern era had ushered in a developing appreciation for the "distinctive character of human existence, which involves an emphasis on man as a knowing-willing-feeling agent."⁵³ While the religious thinkers and figures discussed in this book clearly do not represent the "same" perspective on religious faith, they do, nevertheless, share a common standpoint in the epistemic shift toward the subject as the best expression of authentic faith for the modern age.

This epistemic shift is perhaps nowhere more evident than in Evangelical hymnology. The popular revivalist hymn "He Lives!"⁵⁴ asks what some (not the least, Saint Paul) would consider to be a fundamental epistemological question of the Christian religion: How can the believer be certain of the central apostolic claim that Jesus has risen from the dead? Saint

---

50. Hofstadter, *Anti-Intellectualism in American Life*, 82.
51. Ibid., 83.
52. Evans, *Subjectivity and Religious Belief*, 1
53. Ibid., 7.
54. Ackley, "He Lives," *Covenant Hymnal*, 253. This hymn was originally copyrighted in 1933 by Rodeheaver Company of the famed American revival tradition based in Winona Lake, Indiana. Rodeheaver Auditorium at Grace College and Seminary was built as a semi-permanent version of the classic revival tent, and made famous for hosting the evangelistic crusades of Billy Sunday (for whom Homer Rodeheaver was musical accompanist), among others. See McLoughlin, *Modern Revivalism*, 421–22; also see Hofstadter, *Anti-Intellectualism in American Life*, 114–16.

Paul seemed to think affirmation of the objective fact of the resurrection to be the pivot of the gospel,[55] and most historic, orthodox Christians have agreed.[56] For the writer of the First Epistle to the Corinthian church, the

---

55 First Corinthians 15:1-19. especially vv. 3-6, 14, 17: "I handed on to you as of first importance what I had in turn received: that Christ died for our *sins, in accordance with the Scriptures*, . . . *was raised* on the third *day in accordance with the Scriptures, and that he appeared to Cephas, and then to the twelve* . . . *to James, then to all the apostles* . . . if Christ has not been raised, then our proclamation has been in vain and your faith has been in vain . . . if Christ has not been raised, your faith is futile." The appeal seems twofold: first, the authority of the prophetic word in Scripture, and second, the transforming effect of the resurrection on the community of disciples.

56. Parallel to the modern propensity to ground faith in subjective experience, we find the concurrent attempt to defend (or discredit) faith on the basis of the new-found historical awareness of the Enlightenment. The rise of historical criticism and modern searches for the "historical Jesus" represent (alongside the subjective justification of religious belief) the mere fact that a crisis of faith has been introduced into the Western world by the Enlightenment's historical consciousness. Ephraim Radner posits a compelling theory, namely, "that the historical-critical study of Jesus has been fueled, since its inception in the seventeenth century, in large part by a desire to resolve this incoherence that is rooted at the center of modern Western Christianity . . . [i.e.,] an ecclesially untenable diversity of Christian commitments and practices." Radner argues that "the attempt to ground belief in Jesus as Lord on the basis of Jesus' historical factuality arose only in and not before the seventeenth century," and is something of an oddity in the history of Christendom, for "it really did not occur to Christians to ground their faith on the critical study of history for almost sixteen hundred years." This is not, he argues, because the historical reality of Jesus was unimportant until after the Reformation, but that "for sixteen hundred years the establishment of that historical reality was not deemed to be a significant ground for believing" in Jesus as risen Lord. "Today philosophers argue over whether or not our beliefs need to be 'founded' on a certain epistemology: we have arguments over the 'Jesus of faith' and the 'Jesus of history.'" Radner dismisses the prospect that ancient people were simply "credulous or superstitious, or, more fashionably, pre-critical (which sounds suspiciously like uncritical)" by noting that Origen's apologetic work *Against Celsus* reveals that virtually every "modern" historical criticism against the credibility of the Gospels was already in use by pagan skeptics. And yet, Radner suggests that the apologetic arguments of Origen "rarely coalesce into an integral historical defense for the Church's picture of Jesus." Instead, Origen and, on the whole, other early Christian apologists "were amazingly insouciant to the historical doubts or concerns about Jesus that critical study might resolve." This insouciance "was due in large part to another approach, which they saw as far more persuasive and, in the end, coherent with the truth they were attempting to commend to an unbelieving world. A survey of the extant apologetical works of the early church supports the gross generalization that Christian thinkers defended their faith in Jesus on two grounds: the consistent moral conversion and moral superiority of Christians compared with non-Christians, and the compelling witness of the Old Testament prophecies to the general history of which these Christians saw themselves a part. Particularly odd is that in many early apologies, such as those of Athenagoras, Aristides, or Theophilus, Jesus as an historical person is not mentioned at all." In brief, God, in Christ, was establishing His

truth of the resurrection was grounded in the eyewitness testimony of chosen apostles and the prophecies of the Hebrew Scriptures, which were seen

---

kingdom order in the world, and the church was part (indeed, the inaugural manifestation) of that order. Radner suggests that the apologetic stance of the church remained "stable though much constricted" during the time from the church fathers to following the Reformation. But, a radical change of perspective took place in the sixteenth century, and "by the seventeenth century, the significance of the Christian faith began to be explicated in a new fashion. The difference between the seventeenth century and this long period before lay in a novel realization: the historical coherence between Scripture and the church, which formed the access to an apprehension of Jesus Christ, had become fractured. Whatever the troubles of the church in the past, the sixteenth century proved an absolutely devastating contradiction to the prevailing apologetic reliance on communal holiness wrought within the sphere of God's historical providence. The permanent disintegration of the Christian community into antagonistic and competing groups wholly subverted the mutual relation of both sides of the affirmation—scriptural providence and ecclesial virtue. This is a well-worn observation that has been reasserted in our own day by prominent intellectual historians such as Richard Popkin and Stephen Toulmin. But the practical theological consequences of the sixteenth-century church's loss of scriptural and historical credibility, which we continue to live, have still been underestimated. Protestant apologists adjusted to the new situation by cutting loose scriptural authority from ecclesial virtue: Catholics, on the other hand, tidied up the integrity of providence by simply excising Protestants from the realm of "church" itself. . . . Most importantly, a conviction was lost in the process—the conviction that the Christian community's historical experience, because of its conformity to the scriptural narrative and claims, provided the window of access to a clear knowledge of Christ Jesus. The devotional legacy of this evolution, with its radical individualism and loss of communal humility, still haunts us." Radner concludes that the apologetic legacy was even more baleful: "for with the deep skepticism set loose about the historical coherence of Scripture and church, other avenues were sought after [for] . . . access to the person of Jesus. Indeed, by the seventeenth-century history itself, with its newly recognized embedded divisions and conflicts intractable to even the Christian church, needed to be bypassed altogether if salvation was to be properly described and thereby sought after. The rise of historical criticism, at least in the realm of scriptural study, represents just such an attempt to bypass the historical experience of the church in its relation to scriptural prophecy. It is an effort to get back at the 'origins': the origins of Jesus, the origin of his teachings, the origins of his intentions. If Jesus could be described independently of the ecclesial contradictions that had asserted themselves in the sixteenth and seventeenth centuries, independently of what Catholics, Calvinists, Anglicans, Quakers, or Baptists said, then perhaps the still vaguely apprehended salvation he promised might yet be salvaged." Radner, "We Believe in One Lord, Jesus Christ," 13–21.

as objective[57] and public truth.[58] However, it seems that the hymn-writer's answer could be readily embraced by nearly any post-Enlightenment brand of Protestantism; liberal, existentialist, and Evangelical alike. Over a century of higher criticism of the Christian Scriptures seemed to make the objective foundations of the gospel message a precarious place to stand. Nevertheless, for the post-Enlightenment Protestant Christian, epistemic certainty of the resurrection of Christ is still considered possible at a different, far more personal, level. The hymn asks: "You ask me how I know He lives?" The answer, for the modern individual shaped by the epistemic reversal of the Enlightenment (be they liberal, existentialist or Evangelical), seems to be the same: "He lives within my heart!"[59]

---

57. Jewish Professor Will Herberg contrasts the traditional "Judeo-Christian" view of faith with the modern: "Jewish-Christian faith is God-centered. All being finds its beginning and its end in God, and its unity, reality, and order in its ordination to Him. . . . But it also knows that man's actual life is corrupted by idolatrous self-love . . . . We are always prone to idolize ourselves and our works. . . . But—and this is the challenging word of Jewish-Christian faith—so long as he pursues this search in self-sufficiency, relying on his own virtue, wisdom, or piety, it will not be God that he finds, but an idol—the self, or some aspect of the self, writ large, projected, objectified, and worshipped." Herberg, *Protestant–Catholic–Jew*, 254–56. Herberg challenges the modern notion of faith as strictly individualistic and subjective by citing Alan Richardson favorably: "the individual . . . approached God in virtue of his membership in the holy people. . . . In the whole of the Bible, in the Old Testament as well as the New, there is no such thing as a private, personal relation between an individual and God apart from membership in the covenant-folk." Richardson, "Instrument of God," 278.

58. Saint Paul, speaking to Festus about King Agrippa in Acts 26:26, states, "For I am persuaded that none of these things has escaped his notice, for this has not been done in a corner." The Apostle apparently deemed his teaching to be "nothing but what the prophets and Moses said would take place: that the Christ (would be) the first to rise from the dead" (Acts 26:22, 23). More than a call to ground faith in a subjective experience of Jesus, Paul seems to appeal to the objective character of the Scriptures and the apostolic eyewitness testimony as the basis for epistemic certainty.

59. Ackley, "He Lives"

1

Fides Qua Creditur

The Enlightenment Mind and the Theology of the Heart

> *"Say first, of God above, or man below,*
> *What can we reason but from what we know?*
> *... Know then thyself, presume not God to scan,*
> *The proper study of mankind is man."*
>
> –Alexander Pope, *An Essay on Man*[1]

The Enlightenment "Cast of Mind"

PERIODS OF THOUGHT ARE notoriously difficult to pinpoint or define with complete accuracy. The age optimistically dubbed "the Enlightenment" is certainly no exception. From the late seventeenth and early eighteenth century "a profound alteration of culture had been taking place which John Randall has called the making of the modern mind." Its roots are deep in the past, but it began to manifest itself in the Renaissance and then appeared with new vigor and coherence in the last half of the seventeenth century."[2] While resisting precise definition, the age of Enlightenment might be best characterized as an aggregation of similar ideas and perspectives—or perhaps more accurately—*sympathies* regarding the potential of human intel-

---

1. Pope, "An Essay on Man," Epistle I.1; II.1.
2. Christian, *Friedrich Schleiermacher*, 19.

lectual autonomy. While these attitudes find root in the thought of such thinkers as Francis Bacon (1561–1626) and Rene Descartes (1596–1650), arguably, with seeds planted in the Protestant Reformation, the Enlightenment's principal thinkers nevertheless belong to the eighteenth century. More telling than mere points in time, however, is what Colin Gunton refers to as "the *cast of mind* which seems to be characteristic of an era of human self-confidence" in the Enlightenment which leads to an eventual "tearing apart of belief and knowledge."[3] "This new world view, largely secular, scientific, optimistic in outlook, confronted Christian faith with a challenge of major proportions. Virtually none of the presuppositions of traditional theology remained untouched."[4]

Often the designation "Age of Reason" is used as a synonym for the period of the Enlightenment. This is somewhat deceptive.[5] The moderns did not possess sole custody of reason any more than the medievals were inflexible fideists; for indeed, medieval thinkers had made abundant use of the tools of reason and logic in service to holy church. Philosophy may have been reckoned a handmaiden to theology, the "Queen of sciences," by most medieval philosophers, yet an extremely important attendant she was nevertheless. The Christian thinkers of this era, for the most part, were neither irrational nor anti-rational.[6] The so-called "Dark Ages" were by no means "dark" in terms of the absence or even the devaluation of reason. The difference between the Enlightenment and the "Christian" era of thought was the status of *autonomous* reason. The medieval philosophers, for the most part, affirmed the importance of reason, but they also shared a profound commitment to the appropriate limits and place of human reason as it stood in relationship to revealed divine truth. Indeed, this is the sticking point, for

---

3. Gunton, *Enlightenment & Alienation*, 3–5

4. Christian, *Friedrich Schleiermacher*, 20.

5. "In fact, the Enlightenment is now recognized to be intellectually heterogeneous, including a remarkable variety of anti-rational movements such as Mesmerism or Masonic rituals. Nevertheless, an emphasis upon the ability of human reason to penetrate the mysteries of the world is rightly regarded as a defining characteristic of 'Enlightenment.' The term 'rationalism' should also be used with caution when referring to the Enlightenment. In the first place, it should be noted that the term is often used in an uncritical and inaccurate way, designating the general atmosphere of optimism, grounded in a belief in scientific and social progress, which pervades much of the writing of the period." McGrath, "Enlightenment," 150.

6 Tertullian is the exception, rather than the rule, in his rather vocal disdain for the wisdom of the "disciples of Athens," as is Peter Abelard, at the other end of the spectrum, in his decidedly rationalist challenges to Scripture and church tradition.

one of the more obvious categories of differentiation between the medieval and modern mindset is neither the importance nor validity of reason, but the simple question of priority and placement: What is the proper position of reason in relation to supernatural revelation? In the face of a discrepancy or antinomy, which is the final arbiter of truth? For the medieval thinker (to turn Kant's phrase on its head) reason must remain submissively within the bounds of revealed religion, while for the Enlightenment thinker that relationship of servitude was shifting and would soon be reversed.

Some would trace the seminal form of this modern shift backwards as far as Reformer Martin Luther,[7] who appealed, not merely to holy Scripture, but to his own conscience and reason in his rejection of the authority of the Roman Church, or even to second generation Reformer John Calvin's *testimonium internum Spiritus Sancti*, a veridical experience by which the elect believer is granted personal assurance of faith through the ministrations of the indwelling Holy Spirit of God.[8] Both Luther and Calvin were concerned with discerning what could be held as an infallible sole authority in matters of faith and piety in the absence of the traditional authorities of church tradition and the *magisterium*. In the Reformers' assessment, these latter authorities were no authorities at all because they had proved

---

7. Luther made appeal to "clear reason," in addition to the "testimony of the Scriptures" as the basis of his trust in contrast to "either the pope or in the councils alone" because "it is neither safe nor right to go against conscience." This entreaty has been taken by some to be not only the first serious fissure in the mediaeval ecclesial edifice, but as the beginning of the modern marginalization of external religious authority in favor of a more internal or subjective source of confidence (see Lewis Spitz, *The Protestant Reformation 1517–1529*). Yet, while it may be that the modern spirit of rebellion against external authority was initially sparked by Luther's bravado, Luther's assertion that his "conscience was held captive by the Word of God and that he could not go against conscience" was surely not a full-blown "modern plea for the supremacy of the individual conscience or for religious freedom." Hendrix, "Legends about Luther," 50.

8. Likewise, Calvin's understanding of humanity as *homo religiosus* with an innate *sensus divinitatis*, together with his concept of the internal witness of the Holy Spirit, has been seen as a contributing factor in this modern move toward the interiorized justification of religious belief. Abraham, "The Epistemological Significance of the Inner Witness of the Holy Spirit," 442–43. Calvin defined faith as "a steady and certain knowledge of the divine benevolence toward us, which, being founded on the truth of the gratuitous promises in Christ, is both revealed to our minds and confirmed in our hearts by the Holy Spirit." Calvin, *Institutes*, III.2.vii. However, it must be kept in mind that for both Calvin and Luther the Scriptures provided, in the absence of supreme ecclesial authority, what they took to be sufficient objective, infallible religious authority ("founded on the truth of the gratuitous promises in Christ"), even if appropriated subjectively ("both revealed to our minds and confirmed in our hearts by the Holy Spirit").

themselves unreliable and flawed. As Peter Abelard had demonstrated in his controversial *Sic et Non* (1123), the Scriptures, the church fathers and doctors, the church's councils and traditions did not always agree. For Abelard, this simply meant that there was much work to be done by Christian thinkers. But, for the Reformers, these discrepancies and errors were a fatal flaw in the crumbling edifice of medieval Christendom. In such consequential matters as faith, only complete certainty would be satisfactory.

Still, contrary to widespread opinion, the Reformation did not begin with a disdain for the church's tradition or a "full-fledged critique of the traditional hierarchy of authorities."[9] Indeed, Luther's early polemics relied heavily on the teachings of the conciliar rulings of the church and on the papal decrees. His initial concern was to clear up apparent theological discrepancies and pastoral abuses within the teaching and practice of the church itself. Luther's early agenda was not the casting off of tradition or ecclesial authority at all, but the reform of the church by its own principles. However, "within a few years, the momentum of the early protests carried Luther into a full-scale attack on the traditional rule of faith."[10]

Eventually, Luther raised the concern of multiple authorities: How could various church authorities, decrees, and popes all disagree with one another, much less with Holy Scripture, and all be nevertheless equally true and authoritative? This seemed inconsistent with a truthful, infallible God (Who, it was claimed by the church, was the sole source of all these seemingly divergent authorities). Luther's solution was to pare down these many authorities to one, indisputable authority: that of Holy Scripture. The Christian Scriptures, it was argued in the Reformation tradition, bear inherent certitude (*certitudo*) and infallibility (*infalliblitas*) by nature of their divine origin.[11] As such, they bear the attitudes of perfect holiness and truth of statement without adventure of error (*veritas assertionum sine admixtis erroribus*).[12] Since Scripture could not contradict Scripture, the hierarchies and traditions of the church had to give way to the single, incontrovertible authority of the biblical text. Thus, Luther's famous rejoinder at the Diet of Worms in 1521 pits the multiple authority of "the Pope or [Church] coun-

---

9. Stout, *The Flight from Authority*, 41.

10. Ibid., 41.

11. "*Auctor primarius Scripturae sacrae*," the primary author of Scripture, viz. God. God is the source of the *mandatum scribendi*. Muller, *Dictionary of Latin and Greek Theological Terms*, 51.

12. Ibid., 52.

cils" against the sole authority of Scripture as God's Word.[13] If the magisterium or traditions of the church contradict Scripture, then Scripture stands and the other authorities are no authorities at all.

Ironically, it was the Reformation war cry "*Sola Scriptura*" which led, in part, to the multiple authority problem once again, though in another, more convoluted and insidious form. Protestant scholastics saw the Scriptures as the only proper epistemological or noetic *principium theologiae*, without which God could not be legitimately known or theology developed, yet they soon found it necessary to distinguish between the *principium cognoscendi externum* (the external, written word of Holy Writ) and the *principium cognoscendi internum* (the internal principle of faith which is enabled by the Holy Spirit within to respond to the call of Holy Scripture without).[14] For every new sect, every individual heretic would soon make counterclaims to their own "internal certainty" and "conscience" as the basis for some new, deviant teaching. If Luther or Calvin could not agree with Zwingli, what were they to make of the radical reformer Anabaptists or, worse, the likes of Miguel Servetus? The Protestant impetus was originally to challenge the many authorities of Rome and her traditions, but now there were "far more authorities than before, for *every* man recognizes his own inner light. Every conscience constitutes a separate authority. What started out as an appeal to the single authority of scriptural revelation now seems to recognize, implicitly at least, ten authorities in every pew."[15] If the

---

13. Some would question Luther's appeal to "manifest reasoning" and "my conscience" as a hidden subjective authority, as well. In subsequent Protestant thought and practice, these certainly have played such a role. Erasmus noted this as a potential problem in pointing out that reliance on Scripture alone is impossible, since there will always be disputes about the meaning of the text. In such a case, the magisteria and traditions of the church provide a far more reliable source of authority than individual reasoning, or conscience ever could offer. See Popkin, *The History of Scepticism*, 4–6.

14. Muller, *Dictionary of Latin Greek Theological Terms*, 245–46. This distinction between "*principium cognoscendi externum*" and the "*principium cognoscendi internum*" is parallel to the concept of the "*testimonium internum Spiritus Sancti*" in which the truth of Scripture is attested inwardly by the presence of the Holy Spirit. Muller writes, "the Reformers and the Protestant scholastics were adamant in their belief both that *the testimonium* is necessary to the subjective receipt of the truth of Scripture, and that *the testimonium* only ratifies the truth of the text and adds *no* new Revelation. But while the Reformers and their Protestant scholastic progeny would vehemently reject the prospect of subjective *revelatio immediata* (unmediated, immediate revelation) or *revelatio nova* (new revelation), some of the radical wing of the Reformation and various groups of religious enthusiasts would eagerly take this next step toward subjectivity."

15. Stout, *The Flight from Authority*, 44.

external authority and historic traditions of the church were no longer a trustworthy guide in spiritual matters, then in a very real sense the Bible-wielding individual is promoted to that role him or herself. Add the impetus of a new Protestant appreciation (and later a Pietist reconstruction) of the biblical principle of the "priesthood of all believers," and one finds sufficient fortification for the Evangelical problem of "multiple authorities."

William J. Abraham even detects a conceivable connection between the Reformation view of faith and the Cartesian project: "It is worth speculating whether Descartes's doctrine of the *cogito* with its quest for a single source of certainty, its radically inward turn, and its emphasis on self-evidence, may not be a secular reproduction of a reduced and inadequate account of the experience of the Holy Spirit."[16] Likewise, Jeffrey Stout offers, "Just as Luther sought the sort of justification that would be a match for the radical sinfulness he had discovered in his own will and heart, traditional epistemology has sought the sort of justification that would be a match for the radical skepticism implicit in its own . . . Cartesian doubts."[17] If these authors are correct, then, we find the seeds of the modern inward epistemic turn unconsciously embedded within the Reformation challenge to church authority. Thus,

> For Descartes, as for Luther before him, what most matters in life is no longer played out in the dimensions of community and tradition. One discovers truth in the privacy of subjective illumination, and this truth is underlined by a kind of self-certifying certainty. Community, tradition, authority: these have all started to give way to the individual, his inwardness, his autonomy.[18]

If this modern revolution was conceived in the challenge to authority of the Reformation period, then it was surely birthed by Descartes. Likewise, it was nurtured by Locke, and would soon come of age in the thinking of Immanuel Kant. Taking a cue from the Cartesian *cogito*, Western intellectual culture soon found itself in the throes of an intellectual revolution. The Enlightenment era would be characterized by casting off the bonds of

---

16. Abraham, "Epistemological Significance of the Inner Witness of the Holy Spirit," 442–43.

17. Stout, *The Flight from Authority*, 26

18. Ibid., 49–50. Stout observes, "Appealing to intuition as the basic tool for the reconstruction of *scientia*, Descartes lands in the same kind of dialectical corner as the Protestant proponents of inner persuasion. In both cases we want to know how to tell genuinely objective certainty from mistakenly heartfelt conviction."

external epistemic supervision in favor of a far more interior (and, now it was assumed, more trustworthy) authority: the individual self. Historian Peter Gay speaks of the Enlightenment era in terms of the recovery of nerve,[19] during which the almost forgotten Roman proverb "*faber suae quisque fortunae*"[20] came to signify the new spirit of the age. There was a new enthusiasm abroad, grounded in a new-found confidence in human self-governance and noetic potential. European thinkers now courageously dared to rely on the individual's own intellectual potential rather than on (or, at least, in addition to) traditional religious authority and guidance. In this intellectual "Copernican revolution," as Kant would christen it, the knowing self had been situated at the epistemic center of the universe.

This radical epistemological shift might indeed be the principal heritage of the Enlightenment period, and an ongoing characteristic of modernity. Still, as one historian suggests, this intellectual revolution was clearly not wholly homogeneous. The reorientation of Enlightenment epistemology manifested itself in a range of distinct ways throughout European culture: "The specifics of such use of the understanding varied significantly from the Enlightenment of one nation or period or school of thought to that of another."[21] This means, of course, that "no definition of the Enlightenment fits all the men usually assumed to belong to it."[22] Such is also the case with "all the cultures in which it appeared on both sides of the Atlantic during the seventeenth and eighteenth centuries. Within those cultures, moreover, it affected different aspects of life and thought in quite different ways: education and politics, science and the arts, philosophy and religion."[23]

Descartes and the Turn Within

Nevertheless, even with such variegation of effect, it is generally agreed that common to the Enlightenment era is a prevailing ethos of noetic autonomy in which the knowing subject is elevated to a place of supreme epistemic importance. And most find this ethos, as the primary signal of the onset of the modern age, in the philosophical writings of Descartes. Nearly from

19. Gay, *Enlightenment*, 6.
20. "Man is the architect of his fortune," ibid, 7.
21. Pelikan, *Christian Doctrine and Modern Culture*, 60.
22. May, *The Enlightenment in America*, xiii.
23. Pelikan, *Christian Doctrine and Modern Culture*, 60.

the moment Descartes penned the words "*Cogito ergo sum*," the status of the knowing self in Western thought would never be the same. Richard Kroner writes, "In this Descartes finds the ultimate source of certainty."[24] For Descartes, it was the *a priori* human capacity for reasoning (ironically, a traditional idea which placed him directly within the grand rationalist legacy of Plato and Augustine—a set of assumptions that Descartes never chose to doubt!) that made the turn inward a sure course to certitude. For others thereafter, however, it would not be the inward turn to reason that would became the cornerstone of assurance, so much as it was the merely the inward turn to the subject. The self, reasoning or not, would soon be deemed a far more reliable epistemic authority than anything external to the self.

Among subsequent Western thinkers, then, the individual subject would be soon enthroned to a position previously reserved only for the church, the Scriptures, or even God Himself. Jesuit-trained and devout Catholic René Descartes "might have winced at such blasphemous progeny but he would have found it hard to deny his paternity."[25]

> It is to continental rationalism that we owe the development of the notion that the human subject is passive in the act of perceiving the world. The world, so to speak, hits him from without, via the five senses of sight, touch, hearing, taste and smell. . . . [T]he beginning of philosophical wisdom for Descartes was a strengthening of Plato's case against the reliability of what we learn by the senses. Sense perception cannot be relied upon because of its inherent questionableness . . . . And so Descartes turned away from the slippery world outside to the world within, the world of rational ideas and mathematical certainty.[26]

Kroner adds that for Descartes "inwardness is . . . interpreted as the unique position of the thinking subject in contrast to the objects thought. No thinker before Descartes brought the principle of modern philosophy, its epistemological subjectivism, so emphatically and definitely to light. In that respect he was the true initiator of philosophy in the modern world."[27]

Descartes' epistemology looks inward due to his conviction that sense experience coming from without (while real) may not be trusted, since

---

24. Kroner, *Speculation and Revelation in Modern Philosophy*, 84.
25. Hampson, *The Enlightenment*, 28.
26. Gunton, *Enlightenment & Alienation*, 16.
27. Kroner, *Speculation and Revelation in Modern Philosophy*, 88.

the senses can be easily misled and are often mistaken, and are unable to provide mathematical certainty; Descartes shares the Reformers' desire for certitude and a single fount of unerring authority. Yet that authority would not be the Scriptures, but the rational self. "There is certainly . . . in me a certain passive faculty of perception, that is of receiving and recognising the ideas of sensible things, but that would be useless to me . . . if there were not . . . another faculty capable of forming and producing these ideas."[28] Thus, Descartes' lack of confidence in the passive senses and corresponding trust in his own reasoning abilities leads him from "the valley of doubt on to a plateau from which he may confidently survey the world as a place which can be known and understood," yet "he has paid a price for his success."[29] Namely, the "permanent and irredeemable loss of confidence in the senses" gave birth to the characteristically modern mistrust of any knowledge with origins outside of the reliable self.

Descartes' starting point of universal doubt has been called, in Michael Oakeshott's memorable phrase, an attempt "to live each day as if it were his first"[30] which would become a "tradition that would rather not be a *tradition* at all."[31] The crisis of traditional authority "gave rise to new forms of skepticism with which philosophers have been preoccupied almost to the present day."[32]

Believing and Knowing in Locke

Michael Polanyi attributes to John Locke (1632–1704) the pervasive modern notion that believing (or faith) is merely a subordinate kind of knowing.[33] "Belief here is no longer a higher power that reveals to us knowledge

---

28. Descartes, *Philosophical Works*, 1:191.
29. Gunton, *Enlightenment & Alienation*, 17.
30. Oakeshott, *Rationalism in Politics*, 3.
31. Stout, *Flight from Authority*, 7.
32. Ibid., 7–8.
33. The idea can be traced back to Plato's *Timaeus*, in which πιστις corresponds not to the unseen, spiritual realm of the forms, but to the inferior, illusory realm of material objects. Thus, faith is inferior to reason, because the object of knowledge is inferior. Thomas Aquinas turns this distinction on its head with the notion that, while faith is an inferior *type* of knowing than reason, the *content* or *object* of faith (Divine revelation) is actually superior. Nevertheless, Locke is the source of the modern version of the subordination of faith to reason. He writes: "Traditional Revelation may make us know propositions knowable also by reason, but not with the same certainty that reason

lying beyond the range of observation and reason, but a mere personal acceptance which falls short of empirical and rational demonstrability."[34] With a newly "enlightened" confidence in the presumed certainty of the natural sciences and the potential of human reason, religious faith was on a sure course to being considered epistemically inferior. "All belief was reduced to the status of subjectivity: to that of an imperfection by which knowledge fell short of universality."[35]

Locke's empiricism is typically seen as standing in marked contrast to Descartes' rationalism. While Descartes taught that human reason provided an innate, *a priori* foundation for knowing from birth, Locke rejected this "received doctrine" that "men have native ideas, and original characters, stamped upon their minds in their very first being."[36] Instead, Locke saw the human mind as *tabula rasa*, a blank slate or "white paper void of all characters, without any ideas"—an empty cabinet which comes to be furnished by sense experience and reflection on sense experience.[37] Locke affirmed the characteristically Aristotelean *a posteriori* conviction that "there is nothing in the mind which has not previously come through the senses." Yet for all these important differences, Locke and Descartes do have some important ideas in common. Among those shared notions are the concept that human sense perception is passive while the reason is active, but more significantly, Locke and Descartes share the uniquely modern orientation toward the knowing self as a reliable source of truth:

> The understanding seems to have the least glimmering of any ideas which it doth not receive from one of these two. *External objects* furnish the mind with the ideas of sensible qualities, which are all those different perceptions they produce in us; and *the mind* furnishes the understanding with ideas of its own operations.[38]

---

doth. . . . For whatsoever truth we come to the clear discovery of, from the knowledge and contemplation of our own ideas, will always be certainer to us than those which are conveyed to us by traditional revelation. For the knowledge we have that this revelation came at first from God, can never be so sure as the knowledge we have from the clear and distinct perception of the agreement or disagreement of our own ideas." Locke, *An Essay concerning Human Understanding*, 120.

34. Polanyi, *Personal Knowledge*, 266.
35. Ibid.
36. Locke, *An Essay concerning Human Understanding*, 9.
37. Ibid.
38. Ibid., 11.

Locke's confidence in human capacity for truthful reflection on experience leads to his profound emphasis upon the necessity for empirical verification of all religious faith-claims. As the once seemingly monolithic culture of Christendom faced a deluge of irreconcilable religious claims from the newly discovered world religions (as Western explorers rapidly pushed the frontiers of the world into previously unexplored territory), as well as the phenomenon of perpetual fracturing of denominations and sectarianism among Protestants, and, most distressingly to Locke, the private revelatory claims of religious "enthusiasts" (what most contemporary religionists would now call "charismatics"), Locke attempted to bring some order to the chaos.

> Locke... searched in the Scripture for a universal access to a moral life that might somehow bypass the real antagonisms and particularities of the now warring factions of disintegrating Christianity, particularly obvious in seventeenth century England. Although Locke was not a historian, he felt that an apprehension of the "real" Jesus of the Scriptures, discerned on his own independent terms, would yield a doctrine wholly comfortable to universal human reason, and hence immune to the sectarian strife to which many of his own writings are responses.[39]

By issuing what some would call an "evidentialist challenge," he believed that the authentic claims of historic Christian orthodoxy could be bolstered against the swelling gales of contradictory and pluralistic faith claims. According to Locke, "no proposition can be received for divine revelation, or obtain the assent due to all such, if it be contradictory to our clear intuitive knowledge."[40]

As Locke contrasts "the measures and boundaries between faith and reason," he defines reason as "the discovery of the certainty or probability of such propositions and truths, which the mind arrives at by deduction made from such ideas, which it has got by the use of its natural faculties," namely, "by sensation or reflection."[41] On the other hand, faith "is the assent to any proposition, not thus made out by the deductions of reason, but upon the credit of the proposer, as coming from God, in some extraordinary way of communication,"[42] namely, revelation. The "dominion of faith

---

39. Radner, "We Believe in One Lord, Jesus Christ," 22.
40. Locke, *An Essay concerning Human Understanding*, 121.
41. Ibid., 118.
42. Ibid.

reaches" insofar as it does no "violence or hindrance to reason."[43] Locke describes the necessity of setting up such boundaries between faith and reason, for otherwise "no enthusiasm or extravagancy in religion can be contradicted,"[44] and religion, which should elevate us above the beasts, would give way to Pandemonium. Locke quips, "*Credo, quia impossibile est*: I believe, because it is impossible, might in a good man, pass for a sally of zeal; but it would prove a very ill rule for men to choose their opinions of religion by."[45]

> Whatever God hath revealed is certainly true: no doubt can be made of it. This is the proper object of faith: but whether it be a *divine* revelation or no, reason must judge; which can never permit the mind to reject a greater evidence to embrace what is less evident, nor allow it to entertain probability in opposition to knowledge and certainty. There can be no evidence that any traditional revelation is of divine original, in the words we receive it, and in the sense we understand it, so clear and so certain as that of the principles of reason: and therefore, nothing is contrary, and inconsistent with, the clear and self-evident dictates of reason, has a right to be urged or assented to as a matter of faith, wherein reason has nothing to do.[46]

Unlike the medievals, for whom, in spite of varying views of the relationship between faith and reason, the primary question was, nevertheless, "how can reason be reconciled to faith?" now the question was reversed, "how can faith be reconciled to reason?" Nearly everyone from Tertullian to Augustine or Anselm to Aquinas would see reason in varying degrees as valuable, but faith as essential. Locke insists, however, that reason must be the "last judge and guide in everything."[47] C. S. Lewis, Oxford's celebrated scholar of medieval and Renaissance literature, noted this characteristic shift within the worldview of modernity by the following colorful contrast:

> The ancient man approached God (or even the gods) as the accused person approaches his judge. For the modern man the roles are reversed. He is the judge: God is in the dock. He is quite a kindly judge: if God should have a reasonable defence for being

---

43. Ibid., 124.
44. Ibid., 125.
45. Ibid.
46. Ibid., 124.
47. Ibid., 133.

the god who permits war, poverty and disease, he is ready to listen to it. The trial may even end in God's acquittal. But the important thing is that Man is on the Bench and God is in the Dock.[48]

The subtlety of the shift within Locke is sometimes obscured by his unshakable commitments to Protestant Reformed theology, not to mention his optimism that whatever legitimate test human reason might put to Christian truth, biblical orthodoxy will prevail. Nonetheless, Locke made a permanent contribution to the modern assumption that faith claims, if they are to be taken as veritable, must meet the test of human intellect. Ironically, though Locke intends to undermine the religious enthusiasts' subjectivity by appeal to reason, he has unintentionally contributed the inward turn which would become the mainstay of most modern assessments of faith.

The "Copernican Revolution"

In the sphere of religion, and in particular within Protestant Christendom, these influences of Enlightenment epistemology are perhaps among the most dramatic and most keenly felt. Christian thinkers faced in the Enlightenment a "revolution of man's autonomous potentialities over against the heteronomous powers which were no longer convincing."[49] The powers which had, of late, come to be considered implausible were, "namely, the heteronomous authority of the church and of its dogma and ultimately the objective authority of Scripture and transcendent revelation itself."[50] Gunton writes:

> The first distinguishing characteristic of the cast of mind encouraged by the Enlightenment can be evoked with the help of a contrast. Augustine had taught that "unless you believe you will not understand," a view that was both developed and criticized by different thinkers in the centuries after him. In the Enlightenment, it was reversed. "If you believe you will not understand" has some claim to represent one of its chief mottoes. The Enlightenment was right to attack credulity and superstition. But in the process it produced a view of the human mind that falsified its relation to the world, especially in suggesting that there could be attained

---

48. Lewis, *God in the Dock*, 244.
49. Tillich, *Protestant Theology*, 2:27.
50. Pelikan, *Christian Doctrine and Modern Culture*, 60.

an absolute objectivity and impartiality: a God's-eye-view, so to speak, of reality . . . .[51]

The result, in Gunton's assessment, is the alienating rending asunder of faith and knowing for Enlightenment thinkers. What follows "alongside the over-estimation of the capacity for detachment [is] an exaggeration of the part played by the mind in the organization of its knowledge. The bare objectivity of the world is met by the self-assertion of the subject."[52] To be sure, these ideas take solid formation in that zenith of Enlightenment thinkers, Immanuel Kant. "Kant takes it as axiomatic that the pattern outlined by Locke is correct. Knowledge, to be knowledge, must be certain, in no way indulging in the uncertainties of belief."

Kant mused that "it is so easy not to be of age."[53] The demands of Enlightenment noetic autonomy are rigorous and most people are clearly not up to the challenge. Far too many respond with apprehension and timidity, which is why "after nature has long since discharged them from external direction (*naturaliter maiorennes*), [humankind] nevertheless remains under lifelong tutelage, and why it is easy for others to set themselves up as their guardians."[54] Most people prefer the comfort of being under somebody else's intellectual custody. Kant posits that "if I have a book which understands for me, a pastor who has a conscience for me, . . . I need not trouble myself. I need not think, if I will only pay—others will readily undertake the irksome work for me."[55]

"Reasons of the Heart"

What had been conceived as the Reformation's challenge to ecclesiastical corruption had now given birth to a full-scale assault on the veracity of biblical revelation, and eventually upon theism itself. With the objective character of transcendent revelation under scrutiny and, sometimes, full attack, many Christians found themselves regrouping around a means of justifying religious belief which was, by its very nature, far more difficult to expose to

---

51. Gunton, *Enlightenment & Alienation*, 3.
52. Ibid., 4.
53. Kant, "What is Enlightenment," 85.
54. Ibid.
55. Ibid.

rational criticism. Certainty of faith, for many, came to be grounded solely in "reasons of the heart" as Pascal had so eloquently put it.[56]

> Major Protestant thinkers in the nineteenth century attempted to identify a sphere of human nature within which faith could be located and validated without appeal to the transcendental theological claims which the Enlightenment had dismantled. By locating faith in the affective religious consciousness . . . or the moral sense. . . . this move beyond rationalism tended to reinforce the subjectivity of faith. . . . Whilst anthropologically rich, their accounts are again hesitant in description of the objective referents of faith.[57]

Faith had always been a central concern of theology within the churches of the Reformation heritage. Protestant Scholastic theologians had made a cautious distinction between the content of faith *(fides quae creditur*—faith "objectively considered"[58]) and the experience of believing *(fides qua creditur*—faith "subjectively considered"[59]). The Scholastics were clear, however, that the only sure epistemic foundation was faith firmly established in the *fides quae* (objective content of faith) rather than in the *fides qua* (subjective[60] experience). But as the Protestant tradition became

---

56. Blaise Pascal, *Pensees* (#423). Pascal notes, "It is your own inner assent and the consistent voice of your reason rather than that of others which should make you believe" (#505). And yet Pascal intends to find a *via media* between the Cartesian demand for certainty and sheer skepticism: "We must know when it is right to doubt, to affirm, to submit. Anyone who does otherwise does not understand the force of reason. Some men run counter to these three principles, either affirming that everything can be proved, because they know nothing about proof, or doubting everything, because they do not know when to submit, or always submitting, because they do not know when judgment is called for" (#170).

57. Webster, "Faith," 209.

58. Muller, *Dictionary of Latin and Greek Theological Terms*, 117.

59. Ibid.

60. C. Stephen Evans provides a helpful clarification for what many deem to be the "problem-laden" term "subjective": "The term 'subjective' has at least two distinct, though sometimes confused, meanings. There is first a pejorative sense which connotes arbitrariness and bias on the part of an individual. When a teacher is accused of being a subjective grader, the charge is that he is irresponsible and biased: he lacks objectivity. But there is a second sense of the word which lacks these pejorative connotations. We sometimes say that a person who is not very understanding of his fellows is too objective. He seems cold and heartless because he treats the people around him as if they were simply objects to be manipulated. Such a person, we might be inclined to say, needs to gain an understanding of those around him from a *subjective* point of view. He needs to understand that other individuals are persons in their own right, with feelings, desires, and needs of their own. He needs to see things from the other person's point of view.

profoundly influenced by Enlightenment epistemology, there was a growing disposition which ceaselessly emphasized, instead, what Avery Dulles calls the "affective-experiential" dimension of religious faith, in which "the sign is played off the thing signified, the form is set against the content, *fides qua* is magnified at the expense of *fides quae*."[61] In the most extreme forms, this approach to faith can become wholly detached from the objective tradition, preferring the *experience* of faith over actual *content* and "the immediacy is understood as a substitute for the authoritative mediation of the content of faith through historical revelation, prophetic and apostolic testimony, Scripture, Tradition, and the living Church."[62] Dulles notes that "some experientialists fall into an individualistic empiricism that undermines the social and ecclesial character of faith."[63]

Reinhard Hütter makes the same distinction by contrasting the "Cognitive-Propositional model" of theology with the "Affective-Experiential model"[64] as delineated by Yale theologian George Lindbeck in *The Nature of Doctrine: Religion and Theology in a Postliberal Age*.[65] The cognitive-propositional model is largely the position of Protestant Scholastic orthodoxy (what Hütter sees as *fides quae creditur* without *fides qua creditur*), a model which

> places cognitive aspects completely in the foreground "and stresses the ways in which church doctrines function as informative proposition of truth claims about objective realities." It understands religion as being similar to philosophy and science insofar as the latter produce worldviews commensurate with truth. Accordingly,

---

This point of view is that of the subject. In this sense of the word, 'subjective' implies that which pertains to a subject. It does not necessarily connote bias, arbitrariness, or lack of rationality." Evans, *Subjectivity and Religious Belief*, 4–5. It is in this latter sense of "pertaining to a subject" that the word "subjective" will be used within this thesis. However, this is not to suggest in any of the cases discussed within these chapters that the concept of religious belief never degenerates into the more pejorative sense of "subjective" suggested by Evans. That judgment is simply beyond the scope of this book. The primary interest here is the historic transition toward the grounding of religious belief and epistemic assurance primarily in the experience of the subject (*fides qua creditur*) rather than in what was understood by medieval and ancient Christian thinkers to be the objective revealed content of faith (*fides quae, creditur*).

61. Dulles, *The Assurance of Things Hoped For*, 148.
62. Ibid., 176.
63. Ibid.
64. Hütter, *Suffering Divine Things*, 42–43.
65. Lindbeck, *The Nature of Doctrine*.

the model also understands theology as an undertaking comprehensively and coherently formulating truth claims from sources of revelation and/or reason.[66]

The preliberal model saw religion in "analogy to metaphysics," while the liberal model "understands it in analogy to aesthetics."[67] By contrast to the cognitive propositional model, the experiential-expressive model (for Hütter, *fides qua creditur* without *fides quae creditur*) represents a manifest change

> in European theology from pre-Kantian, classical orthodoxy to post-Kantian theology of the sort exemplified by Schleiermacher. Whereas the first model took its orientation from an "objective" reality, the second is characterized by the "turn to the subject" and by the latter's constitutive role for all explicit "religion." This model understands religions as different systems of expression of inner feelings and attitudes and of existential orientations. These symbolic systems have a strictly nondiscursive, nonpropositional character: that is, they make no immediate and definitive statements about reality, offering instead the interpretive expression of individual "inner-pre-reflexive experiences."[68]

In the world following Kant, this "affective-experiential" brand of religious faith has become its own kind of orthodoxy—dominating both the Protestant liberal and Protestant Evangelical lines of the Reformation tradition. In this respect (among others), the designation "liberal" and "modernist" as it is typically applied merely to the tradition dependent upon Schleiermacher is far too narrow a demarcation. In regard to the appropriation of a decidedly interior and subjective stance on faith, the Protestant Evangelical tradition shares this modernist trait.

In the face of apparent failure for the Aristotelian synthesis within Scholastic theology to safeguard religious faith against the assault of modern science, "many defenders of the faith in the eighteenth century saw . . . that God was opening one door for faith after having closed another."[69] Jaroslav Pelikan suggests that Enlightenment believers discovered that the internalized faith of subjective religious experience

---

66. Hütter, *Suffering Divine Things*, 42–43, citing Lindbeck, *The Nature of Doctrine*, 16.

67. Ibid., 43.

68. Hütter, *Suffering Divine Things*, 43, citing Lindbeck, *The Nature of Doctrine*, 17.

69. Pelikan, *Christian Doctrine and Modern Culture*, 118.

could stand even when the supposedly transcendent grounds of faith . . . were being subjected to persistent attack. . . . When the promoters of this inner life spoke of "theology," they did not mean human "enlightenment [*Aufklärung*]" but "divine illumination [*göttliche Erleuchtung*]." To the motto of the Enlightenment, "Dare to know!" they opposed the motto of the gospel, "Dare to believe!" . . . [S]o the argument from morality to religion and from the subjective experience of the soul to the reality of God was no less legitimate than the traditional cosmological arguments for the existence of God.[70]

This Enlightenment trend toward subjective inwardness, or non-theoretical justification[71] of religious belief, can be found in nearly all versions of eighteenth- and nineteenth-century Protestant thought. Wayne Proudfoot writes that "authors as diverse as . . . Immanuel Kant, Schleiermacher, and Søren Kierkegaard each proposed redescriptions of religious belief and practice designed to insulate them from conflict with developing scientific knowledge."[72] When Enlightenment science appeared to make theoretical knowledge of God impossible or, at least, indefensible, the argument shifted from "the sheer fact that the world exists" to a decided interest in "certain pervasive features of human existence . . . desires, needs and felt obligations."[73]

While it is true that religion "has always been an experiential matter," there is a sense in which both "religious" and "experience" are "relatively recent concepts, whose provenance is in the modern West . . . in the past two centuries"[74] growing out of the need to explain the expressions of spirituality in the religions of the world. As a result, there has been an emerging appreciation for the nature and study of religious experience, which has been central "for the liberal tradition of religious thought which stems largely from the work of Friedrich Schleiermacher" and yet with roots in a "line of thinkers beginning with Descartes and culminating with Immanuel Kant."[75]

70. Ibid., 118–19.

71. Evans uses the concept of "non-theoretical justification of religious belief," which begins with the self as a responsible agent, synonymously with the phrase "subjective justification of religious belief." *Subjectivity and Religious Belief*, 4.

72. Proudfoot, "From Theology to a Science of Religions," 150.

73. Evans, *Subjectivity and Religious Belief*, 4.

74. Proudfoot, *Religious Experience*, xii.

75. Ibid., xii-xiii.

The "non-theoretical justifications of religious belief which derive from these aspects of the human subject"[76] appear to be a common thread running through such diverse, yet distinctly modern traditions as Protestant liberalism, Christian existentialism, and, surprisingly, Anglo-American Evangelicalism. For, in varying degrees, all of these religious perspectives are simultaneously reactions to and adaptations of the epistemic heritage of the Enlightenment. "The answers given by the philosophers of the early modern era, from Descartes to Kant, can be seen to form a general, though not unanimous, development . . . [which] form[s] the often unconsciously learned framework of the contemporary understanding of the world."[77] Indeed, even as each responded in its own distinctive way to the religious skepticism born of the age of Enlightenment, these traditions tended to readily adopt the Enlightenment relegation of faith to the realm of subjective experience. The centrality of the knowing subject became the prevailing epistemological assumption at the heart of these otherwise radically different approaches to Protestant thought.

> Major Protestant thinkers in the nineteenth century attempted to identify a sphere of human nature within which faith could be located and validated without appeal to the transcendental theological claims which the Enlightenment had dismantled. By locating faith in the affective religious consciousness . . . or the moral sense . . . this move beyond rationalism tended to reinforce the subjectivity of faith. . . . Whilst anthropologically rich, their accounts are again hesitant in description of the objective referents of faith.[78]

Immanuel Kant "held that religious doctrine ought not be viewed as knowledge, but that it is rational in the sense that it plays an indispensable role in the moral life."[79] Belief, as opposed to knowledge, could only be justified subjectively. Friedrich Schleiermacher, the "pioneer" of modern liberal theology, appealed to "pious feeling" as the basis of true faith as he defended Christianity to its "cultured [Enlightenment] despisers." Schleiermacher criticized Kant "for portraying religion as derivative from morality," and argued that faith must be "grounded in an autonomous moment of experience that is distinct from both science and morals." Søren Kierkegaard, the father of modern existentialist thought, sought to rescue Christian faith

---

76. Evans, *Subjectivity and Religious* Belief, 4.
77. Gunton, *Enlightenment & Alienation*, 11.
78. Webster, "Faith," 209.
79. Proudfoot, "From Theology to a Science of Religions," 150.

from the ravages of Enlightenment scientific inquiry by stressing faith as "passionate inwardness." Proudfoot says: "Even Kierkegaard's description of the absolute paradox, and of faith as inwardness, can be seen as part of this strategy to portray religion within the limits of reason alone."[80]

> These protective strategies, in which religious doctrine and practice are redescribed so as to preclude conflict with science, have generally taken the form of a shift from theology to some kind of phenomenology, in which the religious life is described and identified exclusively from the subject's perspective. The two chief concepts employed, and in fact constructed, for this purpose by Protestant thinkers, have been religious experience and faith. A broadly phenomenological description is given of faith, or of a moment of experience that is identified as religious, and the claim is made that it is autonomous and thus cannot be reduced to nor does it encroach upon the proper domains of physics or psychology.[81]

The Pietist Impulse

Pietism was an (often informal) revival movement whose chief protagonist was Philipp Jakob Spener (1635–1705). Spener was a Lutheran clergyman noted for his deep, mystical devotion coupled with practical, religious sentiment. When invited in 1665 to compose an introduction for a new edition of the popular book *Von Wahren Christentums* ("Of True Christianity"), a collection of sermons by celebrated Lutheran mystic Johann Arndt (1555–1621), Spener produced what promptly became something of a manifesto for the Pietist movement: the short treatise *Pia Desideria* ("Pious Longings"). Spener's preface was published separately within a just a few months, and was read extensively throughout Europe. Pietism was a reform movement within the Reformation whose day had come:

> Beginning late in the seventeenth century, Protestant theology, especially the Lutheran theology of the North German states, enjoyed a slow but distinctive revival of energies. Lutheranism had long lost the crusading fervor and intellectual vigor of its founder and settled down into a rigid, obtuse, authoritarian

---

80. Ibid.
81. Ibid., 150–51.

clerical hierarchy more interested in the minutiae of observance and quibbles on dogma than the great tenets of faith.[82]

By contrast, Pietist Spener taught that the essence of religion was a practical and personal faith aimed at meeting the subjective needs of the "inner person." "The value of a belief, he maintained, depended wholly upon its practical bearing . . . and [Spener] assumed a freer attitude than was customary toward the official symbols."[83] Ceremonious ecclesiastical practice, doctrinal exactitude, or formal assent to creeds did not a true Christian make. According to the Pietist impulse, it was insufficient to claim technical knowledge of doctrine or of the Scriptures; the individual must become a true Christian by means of a subjective experience of the "grace and illumination of the Holy Spirit." To many, this was received as a refreshing antidote to the arid intellectualism to which, they perceived, Protestant Christianity had become captive.

> At the close of the Thirty Years' War, religious life in Protestant Germany was at a low ebb. The control of the Church by the civil government in the various principalities did not make for spirituality. The interpretation of saving faith in terms of intellectual assent, the prevalence of scholasticism, the emphasis upon formal Orthodoxy, the absorption of the leading men of the Church in theological controversy, all tended to depress the religious and moral life of the country . . . .[84]

Pietism was in many ways a revival within the calcified Evangelical traditions of Europe. The charisma of the Reformers seemed to have become routinized, and the spirit of Protestantism had become congested by the stifling atmosphere of fastidious scholasticism and entombed in the mausoleum of establishment ecclesiasticism. Pietism was an attempt to salvage the deeply buried Reformation concerns for warm, personal faith and a return of the Bible to hands (and, hopefully, hearts) of the laity:

> The strength of Pietism lay in its stress on religion not only as inwardness but as a way of life whose dynamic was prayer and the study of scriptures. Theology was valued much less as an intellectual quest than as a means to spiritual enrichment, as a matter of the heart to be tested in experience. Thus the cardinal Lutheran doctrine of justification *sola fide* signified above all the individual's

82. Gay, *The Enlightenment*, 328.
83. McGiffert, *Protestant Thought before Kant*, 155.
84. Ibid.

inner re-birth, its formal definition being something wholly subordinate. Similarly, the Bible was to be read as the source of the believer's personal knowledge of divine revelation.[85]

The thrust of Pietism was the notion that the Reformation had only done a half job: purification of church doctrine was all well and good, but it was imperative to move from doctrine to purity of life. In a notion that was closer to Catholicism than Lutheranism, Spener suggested that sanctification could not be distinguished from justification. Assurance of salvation (justification) must be grounded in more than mere creedal assent, but must find its confidence in the transformed life. "Only when the life is actually changed and the spirit and motive of Christ control one's conduct, has a person any right to think he has been born again and is to be counted of the number of the saved."[86] Spener saw Christian conduct in largely otherworldly terms: "Not, as with Luther, victory over the world, but escape from it was his ideal. Piety was to show itself in devotion to spiritual and supernal things, and in the transfer of affection and interest from one world to another."[87]

Pietism's popular appeal also attested to the desire of many to find respite from the rapidly progressing rationalism and scientism of the age. A significant sign of this retreat is the transposition of orthodox doctrine with subjective religious experience as the primary criterion for membership within the typical Pietistic Christian community. One need not profess belief in certain dogmas to be admitted into fellowship so much as it was necessary to confess the fervent experience of being "born again." Fear that the Christian faith was being destroyed by Enlightenment reason led some to remove faith from the realm of objective verifiability altogether and ground it wholly in the subjective. This was considered a "safe" move because science, by its very nature, could never affirm or deny inward experience. Yet, for many mainstream Protestants, the inward turn of the Pietists appeared to dangerously elevate the doctrine of justification above all others—and at that a radically experiential version of the doctrine, finally making a certain brand of religious experience and enthusiasm the test of true orthodoxy.

Pietism had begun with the intent to leaven the larger church. The pure, regenerate smaller church communities within the larger church body (*ecclesiola in ecclesia*) were intended to be a purifying agent for the

---

85. Reardon, *Kant as Philosophical Theologian*, 7.
86. McGiffert, *Protestant Thought before Kant*, 159.
87. Ibid.

corrupt system. However, in spite of this original aim to affect the whole from within, Pietism soon became viewed as an entity unto itself, as a distinct *collegia pietatis*, "in which their religious life found expression apart from the Church and its organised ministrations."[88] Oddly enough, while the ethic of Pietism called individuals to withdraw from the world, it also (if subconsciously) began to call them to withdraw, to some extent at least, from the church! The visible church became equated, not with the spiritual realm of salvation, but with the inwardly-focused, manageable *collegia pietatis*. "Salvation meant escape from an evil world for a few elect souls who banded together for spiritual communion and mutual edification, and these souls were not the Christian Church, but a small circle within the larger body."[89]

"Creed of the Heart"

Thus, within the reform movement of Pietism, the subjectivism and individualism (fueled by a radically anti-clerical understanding of the "priesthood of believers") itself tended to move toward detachment from the orthodox ecclesial traditions and forms (which it had once intended to temper), ever inclining toward excessive self-absorption. Even the characteristic spontaneity of Pietism often became just as routinized (in subjective demands, as well as moral) as the rigid orthodox Scholasticism against which the Pietists were reacting. Reardon notes: "[I]t came too readily to be assumed that every believer, as evidence of his vocation, should have undergone a certain type of conversion-experience, following a specific pattern."[90] For many, religious emotion became the distinctive mark of God's acceptance.

> Pietism demanded that justification and rebirth be actually experienced and not merely regarded as orthodox Christian doctrines. It was, in short, an attempt to revive Christianity as a living religion. This end it would achieve by two means—prayer, and a diligent study of the Bible.... Pietism, finally, proclaimed a new individualism. Religion was no longer to be the concern solely of skilled theologians, but the heritage of the common man, who was now encouraged to find God for himself. Yet, as often happens, the very strength of pietism became its weakness. The laudable importance

88. Ibid., 158.
89. Ibid., 160.
90. Ibid.

assigned to the Christian experience developed into an exaggerated, almost fanatical demand (bordering upon superstition) for a certain violent and mystical kind of conversion.[91]

Pelikan writes that the Evangelical Protestant preoccupation with "certainty" in salvation had now manifested itself in the worst fears and "perennial Roman Catholic criticism" of the Protestant "subjective scholastic definition of grace" and a "subjective definition of faith as 'assurance.'"[92] "Pietism, whether radical or conservative, was perceived as a threat to Reformation orthodoxy in the doctrine of justification because by its subjectivism it appeared to make that danger a reality."[93]

The churches of the Reformation had issued confessional statements in "confusing variety" and monotonous detail. Many wars with words, not to mention with swords, resulted from the attempts of Protestants to remove themselves from the authority of the despotic medieval church and their perpetual fragmentation from one another. It seemed obvious to many that all this fastidious attention to doctrinal detail and ecclesiastical demarcation did little or nothing to contribute to the creation of authentic Christian faith and life. This state of affairs, coupled with the enthusiastic sense of human autonomy and rational endowment brought on by the impact of Enlightenment epistemological shifts, brought on a serious challenge to orthodoxy. "To many defenders as well as to most critics of traditional belief, the search for the essence of true religion as an objective 'presence of things outside myself' appeared to have bankrupted itself."[94]

Thus, the path was paved for the modern, Evangelical notion of faith, not as confession of a creed, but confession of an experience, a "creed of the heart." As Pietist Zinzendorf comments, "This our confession, this religion of the heart, transforms all those symbolical books whose truth it accepts into sheer creeds of the heart."[95] Zinzendorf even went so far as to suggest that "when a child at its first communion declared, 'I do not understand all of this, but it does give me a good feeling,' that it was 'not so bad,' since 'Scripture calls that a feeling which is often as good as if the

---

91. Greene, "The Historical Context and Religious Significance of Kant's *Religion*," xiii.

92. Pelikan, *Christian Doctrine and Modern Culture*, 142.

93. Ibid.

94. Ibid., 122.

95. Pelikan, *Christian Doctrine and Modern Culture*, 123, citing Zinzendorf, *Public Addresses to the Congregation [Offentiliche Gemelin Reiden Beyreuther]*.

person understood the words themselves."⁹⁶ Heart religion came to be seen as prior to, defining of, and, finally, the ultimate judge of any creedal formulation. Indeed, "if all the symbolical books were to be destroyed, they could be reconstructed from what lay in the hearts of true believers."⁹⁷

> The dichotomy between the authenticity of this private "theology of the heart" and the artificiality of the public and political confessional theology of the public and political confessional theology of the churches, between "private" and "public" religion, was an epitome of the crisis of orthodoxy.... Each in its own way, therefore, the major creeds and confessions of the historic churches all lent themselves to transposition in the light of the theology of the heart.⁹⁸

As the Enlightenment has transformed modern Protestant thought, virtually every branch of this tradition has seen this "transposition" in one form or another, from modernist or liberal Christianity, to existentialist stylings of faith. By the same token, in Evangelicalism's reaction to this "cultural climate," "something of a complete inversion has occurred."⁹⁹ Historically, this "complete inversion" has been well documented in the shape and development of both liberal and existential forms of Protestantism. Ernst Troeltsch noted that the liberal tradition has espoused a "theology of subjective experience in contrast to the theology of objective revelation: the sole value it assigns to Jesus is that of serving as the original stimulator of the religious consciousness."¹⁰⁰

Likewise, Avery Dulles suggests that existentialist theology stresses an "infinite subjective passion that impels the believer to embrace as subjectively certain what is offensive, even absurd, to human speculation."¹⁰¹ Both liberal and existentialist Protestantism have been censured, however, for their seemingly flippant attitude toward historic orthodoxy. In apparent contrast, however, those in the Evangelical tradition have maintained

---

96. Pelikan, *Christian Doctrine and Modern Culture*, 128, citing Zinzendorf, *Remarkable Conversations between a Traveller and Various Other Persons, Concerning All Sorts of Truths Connected with Religion [Isonderbare Gespruche vorkommenden Warheiten]*.

97. Pelikan, *Christian Doctrine and Modern Culture*, 123.

98. Ibid., 122.

99. Ballard, "Evangelical Experience," 52.

100. Troeltsch, *The Social Teaching of the Christian Churches*, 796.

101. Dulles, *Assurance of Things Hoped For*, 80.

a reputation for clinging tenaciously to the objective revelation of historic Christian orthodoxy.

These typical perspectives are based in something of a caricature of the modern age. The clear lines between the "liberals" and "existentialists," who presumably disdain the historic essence of orthodoxy, and the "Evangelicals," who hold orthodoxy fast against the onslaught of modernism, are not easily drawn. One finds upon investigation that commitment to traditional orthodox dogma is surprisingly varied on all sides of this triangle, while a common thread of modernity still runs through all these post-Enlightenment religious expressions. In all cases, from the modern religious agnosticism of Kant, which in some respects spawned both the liberalism of Schleiermacher and the subjectivism of Kierkegaard, to the religious affections of the Anglo-American Evangelical revivalist phenomenon, one discovers the same value of the knowing subject and a driving impulse toward the subjective justification of religious belief. In all cases, one finds the same profound commitment to the "religion of the heart."

2

Within the Bounds of Reason Alone

The Subjective Justification of Religious Belief in the Thought of Immanuel Kant

> *"True religion is to consist not in the knowing or considering of what God does or has done for our salvation, but in what we must do to become worthy of it . . . and of whose necessity every man can become wholly certain without any Scriptural learning whatever."*[1]
>
> —Immanuel Kant, *Religion within the Limits of Reason Alone*

IMMANUEL KANT (1724–1804) is rightly considered both a product and a distinct representative of the historical period of thought commonly known as the "age of Enlightenment."[2] "Enlightenment," according to his

---

1. Kant, *Religion within the Limits*, 123.

2. Kant, of course, insisted that the Western world had far from arrived at a state of enlightenment, yet he believed it was clearly making progress. Kant contrasted the notion of living in "an enlightened age" with the present "age of enlightenment" he believed himself to be living in. Kant, "What is Enlightenment," 90–91. An "age of enlightenment" was an age of inquiry during which "to criticism everything must submit." Kant, *Critique of Pure Reason* (tr. Smith), 9, note a. Enlightenment was an ideal, a hope for Western humanity, but not yet a full reality.

oft-quoted definition, "is man's release from his self-incurred tutelage."[3] In the essay, *Was ist Aufklärung?* Kant argued that in order for Western society to be considered truly enlightened, it would require the persistent, proactive effort of casting off intellectual domination by external authorities. It was Kant's appraisal that the attenuated custody of individual thought under the moral and intellectual supervision of others was now coming (and, indeed, *must* come) to an end. *Aufklärung*, while not yet fully realized in European culture, was, nonetheless offering a kind of official notification that the imperious reign of external authority over human thinking was no longer practicable, much less desirable.

And yet, while this sort of epistemic "declaration of independence" was being published widely by his day, Kant believed that the real "revolution" had yet to be fought. He wanted to be clear, however, that the battleground did not exist merely in the realm of the authorities themselves, but within the will of each self-conscious person. Many demurred at the prospect of such emancipation. Kant insisted that this hesitancy resulted, not from a fundamental deficiency in reasoning abilities, but as a consequence of a long-reinforced reverential fear of the patriarchate. This created a perceptible trepidation, on the part of some, about the unknown liabilities of unconstrained theoretical freedom. It was clear that these apprehensions about the uncharted terrain of intellectual autonomy tended to keep humans in captivity. But this was not the complete story. No doubt the authorities could often be puissant and autarchic, stubbornly refusing to convey such liberty to the individual. Nevertheless Kant laid much of the blame at the feet of the intellectually oppressed themselves. He did not hesitate to suggest that whatever tutelage Europeans had experienced had been largely self-incurred.

Kant insisted that Western humanity was principally responsible for its own indentured servitude. He wondered why so many demurred at the prospect of emancipation from the "land of slavery," refusing to lay claim to this "promised land" of intellectual liberation. The explanation, Kant thought, was found in a deep-rooted laziness and cowardice which constrained the already reluctant individual from making proper use of

---

3. Kant, "What is Enlightenment," 85. *"Aufklärung ist der Ausgang des Menschen aus seiner selbstverschuldeten Unmündigkeit."* Kant, *Was ist Aufklärung?* This short article, written by Kant for the journal *Berlinische Monatsschrift*, was a response (in addition to other authors, such as Moses Mendelssohn and Gotthold Lessing) to the question posed by the publication's editorial staff, "What is Enlightenment?" Kant, "What is Enlightenment," 92, fn. 4.

his understanding without direction from another. Many were reluctant to embrace deliverance because they were far too comfortable in their confinement, for far too long. It was simply easier to remain compliant under the intellectual charge of others rather than take up the arduous (and risky) task of thinking autonomously. "It is so comfortable to be a minor!" wrote Kant, and thus humans had manifested "a lack of resolution and courage to use [religion] without direction from another." It remained to be seen if Europe would be able to marshal sufficient courage and resolution to advance and sustain the Enlightenment impulse.

To Kant, Enlightenment was a proposed "exit" or "way out" (*Ausgang*), which was "conceived of in a negative way as a (continuous) refusal of prescriptive forms of authority."[4] Thus, Kant deemed "*sapere aude!*" to be a fitting Enlightenment motto.[5] "Have the courage to use your own reason!"[6] He proffered this as the shibboleth of the modern epistemic revolution—a heraldic ensign of liberation from the relentless oversight and control of the traditional authorities. This optimistic maxim was put forth as a clarion call for Western culture to bring to an end its protracted noetic adolescence.[7] The summons was to cast aside the intellectual superintendence of others—to take a few steps on one's own—even at the risk of stumbling (and learning from one's missteps). The prospect of widespread "enlightenment" on the continent seemed very hopeful and inspiring indeed.

Nevertheless, despite the sense of expectancy in the air of Europe, Kant knew that such enlightenment would not come easily. Even if many individuals diligently pursued such autonomy, the overseers of thought would not swiftly grant it. Indeed, Kant himself would come into conflict with both the state and religious authorities (which, in most respects, were inseparable)[8] for his novel ideas. When Frederick William II ascended

---

4. Ibid., 263.

5. Want and Klimowski, *Introducing Kant*, 151.

6. Kant uses the word "*Wahlspruch*" which means literally "a heraldic device, but metaphorically a motto or instruction." Ibid.

7. Ibid., 263.

8. *Cuius regio, eius religio*. Apart from the "Radical Reformers," the old "Constantinian synthesis" of church and state remained unchallenged by the primary Reformers and their heirs. The Peace of Augsburg (1555) was an attempt to determine the faith of each region by permitting each lay prince to decide whether his province would be professing Catholic or Lutheran (no other Protestants were recognized). Nevertheless, this "peace" broke down and was followed by the horrors of the Thirty Year War (1618–48) in which this fragmented version of the "Constantinian synthesis" continued to collide with the theological divisions of the Reformation and territorial divisions of the principalities.

to the throne, he appointed a thoroughgoing Pietist named Wollner to the post of Prussian Minister of Education. Wöllner was no admirer of *Aufklärung* principles. This inaugurated a period of strict censorship and ended an era of high culture and intellectual toleration undertaken by the preceding ruler, Frederick the Great (Kant had once referred to the "age of enlightenment" as "the century of Frederick"[9]). Soon, however, Wöllner would charge Kant with violation of official Protestant Lutheran orthodoxy and distortion of the teachings of Scripture for his own philosophical purposes.[10] The result was an official invective from the King of Prussia himself insisting that Kant completely refrain from lecturing or writing on the subject of religion.

Theological conflict resulted in armed conflict in central Europe, bringing not only Catholic against Protestant in battle, but German Protestant against German Protestant. See Walker, *The History of the Christian Church*, 528–34, 551–59. Also, Olson, *Story of Christian Theology*, 448.

9. Kant, "What is Enlightenment," 91.

10. Though Enlightenment thought had been tolerated by Frederick the Great, it had not spread widely. The city of Königsberg, while the home of a university (the Collegium Albertinum, founded 1544), had so declined into "provincial obscurity by mid-eighteenth century" that when crown Prince Frederick the Great visited in 1739, he remarked that the city was "better suited to the training of bears than to become a theatre of the sciences" (Scruton, *Kant*, 3). Still, during his reign, Frederick the Great did much to create a progressive society, and gave the University much intellectual latitude. Kant took full advantage of this freedom in his publications during this period. However, upon Frederick William II's ascendency to the Prussian throne, the antecedent policies of religious toleration were soon curtailed. Initially, Kant was left untouched by the official purge, because, according to one royal advisor, he was perceived as an old man, whom few people actually read, and even fewer understood what they read. However, his essay *Religion within the Limits of Reason Alone* was manageable enough in size, and the writing was lucid enough to finally catch the attention of the censors. Though the *Berliner Monatsschrift* had originally intended to publish the article, Wöllner, the Minister of Education, ordered the essay circumscribed. Soon, however, *Religion within the Limits of Reason Alone* was instead published "under the imprint of the Königsburg philosophy faculty, this escaping censorship on a point of law." Scruton, *Kant*, 8. In 1794, Kant would receive an authorized cabinet order from the Prussian King, declaring, "Our highest person has been greatly displeased to observe how you misuse your philosophy to undermine and destroy many of the most important and fundamental doctrines of the Holy Scriptures and of Christianity. We demand of you immediately an exact account, and expect that, in accordance with your duty, you will employ your talents and authority so that our paternal purpose may be more and more attained. If you continue to oppose this order you may expect unpleasant consequences." Paulson, *Immanuel Kant*, 49. Ever the dutiful citizen, Kant remained silent until King Frederick William II of Prussia died, believing that the king's death absolved him of the royal stricture. Still, he had already had his say.

Though this censure and reproach from the authorities did not surface until the 1790s, Kant seemed already braced for such acrimony in 1784, when he penned *Aufklärung*. As he wrote, Kant intimated that the historic "guardians" of thought still maintained a vested interest in keeping the people under the control of their austere "statutes and formulas, those mechanical tools of the rational employment, or rather misemployment of [mankind's] natural gifts," but, he warned, these "are the fetters of an everlasting tutelage."[11] People could readily find eager guardians who would "kindly" assume moral or intellectual superintendence over them, always willing to think on their behalf: "I need not think, if I can only pay—others will undertake the irksome work for me."[12] Thus, Kant believed that many would find the path of enlightenment to be quite difficult, since they had become so accustomed to having others think for them.

Eventually however, after following the precipitous path of independent thought, the individual would find much reward, and enlightened persons would soon be compelled to "disseminate the spirit of rational appreciation of both their own worth and every man's vocation for thinking for himself."[13] Slow and arduous though the development might be, the Enlightenment impulse had already germinated in the Western world, and maturation seemed inevitable. Kant wrote, "As nature has uncovered from under this hard shell the seed for which she most tenderly cares—the propensity and vocation to free thinking—this gradually works back upon the character of the people, who thereby gradually become capable of managing freedom."[14] So Kant asked himself the question, "Do we live in an *enlightened age*?" To which he categorically answered, "No," not yet. Far too much had to be accomplished before such an appellation would be accurate. "But," Kant readily added, "we do live in an *age of enlightenment*."[15] Principles of Enlightenment thought or practice were not yet in widespread use, yet the allure of these principles was increasingly apparent. The taste for Enlightenment existed, even if it had not yet become popularly widespread. Kant continues:

> As things now stand, much is lacking which prevents men from being, or easily becoming, capable of correctly using their own

11. Kant, "What is Enlightenment," 86.
12. Ibid., 85.
13. Ibid., 86.
14. Ibid., 92.
15. Ibid., 90.

reason in religious matters with assurance and free from outside direction. But on the other hand, we have clear indications that the field has now been opened wherein men may freely deal with these things and that the obstacles to general enlightenment or the release from self-imposed tutelage are gradually being reduced. In this respect, this is the age of enlightenment ....[16]

Religious Belief in an Age of Enlightenment

Immanuel Kant is credited with bringing "the opinions of his age into philosophical focus" while, at the same time, his contribution to philosophy became a significant "starting point for new ways of thought."[17] As such, he is simultaneously a byproduct and vocal advocate of, as well as a creative contributor to, Enlightenment thought. What Kant hoped to contribute to the Western world was a fuller application of Enlightenment principles to practical life; specifically in the realm of morality. Few people were more qualified than the author of *What is Enlightenment?* to discuss the nature and limits of Enlightenment epistemology. Within Kant's thought one can discern a distinctive shift in the modern understanding of how believing relates to knowing, a shift which has significantly influenced post-Enlightenment views of religious faith. Kant introduced an essential revolutionary change in epistemological orientation as he advocated liberation from ancient restrictions placed upon human reasoning. This change established the autonomous human subject as the pivotal figure in the knowing process. Humanity must be freed to think independently—apart from bondage to an external authority—no longer needing governance by "external direction."[18] Yet this call for Western humanity to "grow up" intellectually and decisively cut the proverbial "apron strings" of Mother Church implied a radical new role of authority for the central human subject.

To some this signaled the end of religious faith. It was feared that the epistemic reorientation of the Enlightenment would eliminate the need for the supernatural altogether. German poet Henrich Heine painted an unflattering portrait of Kant as the *Weltzermalmender*, "the great destroyer in the realm of thought."[19] Heine "portrayed Kant as a kind of theologi-

16. Ibid., 90–91.
17. Hampson, *The Enlightenment*, 196.
18. Kant, "What is Enlightenment," 85.
19. Heine, *Religion and Philosophy in Germany*, 107–21.

cal Robespierre, a soulless, ruthless, and incorruptible executioner of the Deity."[20] Kant's agenda, however, was actually far more sympathetic to religious faith than Heine and his ilk might admit. Indeed, his religious writings are somewhat apologetic in nature: Kant simply hoped to justify faith's proper place and role within an age of enlightened reason and science, he thought, to the benefit of both. In that oft-used phrase from the preface of the second edition of the *Critique of Pure Reason*, Kant succinctly summarizes his religious *modus operandi*: "I have therefore found it necessary to deny *knowledge* in order to make room for *faith*."[21]

Kant's Pietist Sensibilities

Immanuel Kant was nurtured in the culture of religious pietism and instructed in the tradition of Continental rationalism. Interestingly, some scholars suggest that both had played a significant role in the cultivation of the Enlightenment spirit. Theodore Greene wrote, "As an attempt to break down the traditional authority and dogmatism of the church, the *Aufklärung* assumed two mains [sic] forms, evangelical pietism and rationalistic deism."[22] Whether this is fully true or not, Bernard Reardon rightly suggests that there were at least some striking parallels between these seemingly otherwise disparate world views:

> That pietism and rationalism were opposed on a number of basic theological issues, in particular the place of revelation and the authority of the Bible, is incontestable, but they also had something in common, chiefly their antagonism to Lutheran orthodoxy, which by the middle of the seventeenth century had on its doctrinal side hardened into scholasticism, and on its institutional side hardened into a formalistic churchiness.[23]

20. Wood, *Kant's Rational Theology*, 15.
21. Kant, *Critique of Pure Reason*, 29.
22. Greene, "Historical Context," xii.
23. Reardon, *Kant as Philosophical Theologian*, 4–5. Reardon notes that "to argue that Enlightenment thinking actually sprang from pietism is a mistake. The influences determining the former were many and complex, and in the main antecedent to the latter's appearance. More satisfactory is it to regard the two movements as in a sense parallel, alike hostile to the prevailing ecclesiasticism and theologism." Ibid., 5. Yet, I would add that these parallel movements of Enlightenment and Pietism have both drunk deeply at the well of modernity, and thus share some common values about the veridical nature of human subjectivity.

Kant, of course, eventually moved significantly from both the Pietism of his youth and the strict rationalism of his formal education. But each left an indelible mark on his mature philosophy, in terms of both what he saw as important and what he eventually rejected.

Immanuel Kant's parents were devout Lutheran Pietists, and family life was marked by a not altogether unhappy, meagre subsistence and pious simplicity. Kant's early nurture and education came from within this strong religious heritage, and even when he came to a more substantial livelihood, he lived with an artless austerity characteristic of his Pietist forebears. His faithful, but formally uneducated, mother was perhaps the strongest intellectual influence in Immanuel Kant's early years. Frau Kant was said to demonstrate a vast "natural intelligence":

> It was this which particularly influenced her son Immanuel or Manelchen as she called him ("Little Manny"). Kant's mother would take him for walks in the countryside and tell him the names of the plants and flowers. At night she would show him the stars, naming them and their constellations. She was a pious woman, and her loving but austere ways also helped shape her son's moral character. This dual insistence on facts and moral obligation was to remain with Kant throughout his life and played a leading role in his philosophy. Kant's most celebrated remark, made over fifty years later, harks directly back to these early days with his mother: "The starry heavens above and the moral law within fill the mind with an ever new and increasing admiration and awe, the more often and the more steadily we reflect."[24]

At age eight, Kant enrolled in the city of Königsberg's *Gymnasium Fridericianum*, which was "run on the strictest pietist lines."[25] Kant remained there until he was sixteen years old, and while he had flourished intellectually, he found the religious instruction and devotional exercises oppressive. Kant certainly did not reject everything he learned from the Pietists. He saw some value in the emphasis upon inwardness. As he wrote to a friend, F. T. Rink, a pastor in Danzig:

> Even if the religious consciousness of that time, and the conceptions of what is called virtue and piety were by no means clear and satisfactory, it yet contained the root of the matter. One may say of pietism what one will: it suffices that the people to whom it was a

24. Strathern, *Kant*, 10–11.
25. Ibid., 19.

serious matter were distinguished in a manner deserving of all respect. They possessed the highest good which man can enjoy that repose, that cheerfulness, that inner peace which is disturbed by no passions. No want or persecutions rendered them discontent: no controversy was able to stir them to anger or enmity.[26]

But Kant never really developed a taste for the rigorous outward forms of Pietism, even though the focus on the interior life and simple existence remained with him to the end. A former classmate, the famous philologist David Ruhnken, wrote to Kant at a later date: "thirty years have passed since the two of us groaned beneath the pedantically gloomy, but not entirely worthless, discipline of those fanatics."[27] Kant shared this uneven and mixed assessment of his Pietist grooming. He relished the mental discipline of some of his mentors, and yet found the restrictive environment to be stifling and oppressive. Kant's dissatisfaction with these narrowly circumscribed intellectual boundaries mirrors his later negative attitudes toward "alien guidance" that drove his appeal for Enlightenment. In a citation gleaned from one of Kant's lectures on education, note the parallel theme as he muses on the subject of youth: "Many people imagine that the years of their youth are the pleasantest and best of their lives: but it is not really so. They are the most troublesome: for we are then under strict discipline, can seldom choose our friends, and still more seldom have our freedom."[28]

Eventually, in reaction to the onerous zeal of his preceptors, young Kant reached a "point where he rejected all prayer"[29] and abandoned churchgoing for life. The external practices of the Pietists, observed Kant, all too readily developed into insincere conventionalism. Peter Gay says, "Pietism, with its democratic confidence in religious experience, its impatience with doctrine and ratiocination, secured wide support, but gradually it hardened into an orthodoxy of its own."[30] Likewise, Pietism's "extravagant demands for visible conversion and effusions of religious feeling gave birth to scenes of revivalist enthusiasm and to sentimental poetry of embarrassing banality."[31] Kant learned from some respected teachers of the

26. Paulson, *Immanuel Kant*, 28, quoting Rink, *Ansichten aus Immanuel Kants Leben*.
27. Scruton, *Kant*, 2.
28. Ibid.
29. Friedrich, *The Philosophy of Kant*, xvi.
30. Gay, *The Enlightenment*, 328.
31. Ibid.

Pietist tradition, but he had no taste for what his classmate Ruhnken had pinpointed as the repressively pedantic and somber religious codes of the "fanatics" at the *Fridericianum*.[32]

Most of the religious orientation of this movement was readily forsaken by the adult Kant. Yet certain elements of Pietism "left a permanent impression on Kant's own outlook," not the least of which were "its ethical and philanthropic concern, and its belief that the real value of Christian doctrine is to be assessed in moral terms . . . despite his later reaction against what he came to see as a rather mawkish religiosity forced upon him in his youth."[33] Peter Gay states that even Kant did not hesitate to affirm that at best Pietism offered its devoted "that calm, that cheerfulness, that inner peace that is disturbed by no passion."[34]

> As a consequence even Kant—who repudiated all but the most abstract religion, who condemned enthusiasm and refused to engage in any religious observance—paid Pietism the unconscious tribute of incorporating some of its teachings into his work: its love of peace both in public and domestic life, its inner sweetness, and its conviction that religion depends not on dogma or ritual or prayer but on experience.[35]

Kant's "unconscious tribute" to his Pietist heritage may seem at first glance quite inconsistent with his other commitments to a "religion within the limits of reason alone." But it must be understood that Kant used "rational" with a quite limited meaning. This was true for his "rational religion," as well as within the rest of his philosophy, but in contrast to contemporary thought. "It is as if he had sought to mediate between pietism and rationalism, between mysticism and science, by restricting both to their respective spheres in the mind of man."[36] Protestant scholastic orthodoxy, as it had developed within the *milieu* of the Aristotelian renaissance of reason, depended much upon the construction of a Christian doctrine along rational lines, as well as the rational defense of the faith. Pietism was suspicious of this synthesis of worldly wisdom with "pure doctrine,"[37] fearing the consequent deposition of faith. Distinct from, though surprisingly similar in

---

32. Friedrich, *The Philosophy of Kant*, xvi.
33. Ibid.
34. Gay, *The Enlightenment*, 328, citing Cassirer, *Kant's Life and Thought*, 18.
35. Ibid., 328–29.
36. Friedrich, *The Philosophy of Kant*, xv.
37. Spener, *Pia Desideria*, 22.

many ways to, Kant's Enlightenment rejection of dogmatic rationalism, Pietism was "a prophecy of a new age to come."[38]

> The vitalising of Christian piety, the breaking of scholasticism's control, the recognition of religious experience as the chief basis of theology, the emphasis upon the will instead of the intellect in religion, the prominence given to the emotions, and above all the individualism of the whole movement and its hostility to ecclesiasticism, sacramentarianism, and sacerdotalism, meant much for days to come. Pietism was one of the forces which brought the modern age in the religious life of Germany.[39]

Kant, though for different reasons, would likewise challenge the syllogistic justification of religious belief, anticipating the eventual demise of faith under the crushing force of rationalism. Thus, he shared with his Pietist primogenitors a disdain for scholasticism and an appreciation for the subjective power of faith.

That Kant retained even the most minute elements of his youthful Pietism is both remarkable and fortuitous for the direction of modern philosophy. "Most educated Lutherans repelled by orthodoxy bypassed Pietism altogether," yet the young Kant managed to construct a "peculiar alliance between rationalist proofs and Pietist religious sensibility."[40] The mature Kant, sufficiently roused from the respite of rationalism, still clung to the essence of Pietism, yet without the traditional dogmatic substance. In the end, Kant posited an alternative which both exploited and surpassed "the anti-intellectualism of the Pietists and the intellectualism of religious metaphysicians"[41] —the two prominent trends in the German Lutheranism of his day.

> [T]he influence of pietism upon Germany was considerable; in its individualism, its emphasis upon the practical side of religion, and its opposition to the dogmatism of the church, it helped to prepare the way for, and indeed formed part of the vanguard of, the *Aufklärung*. . . . [I]ts influence on Kant's life and teaching was profound.[42]

---

38. McGiffert, *Protestant Thought before Kant*, 161.
39. Ibid.
40. Gay, *The Enlightenment*, 329.
41. Ibid., 328.
42. Greene, "Historical Context," xiv.

The Synthetic *A Priori*

The Pietist Lutheran Church and the pastor of Immanuel Kant's youth funded his matriculation at the University of Königsberg, as both Kant's parents were deceased. It was taken for granted that he would become a divinity student, and be ordained as a Lutheran pastor.[43] But Kant soon tired of theological studies[44] and turned to the reading of physics, mathematics, and philosophy. However, the concerns of theology never left Kant: all of his major philosophical works deal with the question of God's knowability. "One must believe," wrote Berkhof, "that it was his deepest desire to save God for an enlightened culture and thus to save the Enlightenment itself."[45] Upon graduation, Kant tutored students as a private docent (unsalaried) in a variety of subjects, ranging from natural theology and "philosophical encyclopædia" to anthropology and geography.[46] Though in his entire life Kant never travelled very far beyond the boundaries of his native city, he was a fathomless catalogue of trivial details (often surprisingly accurate, sometimes laughably misinformed) about remote regions and cultures which he had never seen with his own eyes. But for all this academic range (Kant was once even offered a professorship in poetry!), it was the study of philosophy that fired his imagination. In 1770 Kant was appointed professor of logic and metaphysics, a post he held until he retired some twenty-seven years later.[47]

Kant's philosophical mind was formed within the strong tradition of continental rationalism that dominated German universities at the time. While a student at the University, he developed a commitment to the necessity of pure mathematical reasoning and the rationalist philosophical method of such thinkers as Newton, Spinoza, and Leibniz. In the same vein, the writings of Baron Christian von Wolff made a profound impact on the rationalism of young Kant. Wolff had done for Germany (though in a less sophisticated way) what John Locke had done for Britain and North

---

43. Brown, *Christianity and Western Thought*, 1:309.

44. Kant's Latin studies led him to the reading of Lucretius and in particular his poem *De Rerum Natura*, which moved Kant toward a more naturalistic or at least deistic, view of reality. The naturalism of Lucretius offered young Kant the capacity to extricate himself from the highly dependent Pietism of his adolescence. Brown, *Christianity and Western Thought*, 1:309.

45. Berkhof, *Two Hundred Years of Theology*, 1.

46. Scruton, *Kant*, 4.

47. Thilly, *History of Philosophy*, 395.

America. He had constructed a rational approach to religion which attempted to reconcile reason and revelation (though, unlike the medieval Christian solution, a revelation which was clearly judged by reason). Christian Wolff was immensely popular in German intellectual circles, though he was, by most accounts, a "facile popularizer" of Locke presenting a softened, "vulgarized" version of Leibniz to a cautiously modern audience who likely "found Leibniz's own writings too demanding."[48]

> Wolff had a genius for taming rebellious ideas and grouping them under clear, memorable rubrics: he was a systematizer of military thoroughness, assigning a firm place to the most exalted of spiritual problems and the most trivial of mundane details. He was, we might say, an extreme moderate who allowed men to enjoy the security of religious tradition as they ventured into the excitement of modernity. Revelation, he taught, transcends reason but never contradicts it: there are a few—only a few—mysteries reserved to the sphere of the supernatural, but, Wolff assured his readers, men, preserving their awe before Christian marvels, could discover religious truth by their reason.[49]

Wolff's "comfortable Christian rationalism" presented to German society a "gently modernized Protestant orthodoxy: it was a perfect compromise for literate Christians anxious to justify nonrational beliefs with rational proofs."[50]

For young Kant, however, the comfort of rationalism would not endure for very long. Peter Gay wryly remarked, "Wolff . . . had put him to sleep,"[51] but his reading of skeptical empiricist David Hume soon awakened Kant from the "dogmatic slumber"[52] of scrupulous rationalism. Kant began to see that the deterministic conclusions of Spinoza and Leibniz ran counter to the human experience of freedom. Since it was a basic concern of Kant that philosophy should never be abstracted from human experience, he thought it necessary to affirm both reason and experience as true given their respective contexts of meaning. This *via media* proposed a resolution to the seemingly irreconcilable philosophical and extreme positions

---

48. Gay, *The Enlightenment*, 329.

49 Ibid. Wolff's carefulness and conservatism aside, even he (like Kant) came under the suspicion of the Prussian Ministry of Education. Under Frederick William, Wolff was censured, and was "exiled on suspicion of unorthodoxy." Hampson, *Enlightenment*, 63.

50. Gay, *The Enlightenment*, 329.

51. Ibid.

52. Kant, *Prolegomena to Every Future Metaphysic*, 45.

of rationalism and empiricism. "That all our knowledge begins with experience there can be no doubt," Kant acknowledges. "But, though all our knowledge begins with experience, it by no means follows that it all arises out of experience."[53] He goes on to suggest:

> [O]n the contrary, it is quite possible that our empirical knowledge is a compound of that which we receive through impressions, and that which the faculty of cognition supplies from itself (sensuous impressions giving merely the occasion), an addition which we cannot distinguish from the original element given by sense, till long practice has made us attentive to, and skillful in separating it.[54]

Kant's unique epistemological solution seeks a resolution between the seemingly antithetical "analytic *a priori*" of continental rationalism and the "synthetic *a posteriori*" of British empiricism.[55] The appeal of the rationalist tradition was found in that it had optimistically offered the prospect of mathematical certitude in philosophy, but was impractical in that it supplied no possibility for new knowledge within its tight geometric determinism. Rationalism tended to be confident, but often blindly uncritical of the limitations of reason. By contrast, the less pretentious empiricist tradition offered hope for gaining new knowledge beyond the merely trivial, but could never hope for real certitude. Empiricism promises only varying degrees of probability, because knowledge is arrived at by means of ever-changing impressions of sense data only to be imposed on a mind which is, until it receives the apperceptions of sensation, a blank slate. All knowledge begins with experience, but it also ends there.

Kant was critical of the short-sightedness of both systems. Agreeing, in part with the empiricists, Kant argued that "all our knowledge begins with experience," but, "it does not follow that it all arises out of experience."[56] He thought that *a priori* reasoning is useless if it is incapable of accounting for sense experience. Furthermore, sensation apart from some capacity to "make sense" of the experience is equally useless. "Knowledge is the prod-

---

53. Kant, *Critique of Pure Reason* (tr. Smith), 41.

54. Ibid, 41–42.

55. Kant defines analytic and synthetic in this way: "Either the predicate B belongs to the subject A, as something, which is (covertly) contained in this concept A; or B lies outside the concept A, although it does indeed stand in connection with it. In the one case I entitle the judgment analytic—in the other synthetic." *Critique of Pure Reason*, 48. By *a priori* Kant meant that knowledge is "absolutely independent of all experience," and by *a posteriori*, knowledge "gained solely from experience . . . ." Ibid., 43.

56. Ibid., 41.

uct of an interaction between our *percepts* mediated by sense-experience and the *concepts* which arise in our minds as the means of ordering and interpreting the percepts. Percepts without concepts are blind; concepts without percepts are empty."[57] True knowledge requires *both* understanding *and* sensation; thoughts alone are incapable of sensing, and the senses alone are incapable of thinking. "Only through their union can knowledge arise."[58] Sense experience provides raw data which comes from without, but the mind within is active in processing that data by means of an endowed aptitude to classify such material. It is perhaps anachronistic, but helpful, to think about the mind as a new computer, programmed with word-processing capacity, but without actual data until the physical experience of tapping the keyboard occurs. Once the data of experience is entered, it is properly arranged and distributed by the "program" of the mind. This is similar to Kant's notion of a synthetic *a priori*, his theoretical alternative to the epistemic obstructions he found in both traditions of rationalism and empiricism:

> We demand in every concept, first the logical form of a concept (of thought) in general, and secondly, the possibility of giving it an object to which it may be applied. In the absence of such an object, it has no meaning, and is completely lacking in content, though it may still contain the logical function which is required for making a concept out of any data that may be presented. Now the object cannot be given to a concept otherwise than in intuition; for though a pure intuition can indeed precede the object *a priori*, even this intuition can acquire its object, and therefore objective validity, only through the empirical intuition of which it is the mere form. Therefore, all concepts, and with them, all principles, even such as are possible *a priori*, relate to empirical intuitions, that is, to the data for a possible experience.[59]

In the course of knowing, then, empirical data does not enter a mere vacuum or encounter a passive *tabula rasa*. According to Kant, the mind brings something to the sense experience and is fully active in shaping knowledge. As such, while Kant agreed with Hume and the empiricists that there are no such things as innate ideas, he disagreed that all knowledge is thereby derived from sense experience. Rather than see knowledge as

57. Heron, *A Century of Protestant Theology*, 17.
58. Kant, *Critique of Pure Reason* (tr. Smith), 93.
59. Ibid., 43.

conforming to our experience, Kant suggests that experience instead conforms to our knowledge. The mind organizes sense experience, thus providing a basis for certainty (also contra Hume). It does this organization by means of the a priori categories of the mind. Even space and time are a subjective framework imposed on our experience, shaping the way we interpret reality. Kant saw space and time as "forms of intuition"[60] which belong to our *a priori* intuition, for "they apply to objects only insofar as objects are viewed as appearances, and do not present things as they are in themselves. The sole field of their validity: should we pass beyond it, no objective use can be made of them."[61] These categories function much like spectacles that cannot be removed. With these subjective categories we can perceive the sense data (*phenomena*) of the world, but we can never perceive *das Ding an sich,* or reality in itself (*noumena*). "While much can be said *a priori* as regards the form of appearances, nothing whatsoever can be asserted of the thing itself, which may underlie these appearances."[62]

While the mind does not contain actual innate *ideas* as the rationalists had suggested, it does, says Kant, contain *a priori* "categories" or "pure concepts of the understanding"[63] which aid in synthesizing human experiences into meaningful information. Such mental categories would be void of content prior to sensation, but, upon receiving raw sense data, they can immediately make certain determinations about the experience, bringing about true knowledge. For Kant, these determinations are: quantity (one/many), quality (positive/negative), relation (cause/effect, or, subject/predicate), and modality (possibility/impossibility).[64] These categories bring unity and significance to what would otherwise be indistinct and unintelligible sense experience. Such categories, along with the forms of sensibility or intuition (space and time), are lenses which affect the way we view and interpret reality. Working together, these functions produce a *Weltanschauung*—a coherent, integrated worldview sorted out from the variety of sense experiences received by the individual knower.

60. Ibid., 59.
61. Ibid., 80.
62. Ibid., 87.
63. Ibid., 111–19.
64. Each of these four concepts are broken down into three further categories respectively: unity, plurality, universality, reality, negation, limitation, substance, cause, togetherness, potentiality, actuality, necessity. Kant, *Prolegomena to Any Future Metaphysic*, 76.

Of course, this implies an essential unity in the knowing and sensing subject. The dualistic "ghost in a machine" of popular Cartesian thought simply would not do. In other words, the appropriation of sensory data and its subsequent categorization must occur within the same, wholly unified, subject. This Kant calls the "transcendental unity of apperception."[65] By "transcendental" Kant means "all knowledge which is occupied not so much with objects as with the mode of our knowledge of objects insofar as this mode of knowledge is to be possible *a priori*."[66] This refers to knowledge which is beyond direct experience, yet nevertheless is a necessary condition for the type of experience humans do have. Kant adds:

> All transcendental ideas . . . can be arranged in three classes: the first containing the absolute unity of the thinking subject; the second containing the absolute unity of the series of conditions of phenomena; the third the absolute unity of the series of the condition of all objects of thought in general. The thinking subject is the object-matter of psychology, the system of all phenomena (the world) the object-matter of cosmology, and the being which contains the highest condition of the possibility of all that can be thought (the Being of all being), the object-matter of theology.[67]

It is "transcendental illusion,"[68] says Kant, to regard these non-sensory ideas as objectively knowable and thus to attempt to prove them rationally or develop them into sciences. The "transcendental unity of apperception"[69] is understood to be a reality not because it is experienced *per se*, but because reality is necessarily experienced by means of it. It is assumed, not as one would determine that the lamp is on because it can be seen, but as one would conclude that the lamp is on because *by the lamp* one can see everything in the room. Indeed, the categories of the mind "are the essential postulates or presuppositions of all experience and reflection, and without them no coherent understanding would be possible."[70]

---

65. Kant, *Critique of Pure Reason* (tr. Smith), 25.
66. Ibid.
67. Ibid.
68. Ibid.
69. Ibid.
70. Heron, *A Century of Protestant Theology*, 17.

A Copernican Revolution in Epistemology

Richard Kroner suggests that "in Kant the modern principle of an anthropocentric philosophy reached its climax. . . . He . . . destroyed not only the cosmocentric scheme of ancient speculation and the theocentric one of medieval speculation, but also that of Descartes, Spinoza, and Leibniz."[71] Kant insisted that knowledge of objective reality is inherently limited by *both* the nature of experience *and* the categories of the mind. Neither the raw data of sensation nor the organization of that data in the mind can finally bring the knower full comprehension of the essential nature of objective reality. For, as soon as reality is experienced, meaning has already been thrust upon it by the categories of the mind. Thus Kant found it helpful to distinguish carefully between "*noumenal*" reality and "*phenomenal*" reality. *Phenomena* is the realm of sensation: the world as we experience it. *Noumena* is the thing-in-itself (*das Ding an sich*) which can never be known *apud se* ("in itself"). To know any thing at all means that the knowing subject is involved, thus making it impossible to have knowledge independent of the subjective process of signification which, by its very nature, brings something of the knower to the thing known. Therefore, knowledge cannot strictly be about the world as it is in itself, but only about the world as it is experienced and made sense of.

The resultant epistemic reversal places the noetic focus upon the subject rather than the object of knowledge. This is Kant's self-proclaimed "Copernican Revolution." For much as Polish astronomer Nicholai Copernicus (1473–1543) had challenged the then-orthodox Ptolemaic geocentric cosmology with his heliocentric view of the universe, Kant proposed an equally dramatic turnabout in epistemology: a shift of emphasis *from the object of knowledge to the knowing subject*. Kant writes:

> We here propose to do just what Copernicus did in attempting to explain the celestial movements. When he found that he could make no progress by assuming that all the heavenly bodies revolved around the spectator, he reversed the process, and tried the experiment of assuming that the spectator revolved while the stars remained at rest. We may make the same experiment with regard to the nature of object. If the intuition must conform to the nature of the objects, I do not see how we can know anything of them *a priori*. If, on the other hand, the object conforms to the nature of

---

71. Kroner, *Speculation and Revelation in Modern Philosophy*, 194.

our faculty of intuition, I can then easily conceive the possibility of such an *a priori* knowledge.[72]

The shift of concern to the subject stands in dramatic contrast to pre-Enlightenment epistemologies which concerned themselves primarily with the object of knowledge. Kant suggests the value of this type of epistemic reversal in the preface to the second edition of the *Critique of Pure Reason*:

> Hitherto it has been assumed that all our knowledge must conform to objects. But all attempts to extend our knowledge of objects by establishing something in regard to them a *priori*, by means of concepts, have, on this assumption, ended in failure. We must therefore make trial whether we may not have more success in the tasks of metaphysics, if we suppose that objects must conform to knowledge. This would agree better with what is desired, namely, that it should be possible to have knowledge of objects *a priori*, determining something in regard to them prior to their being given.[73]

The rigid, mathematical rationalism of continental thinkers Spinoza and Leibniz and the raw skepticism of British empiricist Hume had created a philosophical impasse. Kant broke through the deadlock with his innovative, critical evaluation of human reason. As we have seen, Kant's view of knowledge challenged the commonly accepted view that objects impress themselves upon a passive mind. Instead, Kant proposed that the mind is active in constructing knowledge, as it brings the *a priori* categories (pure reason) of the mind to bear upon the external stimuli of the world of objects. If true knowledge can only be attained by means of the synthetic *a priori* from the phenomena of our experience, then it follows that knowledge of the transcendent (that which is beyond phenomenal experience) is impossible. Hume's immoderate skepticism seemed to have demolished the prospect of metaphysics and transcendental truth with one powerful blow. But Kant thought he could demonstrate, despite Hume's levelling criticisms, the possibility of both metaphysics and belief in God. With the former grounded in pure reason and the latter in practical reason, Kant would forge a new metaphysic (the "forms of our understanding," and the "categories of our understanding" were, in Kant's thinking, inexorably metaphysical).

---

72. Kant, *Critique of Pure Reason* (tr. Meiklejohn), xxix.
73. Kant, *Critique of Pure Reason* (tr. Smith), 22

During what was called the "critical decade" (1770–80), Kant produced three of his major philosophical works, *Critique of Pure Reason*, *Critique of Practical Reason*, and *Critique of Judgment*. In brief, these three works deal sequentially with thought (theoretical reason), will (moral discernment), and emotion (aesthetic feeling).[74] True to the modern Cartesian project, all of Kant's philosophy begins from the premise of self-consciousness. "His three *Critiques* concern themselves respectively with the questions: 'What must a self-conscious being think?' 'What must he do?' and 'What must he find agreeable?'"[75] Kant's undertaking was ambitious to be sure, yet he confidently assured readers, "There is not a single metaphysical problem which has not been solved, or for the solution of which the key at least has not been supplied."[76]

Kant's first *Critique* also deals definitively (many think) with the classical Thomistic proofs for the existence of God. "None of the proofs, it is said, can reach across the chasm between that which the mind *constructs* and the objects which stimulate it to the constructive activity.... The emphasis by the existentialists upon subjectivity ('subjectivity is truth') has its roots in Kant's assertion of the eminent role of the subject in knowledge."[77] Knowledge of God would only be possible if God were immediately available as an object of our senses, or if God were, like one of the categories of understanding, demonstrably necessary to shaping our understanding. Kant saw all of Thomas' "five proofs" as essentially reducible to the same appeal as Anselm's ontological argument (that God, by definition as the perfect Being, must exist, since existence is necessary to perfection).

The cosmological argument, Kant taught, is nothing more than this: "If anything exists, an absolutely necessary being must also exist. Now, I, at least, exist. Therefore, an absolutely necessary being exists. The minor premise contains an experience, the major premise the inference from

---

74. Aristotle had divided up human psychical activity into thinking and willing, which had become the generally accepted view until Kant. See Copleston, *A History of Philosophy*, 1:320–50. To Aristotle's two-fold division, Kant added the third psychical activity of "feeling" to this diversion of the human mind, which soon gained wide approval. In many respects, one could argue that the modern and post-modern world have promoted this latter psychic activity of "feeling to supreme status, beyond reason or will. This is clearly the case in the realm of religious faith." Gilmore, "A Reappraisal of Liberal Apologetics," 369–70.

75. Scruton, *Kant*, 24.

76. Kant, *Critique of Pure Reason* (tr. Smith), 10.

77. Gilmore, "A Reappraisal of Liberal Apologetics," 370.

there being any experience at all to the existence of the necessary."[78] While this argument seems plausible, it is filled with several "pseudo-rational principles."[79] Not only is it a merely masked form of the ontological argument (which Kant deals with in turn), but "the principle of causality" which is evoked "has no meaning and no criterion for its application save only in the sensible world."[80] Kant's criticism of the teleological proof is similar. He sees both cosmological and teleological arguments as "only a disguised ontological proof."[81]

Against the ontological proof, Kant argues that a "necessarily existent Being" is a confusion of *existence* and *attributes*, and "no valid demonstration of God's existence can be founded on the concept of a necessary Being."[82] Kant exposes the ontological argument as a carefully constructed redundancy. For to define God as *ens realissimum* (the ultimately real being), and then to suggest that his existence is demanded by that very terminology is "a miserable tautology." Such a definition is not *synthetic* (truth based in empirical demonstration, but an attempt at being *analytic* (true based in validity of definition). And as such, the ontological proof has no basis in reality.

> We must ask: Is the proposition that *this* or *that thing* (which, whatever it may be is allowed as possible) exists, an analytic or synthetic proposition? If it is analytic, the assertion of the existence of the thing, adds nothing to the thought of the thing: but in that case either the thought, which is in us, is the thing itself, or we have presupposed an existence as belonging to the realm of the possible, and have then, on that pretext, inferred its existence from its internal possibility—which is nothing but a miserable tautology.... But if, on the other hand, we admit, as every reasonable person must, that all existential propositions are synthetic, how can we profess to maintain that the predicate of existence cannot be rejected without contradiction? That is a feature which is found only in analytic propositions, and is indeed precisely what constitutes their analytical character.[83]

78. Kant, *Critique of Pure Reason* (tr. Smith), 508.
79. Ibid., 509.
80. Ibid., 511.
81. Ibid., 524.
82. Heron, *A Century of Protestant Theology*, 17.
83. Kant, *Critique of Pure Reason* (tr. Smith), 504.

Only analytic statements are true by definition, but the ontological argument is existential, and therefore synthetic rather than analytic. Colin Brown explains, "We do not add to a thing by asserting that it exists. Whether a thing exists or not is not determined by definition but by the discovery of grounds from which its existence may be inferred."[84] As Kant says:

> *"Being"* is obviously not a real predicate: that is, it is not a concept of something which could be added to the concept of a thing. It is merely the positing of a thing, or of certain determinations, as existing in themselves. Logically, it is merely the copula of a judgment."[85]

He concludes, "We can no more extend our stock of theoretical insight by mere ideas, than a merchant can better his position by adding a few noughts to his cash account."[86]

Kant's ultimate point here is merely that God simply cannot be "proved" or "known" as a postulate of pure reason, since he cannot be observed as an object of science. "To advance to absolute totality by the empirical road is utterly impossible."[87] However, this does not invalidate God's existence or the possibility of belief. Kant argues,

> If, in connection with a transcendental theology, we ask, *first*, whether there is anything distinct from the world, which contains the ground of order of the world and of its connection in accordance with universal laws, the answer is that there *undoubtedly* is. For the world is a sum of appearances: and there must be some transcendental ground of the appearances, that is, a ground which is thinkable only by pure understanding. If, secondly, the question be, whether this being is substance, of the greatest reality, necessary, etc., we reply that *this question is entirely without meaning*. For all categories through which we can attempt to form a concept of such an object allow only of empirical employment, and have no meaning whatsoever when not applied, to objects of possible experience, that is, to the world of sense.[88]

---

84. Brown, *Christianity and Western Thought*, 1:319.
85. Kant, *Critique of Pure Reason* (tr. Smith), 504.
86. Ibid., 507.
87. Ibid., 523.
88. Ibid., 555–66.

From this, we may "undoubtedly" infer "a wise and omnipotent Author of the world," indeed, Kant says, "we not only may, but *must* do so."[89] But by no means may we "extend our knowledge beyond the field of possible experience," for if we ascribe to the idea of God "a validity that is absolute and objective, we should be forgetting that what we are thinking is a being in idea only" taking our start "from a ground which is not determinable through observation of the world."[90] Thus, says Kant, God's "objective reality cannot indeed be proved, but also cannot be disproved."[91] This equitable solution is possible because of Kant's transfer of theology from the realm of *pure* to *practical* reason.

Kant's second critical work, *Critique of Practical Reason*, continues the concern with the *a priori* aspects of reason, but in this case it is *practical* or moral reason that is the focus. But it must be clear that this is not, for Kant, a second *type* of reason, but the *one* pure reason oriented now toward the object of the will. As with the first *Critique*, the mind is active in an established manner by means of the a priori principles in moral experience. In the case of practical reason, unlike that of theoretical reason, humans could attain metaphysical insight: not *knowledge* per se, but *faith*. While the "categories of the mind" are the subjective tool of pure reason, it appears that the "categorical imperative" is the subjective tool of practical reason, or morality.

Kant's categorical imperative is an unqualified and unconditional deontological obligation for all reasoning beings to do what is right. Within the perimeters of practical reason, we can discern three fundamental ideas upon which this moral imperative is founded: first, the idea of God, the guarantor of moral law in the world; second, the idea of freedom of the will, humans are free moral agents, capable of choosing the good; third, immortality of the soul, which assures us of just reward and punishment in the life to come (if not now). These ideas of God, freedom, and immortality are the basis of religious faith, and the foundation for a properly moral life. The ideas of God, freedom, and immortality are useful and necessary for thinking about our place in the world.

In this assessment, Kant offered a new footing for religious belief: in the moral will—the "law within." This practical moral foundation replaced, for Kant, the theoretically rational, classical proofs for God's existence. It is

89. Ibid., 566.
90. Ibid., 566–67.
91. Ibid., 531.

in this sense that he offers a subjective justification for religious belief. Kant wrote, in his *Critique of Judgment*, that it is impossible to *cognize* God by means of observed causality in the universe (as Saint Thomas attempted):

> However, if I wish to *think* a supersensible Being (God) as an intelligence, this is not only permissible in a certain aspect of my employment of reason, it is unavoidable, but to ascribe to Him understanding and to flatter ourselves that we can *cognize* Him by means of it as a property of His is in no way permissible. For I must omit all those conditions under which alone I know an understanding, and thus the predicate which only serves for determining man cannot be applied at all to a supersensible object; and thereby, a causality thus determined, I cannot cognize what God is. . . . However, according to the analogy of an understanding, I can in a certain other aspect think a supersensible being without at the same time meaning thereby to cognize it theoretically, *viz.* if this determination of its causality concerns an effect in the world which contains a design morally necessary but unattainable by a sensible being.[92]

The Subjective Justification of Religious Belief

Faith is contrasted to knowledge according to Kant, yet it is nevertheless rational. Therefore, faith is linked, not to the theoretical realm of pure reason, but to the practical realm of morality. Faith is reasonable insofar as it directs moral choice and behavior. Faith is related to action, instead of abstract reasoning, for its own good. Kant thought that if faith could be entirely removed from the gaze of theoretical judgments, then it could be rescued from the ravages of Enlightenment scientific inquiry. "The grounds upon which Kant was to show the inability of reason to maintain the existence of God served equally well, he thought, as grounds to show the invalidity of all counter-assertions."[93] Thus, Kant thought it necessary to deny knowledge in the area of religious truth in order to make room for faith—more specifically, a faith which could remain undaunted in an age of mounting rational skepticism. C. Stephen Evans says, "Kant believes that true religion is best served by the critical destruction of dogmatic philosophical foundations:

---

92. Kant, *Critique of Judgment*, 252.
93. Evans, *Subjectivity and Religious Belief*, 31.

by removing spurious claims to religious knowledge, the true character of religious faith can emerge more clearly."[94] Elsewhere, he writes:

> Kant's critique of natural theology has often been viewed as a negative, even shattering analysis. And of course it is negative in the sense that Kant denies that any positive or theoretical knowledge of God is possible. But Kant himself was far from viewing his work as negative in the sense of "harmful to religious belief." As he puts it, "to deny that the service which the *Critique* renders is positive in character, would thus be like saying that the police are of no positive benefit, inasmuch as their main business is merely to prevent the violence of which citizens stand in mutual fear, in order that each may pursue his vocation in peace and security."[95]

In order to appreciate Kant's thinking on this matter, it is necessary to remember that he uses the term "reason" in at least two distinct ways: in his first two critical works, Kant speaks of both theoretical reason and practical reason. These are not merely two separate faculties of reason juxtaposed with one another. Instead, reason is one faculty with two distinct operations or applications. Theoretical reason is used to accrue understanding of the external world (though when Kant uses the word "reason" without qualification he typically means "theoretical reason").[96] "Practical reason, on the other hand, is employed to discern how one ought to behave in the world." Historically, "faith" had been seen as the response to divine revelation (as in Aquinas), but for Kant, faith is more properly connected to a natural morality common to all humans, without need for reference to special revelation.[97] Without denying the prospect of such revelation or the irrationality of such belief, Kant wishes to establish a moral faith not dependent upon special revelation. And in the end, this pure moral faith becomes the final arbiter and highest interpreter even of traditional revelation claims by historic church communities.[98]

Even when Kant's epistemological framework brought him to deny the value of the traditional proofs for the existence of God, he found it

---

94. Evans, *Faith beyond Reason*, 66.

95. Evans, *Subjectivity and Religious Belief*, 30–31.

96. Evans notes, however, that Kant's usage of terms varies "even within the theoretical sphere" where "there is an ambiguity. Kant sometimes uses the term 'reason' for the whole of the theoretical sphere, and sometimes uses it for a specialized part of the process of theoretical inquiry." Evans, *Faith beyond Reason*, 66.

97. Kant, *Religion within the Limits of Reason Alone*, 99–100.

98. Ibid., 100–105.

impossible to deny the existence of a moral law within human experience. In Kant's estimation, this inherent human morality was the essence of religion. Kant thought that human morality was essentially grounded in three ideas which "rise completely above the sphere of all possible experience . . . to which there exists in the whole extent of experience no corresponding object."[99] These transcendental or supersensible ideas of pure reason are: "God, Freedom (of will), and Immortality."[100] Such ideas produce moral behavior (note: it is the *ideas* which affect behavior, not the actual objective realities) because they keep before us the notion of a transcendent judge of human action, that humans are free (and, therefore, responsible) to choose the good, and that these choices have meaning and consequences even beyond temporal existence. God, freedom, and immortality are synthetic *a priori* judgments educed from the practical moral nature of the human subject. These three concepts, while they may not be known theoretically, certainly can be "known" practically as inferences from the moral *a priori*. And it is these three ideas (not so much their objective actuality or knowability) which produce practical morality, which is the *telos* of religion, anyway. In a sense, nothing can be gained by (theoretically) *knowing* about God that cannot be gained by (practically) *believing* in God; but much can be lost. Leaving religion under the scrutiny of modern science might result in the complete annihilation of faith. But removing it to the province of practical morality could preserve faith from judgment. Kant writes:

> For then a cognition of God and of His Being (theology) is possible by means of properties and determinations of His causality merely thought in Him according to analogy, which has all requisite reality in a practical reference, though *only in respect of this* (as moral). An ethical theology is therefore possible, for though morality can subsist without theology as regards its rule, it cannot do so as regards the final design which this proposes, unless reason in respect of it is to be renounced. But a theological ethic (of pure reason) is impossible . . . . It thus makes felt the need of a theology which shall determine the concept of God adequately for the highest practical use of reason, but it cannot develop this and base it satisfactorily on its proofs.[101]

---

99. Ibid., 4.
100. Ibid., 5.
101. Kant, *Critique of Judgment*, 338–39.

The genius of Kant's perspective is that it simultaneously preserved faith for the believer and removed faith from the attacks of the skeptic. Subjective religious belief is as difficult to prove as to disprove. "Kant did not just abolish knowledge to make room for faith: he believed it was *necessary* to do so, and he also felt that in doing so he was building an equally strong case against those who claim to have knowledge which is contrary to the religious position."[102] Kant insisted that knowledge of God cannot be founded upon pure reason as if it were a science. For while God's objective existence cannot be proved, it "also cannot be disproved by merely speculative reason." Thus God is "safe" from the acid tests of scientific inquiry. Richard Kroner summarizes Kant's argument in this syllogism:

> God is the Supreme being
> The knowledge of real beings requires empirical perception
> There is no empirical perception of the Supreme Being
> No knowledge of God is possible.[103]

John Skinner commented:

> The reason why no empirical knowledge of God is possible is because God is not an object. He cannot be reduced to the status of a thing among other things or to the status of an observable reality, and thus He cannot be found through the categories of scientific and empirical knowledge. With the possible exception of the so-called Chicago school, no natural theologian would be so bold as to say that God is an object. Instead, He is the perfect subject.[104]

Plato held belief (πιστις) to be at the level of mere opinion (δοξα, "what seems right"), which is one of the lowest levels of cognition. By contrast, Kant distinguishes between holding a belief (*Glaube*) and merely having an opinion (*Meinen*). "Opinion," he says, "is a consciously insufficient judgment, subjectively as well as objectively."[105] Opinion, then, is to hold something as true without sufficient evidence to warrant such a proposition, yet is not even "subjectively sufficient" to convince oneself that it is "true for me." When hard-pressed, such an opinion would be readily relinquished. Belief, on the other hand, is undaunted by the absence of evidence. While both opinion and belief lack the "objective sufficiency" of

---

102. Evans, *Subjectivity and Religious Belief*, 2.
103. Kroner, *The Primacy of Faith*, 42.
104. Skinner, "Rational Faith in Kant's Philosophy," 182.
105. Kant, *Critique of Pure Reason*, 461.

empirical knowledge ("truth for all"), belief is "subjectively sufficient" and is tenaciously held as a deep conviction ("truth for me").

Although proof for belief in God is "theoretically insufficient," belief still provides significant criteria for praxis. Carl Raschke wrote:

> The practical function of belief, indeed, interests Kant more than its epistemic content; and thus the question of belief in God boils down to how our conviction of his existence might help direct our lives. But the practical aspect of believing in God also depends on our consideration of the peculiarly moral elements in experience.[106]

Of course, not all beliefs carry such moral weight. Raschke adds, "there are certain types of beliefs which indeed we could hardly live without . . . [which] tend to certify in some manner our most deep felt intentions—in point of fact, our *moral intentions*."[107]

Kant's post-critical work *Religion within the Limits of Reason Alone* is an application of the critical judgments specifically to the Christian faith, or empirical religion. "His question is whether empirical (he has in mind mainly the Christian) religion, in its doctrinal, cultic, and institutional existence, can be considered an expression of the religion of reason developed in *The Critique of Practical Reason*."[108] Kant's solution is formally Protestant in that it tips its hat to the "authority" of Scripture, yet it is distinctly modern in the notion that even Scripture is to be judged by reason. Kant says,

> There is therefore no norm of ecclesiastical faith other than Scripture, and no expositor thereof other than pure *religion of reason* and *Scriptural scholarship* (which deals with the historical aspect of that religion). Of these, the first alone is *authentic* and valid for the whole world: the second is merely doctrinal, having as its end the transformation of ecclesiastical faith for a given people at a given time into a definite and enduring system.[109]

In fact, Kant is quite critical of what he calls "ecclesiastical faith" (i.e., historic orthodoxy), seeing the specifics of revelation (those doctrines which move beyond the basic notions of religion in accord with reason) as non-normative, and only having (limited) pedagogical or practical value.

---

106. Raschke, *Moral Actions, God, and History*, 90–91.
107. Ibid., 93.
108. Berkhof, *Two Hundred Years of Theology*, 11.
109. Kant, *Religion within the Limits of Reason*, 104.

"They are 'means,' 'vehicles,' 'husks,' or 'organs' of the religion of reason"[110] (anticipating Adolf von Harnack!). Kant appeals to a broadly "enlightened" view of *catholicity* as the basis for his judgment about the priority of the "religion of reason" (available to all rational humans) over the "ecclesiastical" or "historical faith" (accessible to only a select few). He continues:

> The token of the true church is its *universality*: the sign of this, in turn is its necessity and its determinability in only one possible way. Historical faith (which is based upon revelation, regarded as an experience) has only particular validity, to wit, for those who have had access to the historical record upon which this faith rests . . . whereas only pure religious faith, which bases itself wholly upon reason, can be *accepted* as necessary and therefore as the only one which signalizes the *true* church.[111]

Having rejected the orthodox views of "ecclesiastical faith," as well as the traditional rationalist proofs for God's existence, Kant finally brings the reader to the necessity of belief in God on purely moral grounds. This subjective form of belief, which is so profoundly interwoven with human morality, is consistent with the experience of human freedom. If there were truly a definitive theoretical proof of God's existence it "would lead to a religion of fear and compulsion" because "objective proofs ask only submission."[112] In the beginning of *Religion within the Limits of Reason Alone*, Kant says:

> So far morality is based upon the conception of man as a free agent who, just because he is free, binds himself though his reason to unconditioned laws, it stands in need neither of the idea of another Being over him, for him to apprehend his duty, nor of an incentive other than the law itself, for him to do his duty. . . . Hence for its own sake morality does not need religion at all.[113]

Yet, "[m]orality leads ineluctably to religion."[114] But the religion it leads to is not compulsory, for coerced religion detracts from human freedom, out of which moral choice springs. It is unthinkable, Kant taught, to view the world as not essentially controlled by a moral being or to view hu-

---

110. Berkhof, *Two Hundred Years of Theology*, 12.
111. Kant, *Religion within the Limits of Reason Alone*, 105–6
112. Evans, *Subjectivity and Religious Belief*, 32.
113. Kant, "Preface to the First Edition," *Religion within the Limits of Reason Alone*, 3.
114. Ibid., 5.

mans as not, therefore, morally free. Kant notes: "I *am* morally certain. That is, my belief in a God and another world is so interwoven with my moral disposition that I can run very little risk of forfeiting the latter, moreover, that I hardly fear that the former can be torn away from me."[115]

Thus, Kant finds epistemic justification for belief in God, not in the veracity of faith's object (which would call for requisite objective knowledge), but rather, within himself, the knowing subject (who is free to choose both belief and the good). In this postulate, Kant is virtually the inventor of the modern notion that religious belief must be subjectively justified. Evans notes:

> To show that Immanuel Kant provides an example of a subjective justification of religious belief should not be difficult inasmuch as Kant served us as something of a model in developing the concept. Kant is the pre-eminent example of a thinker who carefully denies any knowledge whatsoever of God's existence or nature, but who equally firmly holds that belief in God is completely and thoroughly rational. "For although we have to surrender the language of *knowledge*, we still have sufficient ground to employ, in the presence of the most exacting reason, the quite legitimate language of a firm *faith*." . . . From the standpoint of theoretical reason, [Kant] has argued that, though knowledge of God's existence is both impossible and undesirable, the idea of God is a concept the reality of which reason must necessarily consider a possibility.[116]

But in doing so, one must abandon the language of objective knowledge and resort to a subjective understanding of religious faith. Kant, then, does not deny faith (though philosophically he cannot affirm it either). Yet by effectively removing belief from the realm of knowledge entirely, and placing it squarely within the subjective experience of the individual, he clearly intends to make room for it. Immanuel Kant, and many following, thought this to be the only way to preserve faith in an age of Enlightenment.

> Kant was the first thinker in the entire history of philosophy who recognized that the "objective" method, which we apply to the knowledge of the world and of nature, had to be resolutely abandoned when we wish to understand man as the thinking and knowing subject, as the "I" that accompanies all thinking, as the self that acts in the scientist, as the ego that is inseparable from the understanding, the reason, and the mind in general. His

---

115. Kant, *Critique of Pure Reason* (tr. Meiklejohn), 502.
116. Evans, *Subjectivity and Religious Belief*, 73.

philosophy was the first "egological" speculation, to use a newly coined word. Man is man precisely because he is not an object, but the subject of knowledge.[117]

Modern philosopher of science Stanley L. Jaki, however, is seriously critical of this subjective turn in Kant as "profoundly un-Newtonian and un-Copernican."[118] Jaki christens Kant "the high priest of epistemological geocentrism" and charges him with "an error far more destructive for science than physical geocentrism could ever be."[119]

> For if the imagined structure of the mind determines the structure of things that are outside the mind, then the *raison d'être* for experimenting and observation will hardly ever become a compelling reason. . . . The Kantian knowledge of things was a construction by the mind of the semblance of things and not a natural grasp of intelligibility embodied in them. As a result, whatever Kant's longing for an intellectual touch with things other than his own mind, the Kantian impossibility of being in touch with the *Ding an sich* meant being trapped within one's own mind.[120]

A century and a half after Kant, Karl Barth would criticize this subjective view of knowing, insofar as it affected theology: "Knowledge of God is a knowledge completely effected and determined from the side of its object, from the side of God. But for that very reason it is genuine knowledge."[121] And yet, showing the inescapable impact of Kant's "Copernican Revolution" on even his own modern theology, Barth adds, "Of course, it remains a relative knowledge, a knowledge imprisoned within the limits of the creaturely."[122] It is said that Kant, as he neared the close of his life, began to sense that his three critical works had not adequately dealt with the concerns and problems of religion and theology. He intended to address this "oversight" in a fourth *Critique* on religion itself.[123] That book was never written. Yet some suggest that Schleiermacher would soon effectively settle the omission on Kant's behalf.[124]

117. Kroner, *Speculation and Revelation in Modern Philosophy*, 194.
118. Brown, *Christianity and Western Thought*, 1:317.
119. Jaki, *The Road of Science and the Ways to God*, 118.
120. Ibid., 118–19.
121. Barth, *Dogmatics in Outline*, 24.
122. Ibid.
123. Ward, *A Study of Kant*, 135.
124. Gilmore, "A Reappraisal of Liberal Apologetics," 372.

3

Schleiermacher's "Higher Order Pietism"

Subjectivity and Protestant Liberal Thought

> "Amid all the diversities of this world's motley spectacle I learned to discount appearances and to recognize the same reality whatever its garb, and I also learned to translate the many tongues that it acquires . . . to look into the inner nature of things."
>
> —F. D. E. Schleiermacher, *Soliloquies*[1]

KANT'S *CRITIQUE OF PURE REASON* (1781) not only made a profound impact on the shape and direction of modern continental epistemology, but it must "also be valued as a radical new beginning for evangelical theology."[2] For, "as a result of its appearance, orthodox scholasticism, rationalism, and supernaturalism found that at a single stroke, the road forward had been blocked."[3] And yet, this path obstructed by Kant's critical methodology was precisely the same "one that Schleiermacher took six years later."[4] Friedrich Daniel Ernst Schleiermacher (1768–1834) is indisputably the "pioneer"

---

1. Schleiermacher, *Soliloquies*, 74–75.
2. Berkhof, *Two Hundred Years of Theology*, 1.
3. Ibid., 1–2.
4. Ibid, 11.

or "father of modern theology."[5] Richard Niebuhr wrote that "Religiously speaking, we must concede the nineteenth century to Schleiermacher."[6] To this, nearly all his critics—both friends and enemies—seem to agree. "No other judgment is possible when one takes account of the development of Protestant thought in the extraordinary epoch that embraces the French Revolution and Immanuel Kant at its beginning and the First World War and Ernst Troeltsch and Adolf von Harnack at its conclusion."[7] Schleiermacher's impact on the course of modern Protestant thought is inestimable.

"A great man," quipped H. R. Macintosh, speaking of Schleiermacher, "condemns the world to the task of explaining him."[8] For those who follow Schleiermacher's lead, as well as for those who are critical of his role in the history of modern theology, it is inescapable that "in one way or another, Schleiermacher is tolerably at the centre of the stage."[9] Karl Barth (1886–1968) maintained great respect for Schleiermacher the theologian, though he was clearly no friend of Schleiermacher's theology or its presumed impact on modern Christendom. Barth believed that Reformed theology had taken a seriously wrong turn with Schleiermacher, and yet he was compelled to acknowledge the significant sway of Schleiermacher's teaching on the modern way of thinking about the Christian faith:

> Schleiermacher is not dead for us and his theological work has not been transcended. If anyone still speaks to us today in Protestant theology as if he were still among us, it is Schleiermacher. We study Paul and the reformers, but we see with the eyes of Schleiermacher and think along the same lines as he did.[10]

The face of the modern Protestant world was forever changed by the contribution of this provocative pastor-theologian. Elsewhere Barth comments that Schleiermacher is the "great Niagara Falls" toward which all modern theology is inevitably drawn.[11] He also notes, "E. Brunner, in 1924, was the first man writing against Schleiermacher whose premises were really different, really free of him (even if they were perhaps only relatively

---

5. Welch, *Protestant Thought in the Nineteenth Century*, 1:1.
6. Niebuhr, "Friedrich Schleiermacher," 17.
7. Ibid.
8. Mackintosh, *Types of Modern Theology*, 31.
9. Ibid.
10. Barth, *Theology of Schleiermacher*, ix.
11. Karl Barth, "Brunners Schleiermacherbuch," *Zwischen den Zeiten* 2, no. 8 (1924) 62.

free of him!)"[12] Like Barth, Brunner's attacks on Schleiermacher were formidable, yet Brunner still confessed Schleiermacher to be the only great theologian of the nineteenth century. All theology after Schleiermacher must inevitably be done in his shadow.

Because Schleiermacher took the task of theology and the *Zeitgeist* of the modern age with equally profound seriousness, he forever changed the character of both the questions and answers of faith for the post-Enlightenment age. In some respects, Barth and Brunner's objections were less with Schleiermacher than with modernity itself. For while Schleiermacher thought the Enlightenment's questions were valid and well worth engaging, Barth and Brunner did not.[13] Schleiermacher was convinced that, for the sake of the survival of Christian faith itself, it was prudent and necessary to address the questions of the age, in the terms of the age. Barth feared that to do so is to concede the battle to modernity from the start. He believed that the line of liberal theological thought all through the nineteenth century up to Ritschl and Troeltsch, could "undoubtedly be reduced to a single common denominator," and that common denominator "was and is Schleiermacher."[14] Indeed, Barth saw the contemporary German theology of his day, including that of Bultmann, as "a new and vigorous Schleiermacher renaissance."[15] So serious was this influence, Barth wrote, that if it were, in truth, a natural direction of the Reformation, he would have abandoned the evangelical tradition and "would in fact rather have become a Roman Catholic."[16]

Admirers and detractors of Schleiermacher alike agree that one specific aspect of his contribution to modern theology is of central importance: "Schleiermacher's emphasis upon the inward has become the stamp of much of modern Protestant theology."[17] To some, this places Schleiermacher firmly within the Reformation heritage as a classic example of the Reformational principle "*ecclesia semper reformanda est*," continuing what Luther and Calvin conceded to be the never-ending task of reforming the church in every age. To others, it is precisely here where Schleiermacher deviates from the Reformers, not to mention from all previous forms of

---

12. Barth, *Protestant Theology in the Nineteenth Century*, 426.
13. Ibid.
14. Ritschl, "Editor's Preface," x, citing Barth, "Nachwort," 300.
15. Ibid.
16. Barth, "Roman Catholicism: A Question to the Protestant Church," 314, n.1.
17. Clements, *Friedrich Schleiermacher*, 39.

Christendom: after all, the Reformers had managed to respond to their culture's concerns while still affirming the historic orthodoxy of the medievals and the ancient church fathers. Nevertheless, Schleiermacher's genius was to be so fully aware of the spirit of post-Enlightenment culture while remaining pastorally sensitive to the spiritual needs of this new era that he could articulate a faith befitting enlightened moderns. Whether he is the deliverer of the faith or its betrayer, whether his theological innovations were for the good or ill of Christendom, Schleiermacher had undoubtedly done something radical and unique in his post-Enlightenment theology, and Western Protestant thought would never be the same.

Kant's Critical Philosophy and the Romantic Circle

"One can say of Schleiermacher . . . that his reading of the works of Kant evoked from him his own most characteristic ideas."[18] Schleiermacher began reading Kant while serving as a private tutor in East Prussia (1790–93), and continued to labor over his thought during his active ministry (1794–1796). Kant's thought convinced Schleiermacher that rational, philosophical knowledge of God was impossible.[19] However, Schleiermacher did not agree with Kant's placement of religion under the realm of morality. "Neither metaphysics nor ethics is the home of religion, nor does either hold the key to its real nature. Where religion is reduced to either, and treated as if it were simply a form of *knowing* or a form of *doing*, it is lost to sight altogether."[20] Schleiermacher wanted to ground religious faith in something deeper and more profound than either knowing or acting. Schleiermacher found Kant useful as a place to begin, but if anything auspicious were to be said about Christian theology at all, it would be necessary to move beyond critical philosophy.

> Apart from contributing to his deepening religious skepticism at the time, Kant's influence was more methodological than substantive. Schleiermacher accepted the basic conclusions of the critical philosophy concerning the limits of speculative knowledge. Confronted with the force of Kant's metaphysical agnosticism, Schleiermacher felt compelled to forgo the metaphysical task in its traditional sense. In fact, the chief value of Kant's philosophy

18. Berkhof, *Two Hundred Years of Theology*, 30.
19. Heron, *A Century of Protestant Theology*, 24.
20. Ibid.

for Schleiermacher in his later years was its usefulness as a tool for tearing Enlightenment theology away from its rationalist moorings.[21]

Schleiermacher found Kant's critical work "useful for clearing away the debris of rational religion"; however, he also found that "Kant could not provide him with a basis for the reconstruction of faith."[22] The ideas of Kant's *Critique of Pure Reason* elicited little negative criticism from Schleiermacher, for it "was and remained self-evident to him that our knowledge is bound up with, and limited to our experience."[23] However, Schleiermacher did aver deep concerns against Kant's *Critique of Practical Reason*. The "world of the categorical imperative seemed to him overstrained and abstract."[24]

> Linked with this way of thinking is Schleiermacher's distaste for the God-concept as a postulate of the (abstract) categorical imperative. For him religion is no derivative; on the contrary, it is expressive of the "immediacy of feeling." It springs from a level higher than objectivizing or acting reason—a level where the unity of life is experience in an inner unity that is prior to the subject-object distinction. These ideas of the young Schleiermacher approached the early Romantic worldview one finds in the tradition of Herder and Goethe.[25]

As the nineteenth century dawned "the feeling was widespread that Enlightenment reason—Kant's pure reason—was a very good way to know but a very unsatisfactory way to *live*, that it was incapable of dealing with the relations of life or of grasping the nature of reality as a dynamic, living whole."[26] Schleiermacher finally did not see Kant's god as a great improvement on the sterile deity of the rationalists or the "absolute" *Geist* of German idealism. Religion, thought Schleiermacher, must affect the individual at the very core of being. It was Schleiermacher's brief association with the Romantic movement of Berlin's salon culture that, in part, satisfied this yearning. This fraternization for a short time offered Schleiermacher a fuller vision of existence which deeply resonated with his spiritual long-

21. Christian, *Friedrich Schleiermacher*, 37
22. Ibid.
23. Berkhof, *Two Hundred Years of Theology*, 30.
24. Ibid.
25. Ibid., 31.
26. Christian, *Friedrich Schleiermacher*, 39.

ings, and nurtured the desire to paint a new portrait of faith in God as a "fundamental, distinct, and integrative element of human life and culture."[27]

To properly define Schleiermacher as a Romantic is ambiguous at best. This ambiguity is due, in large part, to the indistinct character of Romanticism as a movement. It represented a broad and nebulous ethos more than any distinct ideas. If by "Romantic" one means, as many do, "a shallow and noncritical aestheticism, a kind of vacuous religiosity devoid of intellectual rigor and integrity,"[28] then Schleiermacher was decidedly *not* a Romantic. However, "insofar as romanticism represented a partial reaction to the increasingly cold, analytical, and technical reason of the scientific mentality and a corresponding attempt to discover the rich unity behind 'appearances,' Schleiermacher was a son of romanticism."[29] In the Romantic *milieu*, the young Reformed pastor found confirmation of some of his most basic concerns: the desirability of a supportive community of like-minded friends, an aversion to inflexible, ceremonious and rationalist forms of religion, and the supreme importance of *Gefühl* (deep, inner awareness of the individual) as an integral dimension of all human life.

In 1796, when Schleiermacher came to the chaplaincy at the Charité hospital in Berlin, he forged a friendship with Friedrich Schlegel (controversial author of the then-scandalous novel *Lucinde*), who, along with Ludwig Teick, Rahel and Henriette Herz, and Dorothea Veit-Mendelssohn, and others came to be known as the Berlin "Romantic circle." In reaction to Enlightenment rationalism and even to Kant's strong sense of moral duty, this circle focused more on the vigorous sense or feeling of life (*Lebensgefühl*) as the driving force of human existence. "Life is fluid, dynamic, untamed. One revels in nature, feeling, the interior world of the soul, individuality, love."[30] These sentiments led to somewhat progressive views of passion, sexual behavior, fidelity, and divorce, among other things. Schleiermacher found himself writing in defense of Schlegel's erotic *Lucinde*, much to the antagonism of his religious superiors.[31] It was often a topic of passionate debate

---

27. Tice, "Introduction," 12.
28. Christian, *Friedrich Schleiermacher*, 38.
29. Ibid., 39.
30. Berkhof, *Two Hundred Years of Theology*, 32–33.
31. It was partly due to Schleiermacher's defense of Schickel's work in his *"Vertranten Briefe überFriedrich Schlegels "Lucinde"* (1800), that Schleiermacher was "banished" to the parish of Stolp. Reformed court preacher and Schleiermacher's benefactor, Sack, was convinced that the Romantic circle was an immoral and unhealthy influence on young Schleiermacher. The combination of the "disturbing" theology of *Speeches* and

as to whether the ideal of a "higher sensual-spiritual unity" could actually be achieved within the traditional institution of marriage.[32] The place and emancipation of women was important to the circle, as to Schleiermacher himself,[33] and the "question of how such an ideal of unity could be realized in this institution of marriage was passionately discussed."[34] The Romantic Circle briefly re-created, though in a more erudite form to be sure, a kind of "Moravian community" for which the genteel Schleiermacher had never lost the taste.

Yet, this sense of belonging to the circle was precarious at best. Schleiermacher's calling as an ordained clergyman was little appreciated by Schlegel and his ilk. In part, the composition of Schleiermacher's *On Religion: Speeches to Its Cultured Despisers* was aimed at this group, as a justification for his ministerial vocation, and, more importantly, of the importance of Christian faith.[35] His opening lines betray his concern:

> It may be an unexpected and even a marvelous undertaking, that any one should still venture to demand from the very class that have raised themselves above the vulgar, and are saturated with the wisdom of the centuries, attention for a subject so entirely neglected by them. . . . Now especially the life of cultivated people is far from anything that might even have a resemblance to religion.

---

the defense of *Lucinde* brought confirmation to Sack of these assumptions. Berkhof, *Two Hundred Years of Theology*, 38.

32. Ibid., 33. See Berkhof's quotation of R. Huch's observation, "It is amazing how in this period the highest idea of the importance and permanence of love went hand in hand with the most broadminded leniency toward infidelity and all kinds of erotic aberrations" (ibid., 33, n.3).

33. Berkhof writes, ". . . in the matter of the emancipation of women and relations between the sexes the young Reformed pastor was a passionate defender of Romantic convictions, as his *Idee zu einem Katechismus der Vernunft für edle Frauen* (1798) and his *Vertraute Briefe über Friedrich Schlegels "Lucinde"* (1800) show" (*Two Hundred Years of Theology*, 33).

34. Ibid., 33.

35. Berkhof speaks of the Romantic circle as the intended primary audience of the *Speeches*: "These despisers are his closest friends! All of them had turned their backs on Kant and revelled in the All-in-One. In the process they cast their glances in the direction of Spinozistic pantheism and at the same time in the direction of a determined atheism. In the year in which *Speeches* appeared, the Atheism Controversy was at its height, and all members of the group lined up with warm sympathy on the side of the 'persecuted' Fichte. Given the appropriate circumstances, they could be enthusiastic about the 'absolute,' 'the universe,' or whatever its name might be, but never about religion as it was taught by the church." Ibid.

> ... Suavity and sociability, art and science have so fully taken possession of your minds, that no room remains for the eternal and holy Being that lies beyond the world. I know how well you have succeeded in making your earthly life so rich and varied, that you no longer stand in need of an eternity. Having made a universe for yourselves, you are above the need of thinking of the Universe that made you.... All this I know, and yet, divinely swayed by an irresistible necessity within me, I feel myself compelled to speak, and cannot take back my invitation that you and none else should listen to me.[36]

While Schleiermacher shared certain ideals with the Romantic circle, and certainly could speak their language, there must have been a sense in which he was also an outsider. Friedrich Schlegel demonstrated his antipathy toward formal religion in this statement: "Religion is usually only a supplement to, or a substitute for, education [*Bildung*]: and nothing is, strictly speaking, religious that is not the product of freedom. Hence one can say: the freer, the more religious: and the more education, the less religion."[37] From the start, however, Schleiermacher addresses this prejudice toward religion and religious authority by asking the pointed question: If you are willing to be taught by specialists in other fields—if, indeed you seek out the expertise on various subjects of "those who have devoted to it their lives and their powers.... How does it then come about that in matters of religion alone, you hold everything the more dubious when it comes from those who are experts, not only according to their own profession, but by recognition from the state, and from the people?"[38]

In the end, few of Schleiermacher's circle found the book helpful, while many religious authorities found it threatening and heretical. Schlegel said that the book was "too definite and positive in tone."[39] He found the book too decidedly "Christian" for his tastes!

> Goethe was elated with the first three Speeches: "Meanwhile to the degree that the style became more careless and the religion more Christian, this effect changed into its opposite and the whole thing finally ended in a healthy and happy aversion." One has to note that both these cultured despisers of religion discovered

---

36. Schleiermacher, *On Religion*, 1–2.

37. Schlegel, *Athenaeum* 1 (1798) 239, in Berkhof, *Two Hundred Years of Theology*, 33.

38. Schleiermacher, *On Religion*, 2.

39. Berkhof, *Two Hundred Years of Theology*, 37.

Schleiermacher's real intention in and behind the rhetorical form. They rejected the invitation the book held out to them, as did the majority of philosophers.[40]

Meanwhile, many of Schleiermacher's fellow churchmen feared a subversively pantheistic agenda in the *Speeches* along with categorically un-Christian attitudes in the work. Berkhof notes, "Thus those who caught the intention of the book rejected it. But those who should have gratefully welcomed it in their struggle against unbelief . . . did not understand this intention and therefore also rejected it."[41] An indignant Schleiermacher responded (without actually answering) angrily. "An apology for pantheism, a presentation of Spinozistic philosophy? Something that came up only in passing on a few pages is supposed to the main content?"[42] Schleiermacher would not live to see his teachings fully appreciated by either the church or the cultured despisers, and yet the impact would inevitably come.

"Liberal Evangelical"

Friedrich Schleiermacher's theology marks a radical new approach to the knowledge of God in the history of the church. Consistent with the Enlightenment appreciation for the individual, Schleiermacher brings the Christian religion into the modern world with his new theology grounded in the feeling self. Broadly speaking, the natural theologians had built primary theological ideas on the application of Aristotelean logical deductions about the nature of the world (as with Saint Thomas' Five Proofs) or based on the mere notion or idea of God (as with Saint Anselm's ontological argument), while the Reformers grounded theology in the proper interpretation of the biblical text.

> From Thomas Aquinas onwards there were those who tried to combine the two by the simple process of adding them together. And there were philosophers like Kant who held that the two cancelled each other out. Because natural theology was rotten at the foundations, it was incapable of bearing the superstructure of Christian theology. Schleiermacher tried to get the best of both

---

40. Berkhof, *Two Hundred Years of Theology*, 37–38. For an account of the historical effects of *On Religion*, see Dilthey, *Life of Schleiermacher*, Book II, ch. 10.

41. Berkhof, *Two Hundred Years of Theology*, 38.

42. Schleiermacher, *On the* Glaubenslehre, 49.

worlds by steering a middle course between them. He developed what is sometimes called *positive theology*.[43]

Schleiermacher has been called "the founder of the school of liberal evangelical theology."[44] To the contemporary British or American Evangelical, this notion of a "liberal evangelical" may seem oxymoronic, because the contemporary use of this label has been restricted largely to the theologically conservative and doctrinally orthodox. "But," B. A. Gerrish notes, "it has not always been this way. An evangelical in England, like a pietist in Germany, was once a champion of experiential religion against the dead weight of traditional forms. And the Germans, at least, have never forgotten that 'evangelical' is the badge of continuity with Luther and the Reformation."[45] He concludes, "Perhaps, after all, it is not a contradiction but a redundancy—a piece of needless repetition—to say that Schleiermacher was a liberal evangelical. That, historically speaking, is exactly what an evangelical originally was."[46]

Therefore, Friedrich Schleiermacher's "program was 'evangelical' because it was the distinctively evangelical Protestant consciousness (his own) that Schleiermacher made the object of his inquiry: it was 'liberal' because he did not consider himself tied to the old expressions of it . . . ."[47] By contrast, Barth, in his "Concluding Unscientific Postscript on Schleiermacher," could only see Schleiermacher as having lost continuity with the Reformers as well as with orthodox Christianity:

> Until better instructed, I can see no way from Schleiermacher, or from his contemporary epigones, to the chroniclers, prophets, and wise ones of Israel, to those who narrate the story of the life, death, and resurrection of Jesus Christ, to the word of the apostles—no way to the God of Abraham, Isaac, and Jacob and the Father of Jesus Christ, no way to the great tradition of the Christian church. For the present I can see nothing here but a choice. And for me there can be no question as to how that choice is to be made.[48]

In the view of many orthodox and neo-orthodox thinkers, Schleiermacher had dealt a deathblow to historic Christianity in his day, and his

43. Brown, *Philosophy and the Christian Faith*, 110.
44. Fisher, *History of Christian Doctrine*, 512.
45. Gerrish, *A Prince of the Church*, 32–33.
46. Gerrish, *A Prince of the Church*, 33.
47. Ibid., 19.
48. Barth, *Theology of Schleiermacher*, 271–72.

writings are nothing less than heretical. By contrast, in the view of many liberals (or "modernists" as some prefer) Schleiermacher had breathed life into the already cold corpse of the Christian religion, and in his *The Christian Faith*, Schleiermacher had produced a masterpiece of modern Protestant thought on a par with Calvin's *Institutes of the Christian Religion*. One thing is certain: More than any other thinker in his day, Schleiermacher took seriously what it meant to do theology in a post-Enlightenment world by anticipating, asking, and answering many of the distinctive religious questions produced by modern epistemological concerns. According to Rudolf Otto:

> No matter what one's attitude toward Schleiermacher's method and his utterances on religion may be, one is time and time again enthralled by his original and daring attempt to lead an age weary with and alien to religion back to its very mainsprings: and to reweave religion, threatened with oblivion, into the incomparably rich fabric of the burgeoning intellectual life of modern times.[49]

Both professor and pastor at heart, Schleiermacher thought it possible to sustain sincere devotion to God in the modern world, and yet remain intellectually honest in the light of dramatic scientific advance. His critics—the Enlightenment rationalists or the orthodox traditionalists—often found it necessary to sacrifice either their religion or their intellectual integrity to maintain their respective commitments to science or revelation. Schleiermacher thought such sacrifices to be unnecessary, but that it was obvious that "modern habits of thought demand radical theological change, a thorough overhauling of the meanings traditionally ascribed to Christian language."[50]

The Nurture of Moravian Piety

Schleiermacher's theological distinctiveness can hardly be understood apart from the experiences of his life. This is precisely how he would want it. He was concerned foundationally with the practical matters of religious life and experience—or, piety—"not simply with God as a philosophical construct."[51] "Piety," says Schleiermacher in the *Speeches on Religion*, "was

---

49. Otto, "Introduction" in Schleiermacher, *On Religion* (tr. Oman), vii.
50. Gerrish, *Schleiermacher and the Beginnings of Modern Theology*, xiii.
51. Ibid., 7.

the mother's womb, in whose sacred darkness my young life was nourished .... In my spirit it breathed ere it had yet found its own place in knowledge and experience."[52] Schleiermacher's stalwart sense of piety functioned as something of a yardstick for gauging the value of his childhood religion. He took great comfort in the inwardness of Moravian piety as he began to assess the traditional faith of his "fathers" and sort out genuine religious "thought and feeling from the rubbish of antiquity."[53] Even when it was determined that some of the dogmas of orthodoxy seemed less than plausible or useful for modernity, Schleiermacher affirmed that piety "remained to me."[54] Both a son and grandson of clergymen, Schleiermacher was swathed and coddled in religious culture. His father was a Reformed chaplain in the Prussian army, yet through a personal conversion experience he, and his wife, came to be associated with Moravian pietism. Both parents were determined to reproduce in their children their own strong devotional piety and sincere Moravian brand of spirituality. This gave Schleiermacher the unique benefit of a footing in both the substantial intellectual tradition of Calvin and the warm devotional tradition of Spener and Zinzendorf. Yet, if Schleiermacher's parents had to choose a preferred tradition for their son to emulate, it would clearly be the latter. Friedrich, however, managed to benefit greatly from both in style, while moving significantly beyond them both in substance.

Friedrich's mother agonized over the spiritual state of her children "considering the soul-endangering opinions, principles, and habits that are so prevalent in the present times."[55] At age fourteen, Schleiermacher experienced a dramatic, personal conversion experience while he was away at the Moravian boarding school at Niesky. His mother found this deeply reassuring. She finally took comfort in the fact that all her children had been admitted into the tutelage of the Moravians, and had experienced personal conversion according to the Moravian pattern. Schleiermacher's mother died shortly after he entered the Moravian boarding school. But, before she died, she expressed that she was at last contented with the spiritual safety of her brood, her primary duty (that of leading them to Christian piety and

---

52. Schleiermacher, *On Religion* (tr. Oman), 9.
53. Ibid.
54. Ibid.
55. Schleiermacher, *Life of Schleiermacher*, 1:25.

faith) being complete: "Now that all my children are going to the Brethren, I shall be of little more use here, so I may as well lay down and go to sleep."[56]

One of the essential figures of eighteenth-century German Pietism was the aristocratic Count Nikolaus Ludwig Von Zinzendorf (1700–1760).[57] Following an intensely emotional experience of personal conversion and dedication to Jesus, Zinzendorf became a prominent leader of the Moravians. He dedicated one of his estates, Herrnhut, as a center for Moravian Brethren refugees. Thus, the name "Herrnhuter" became a synonym for "Moravian." Like his predecessors Phillip Jacob Spener and Auguste Francke, Zinzendorf revolted "against the formalism of religious life and the aridity of theological teaching . . . in German Protestantism, placing emphasis not so much on the content of faith (*fides quae creditur*) as on the act by which we believe (*fides qua creditur*)."[58]

The Herrnhut brand of Pietism was highly communal with a strong social conscience, in contrast to many other forms of Pietism which often were strongly individualistic and separatistic. It was this brand of pietism that left such a deep impression on Schleiermacher. The heart and soul of Schleiermacher's mature theology would still maintain the elements of a highly personal relationship with Jesus expressed and experienced within the loving relationships of the pious Christian community. Keith Clements says of Schleiermacher's experience at the Moravian theological seminary of Barby: "The warm-hearted devotion to Jesus, with the shared life of rigorous study, vital worship and close personal relationships gave him his primary religious experience and its influence never left him, even though he was to leave the Moravians."[59]

From Doubt to a "Higher Order" Moravian

Young Schleiermacher's early letters from this period are saturated with talk of a companionship with Jesus and ail intense personal love for the Lord, along with the desire for a deeper spiritual experience with God. This

---

56. Ibid., 35.

57. Zinzendorf was heir to one of Europe's leading families, and was destined to high duties in eighteenth century Europe. Since 1662 all males in the Zinzendorf clan bore the title of count in the Holy Roman Empire.

58. Dulles, *The Assurance of Things Hoped For*, 63.

59. Clements, *Friedrich Schleiermacher*, 15.

is the "standard talk of the twice-born pietist—the 'born again Christian.'"[60] Yet, even at this stage, Schleiermacher was plagued with the implications of modern science in regard to religion, and a "strange skepticism" settled on him that the whole of Christian theology rested on philosophically outmoded expressions. Gradually, Friedrich's doubts grew about standard orthodox interpretations of the atonement of Christ, the Trinity, Christ's unique divinity, etc. In a letter written in 1787, young Friedrich confessed his doubts to his father:

> Faith is the regalia of the Godhead, you say. Alas! dearest father, if you believe that without this faith no one can attain salvation in the next world, nor tranquillity in this—and such, I know, is your belief—oh! then pray to God to grant it to me, for it is now lost. I cannot believe that he who called himself the Son of Man was the true, eternal God: I cannot believe that his death was a vicarious atonement.[61]

Upon hearing of his son's unbelief, Schleiermacher's father became incensed. He and Friedrich's mother had done all they knew to steer their son from impious disbelief. They had sent their son to the Pietist school at Barby specifically to ensure that this sort of apostasy would not set in! Gerrish notes:

> The father's reply is terrible: his insensate son has crucified Christ, disturbed his late mother's rest, and made his stepmother weep. The cause for his straying is ambition for the honors of the world. And so the father solemnly disowns his son: "I must, for you no longer worship the God of your father, no longer kneel at the same altar with him."[62]

When young Schleiermacher later laments that he has been slighted and nearly outcast by his Moravian teachers, his father shows no pity: "It is their duty to take care that one mangy sheep does not contaminate the whole flock."[63] Gottlieb Schleiermacher responded to his own son as an apostate, a prodigal. Yet this estrangement would be short-lived. For all the familial turmoil it caused, this period of apostasy showed itself for what it was, a time of youthful investigation and intellectual ferment. Before long,

---

60. Gerrish, *A Prince of the Church*, 24.
61. Schleiermacher, *Life of Schleiermacher*, 1:46.
62. Gerrish, *A Prince of the Church*, 25.
63. Schleiermacher, *Life of Schleiermacher*, 1:62.

Schleiermacher left the intellectually confining atmosphere of Barby and matriculated at University of Halle, at which the Enlightenment influence was keenly felt. It was here that Schleiermacher found he could not simply give way to untempered rationalism and religious skepticism. His religious spirit was too deeply rooted to ignore. The piety implanted by his parents remained rooted and would soon grow to a strong plant—perhaps different in composition, but not in character from the Moravian impulse.

At the time of his ordination, in 1791, Schleiermacher wrote to his father (with whom, by now, he had made amends), confidently asserting his renewed and strengthened faith: "My heart is properly cultivated . . . and is not left to wither under the burden of cold erudition, and my religious feelings are not deadened by theological inquiries."[64] Schleiermacher had not only reconciled with his father, but he had also begun the reconciliation of his feelings of spirituality and his searching intellect. Oddly, it was nothing else than a highly modified version of the old Moravian dichotomy between piety and intellect by which Schleiermacher was now learning that the two need not ultimately conflict. Faith and reason could indeed co-exist, so long as they did not overwhelm and smother one another.

In the spirit of the Pietism of his roots, Schleiermacher found what he thought was the solution to the whole problem of sustaining authentic faith in an age of cultural Enlightenment. The pious sensibilities of the Moravians provided a rudder for navigating the turbulent sea of modernity. Schleiermacher would confess: "Piety . . . helped me as I began to sift the faith of my fathers and cleanse thought and feeling from the rubbish of antiquity. When the God and immortality of my childhood vanished from my doubting eyes (piety) remained to me."[65] Thus, Schleiermacher believed that he had come, in a sense, full-circle from the simple piety of his youth to a seasoned, critical piety of mature faith. And he was all the wiser for having travelled the distance.[66] Some years later, after having revisited the

---

64. Schleiermacher, *Life of Schleiermacher*, 1:95.

65. Schleiermacher, *On Religion*, 9.

66. In his explanatory notes to the first speech, written two decades later, Schleiermacher clarifies this point. He had not actually gone as far as atheism, but his youthful intellectual zeal had compelled him to some significant "house-cleaning" of certain unnecessary anthropomorphisms: "The first conception both of God and immortality, which at a time when the soul actively lives entirely in images is always highly sensuous, does not, by any means always vanish. With most it is gradually purified and elevated. . . . But those who are early involved in a pure contemplative endeavor take another way. There is nothing in God, they say to themselves, opposed, divided or isolated. Wherefore, nothing human can be said of Him. Nothing earthly is to be transferred. . . . The author

old community of Moravian Brethren, he recognized his affinity with these people and with a stroke of nostalgic appreciation he acknowledged his debt and high esteem for this religious tradition:

> There is no other place which could call forth such lively reminiscences of the entire onward movement of my mind, from its first awakening to a higher life, up to the point which I have a present attained. Here it was for the first time that I awoke to the consciousness of the relations of man to a higher world.... Here it was that the mystic tendency developed itself, which has been of so much importance to me, and has supported and carried me through all the storms of skepticism. Then it was only germinating, now it has attained full development, and I may say, that after all I have passed through, I have become a *Herrhuter* again, only of a higher order.[67]

The Moravians had nurtured a sense and taste for the infinite within Schleiermacher, and though it established a decidedly inward focus for both him and Kant, the residual positive effects of Pietism are clearly more evident in Schleiermacher. Kant would abandon all forms of religious piety and retain only the barest forms of Christian theology, while Schleiermacher would remain within the church all his life, a Pietist to the end, "only of a higher order."

To Religion's "Cultured Despisers"

Schleiermacher's better-known and immature work *On Religion: Speeches to Its Cultured Despisers* (or more briefly, *Speeches on Religion*), was first published in 1799. The immediate impact of the book and widespread critical response demonstrated that this relatively obscure hospital chaplain had struck a cultural chord. The need was obvious. The ground beneath European intellectual culture was shifting in seismic proportions, and the structures of medieval Christendom were fast crumbling. Enlightenment thought had forged ahead, producing progress in nearly every dimension of human knowledge and culture. Rudolf Otto remarked that only "one

---

was, therefore, far removed from suggesting that there was ever a time when he was an unbeliever or an atheist. Such a misunderstanding could only arise in those who have never felt the speculative impulse to annihilate anthropomorphism in the concept of the Highest Being, an impulse found most clearly expressed in the writings of the profoundest Christian teachers." Schleiermacher, *On Religion* (tr. Oman), 22, n.2.

67. Schleiermacher, *Life of Schleiermacher*, 1:283–84.

human interest seemed to be laggard amid this universal stir and excitement and it was precisely the interest which for so long had been the first, indeed almost the only one: religion."[68]

What had for centuries been considered the "Queen of the sciences" was now dethroned, and indeed, due to Kant's critical work, it was no longer considered a science (*scientia*, "knowledge") at all. "Instead, a lofty idealism, sparked by great expectations, was the signature of the age which had embraced the teachings of Kant, Herder, and Goethe."[69] Goethe's poetic observation captured the growing, Romantic spirit of the age, Herder contributed to an increased hope and excitement for the human ideal, and Kant "with an inconquerable power," says Otto,

> had awakened men to moral consciousness, and to the dignity of spirit and the moral will. His disciples, therefore, preferred to explain the world and its coherence on the basis of the laws and forms of the mind and the moral will rather than to derive the workings of the mind from the mechanistic interconnections of the physical world.[70]

However, in spite of an apparent rise in this type of "aesthetic sensibility" and "moral teaching," the practical result was that "religion had been driven into a corner," it "seemed superfluous: it was no longer in step with the times."[71] Otto says of the characteristic post-Enlightenment person: "One did not hate religion, but one somehow held it in contempt like something for which one no longer had any use. One was cultured and full of ideals; one was aesthetic, and one was moral. But one was no longer religious."[72] Religion had already had its day in the sun, and now seemed passé, without real purpose, and redundant in an age of human optimism and scientific advance. The sciences, it seemed, had already begun to fulfill most of the needs that religion had once met. With an already full intellectual life, one could hardly find room for matters of religion. Life seemed undiminished without it.

It is to this crowd of "cultured despisers" of religion that Schleiermacher addressed himself in his five speeches: to "the very class that have raised themselves above the vulgar, and are saturated with the wisdom of

68. Otto, "Introduction" in Schleiermacher, *On Religion* (tr. Oman), vii–viii.
69. Ibid., viii.
70. Ibid., viii-ix.
71. Ibid., ix.
72. Ibid.

the centuries."⁷³ These who had prided themselves on wholeness in their intellectual pursuits had, thought Schleiermacher, neglected one very important discipline, or more accurately, one very important dimension to their humanness. Indeed, in their enthusiasm for rediscovering humanity, they had ignored the foundationally human character of religion. Humanity is *homo religiosus*, as Calvin put it: humans undeniably have the *sensus divinitatis*. Thus, to be human is to be religious, and to deny this is to lose the whole picture of humanity—something which ought to be unthinkable for a culture which prided itself on its *humanism* and wholeness.

Religion could not simply be a small category of life that an enlightened could choose to take or leave. It is part of what it means to be essentially human. Against Kant, Schleiermacher criticized the tendency to diminish religion to mere moral action based on a "peculiar way of contemplating the world."⁷⁴ Religion or "piety," wrote Schleiermacher, "cannot be an instinct craving for a mess of metaphysical and ethical crumbs."⁷⁵ Yet, he agrees with Kant that religion cannot interfere with scientific knowing, because it is simply not knowledge. Schleiermacher writes:

> In order to make quite clear to you what is the original and characteristic possession of religion, it resigns, at once, all claims to anything that belongs either to science or morality. Whether it has been borrowed or bestowed it is now returned. . . . [R]eligion is not knowledge and science, either of the world or of God. Without being knowledge, it recognizes knowledge and science. In itself it is an affection, a revelation of the infinite in the finite, God being seen in it and it in God.⁷⁶

In response to historic Western orthodoxy's scholastic propensity to speculate about metaphysics and claim scientific knowledge of God and the infinite, Schleiermacher says simply: "Quantity of knowledge is not quantity of piety."⁷⁷ This is an insight very much consistent with the Pietist perspective on faith. The historic Protestant tendency to equate faith with a series of reasoned and properly affirmed ideas is simply misguided. Schleiermacher says that he does not consider "the conceptions and the doctrines of God and of immortality, as they are usually understood, to be

---

73. Schleiermacher, *On Religion* (tr. Oman), 1.
74. Ibid., 27.
75. Ibid., 31.
76. Ibid., 35.
77. Ibid.

the principle things in religion."[78] True religion must be more than mere confirmation of cold, syllogistic facts about God.

Religion, rather, is the "pious consciousness" of the human being, it is the "sense and taste for the infinite" experienced by every person, says Schleiermacher.[79] And while this "pious feeling" is not to be confused with activity (ethical or aesthetic) or knowledge (metaphysical or scientific) it does not live in isolation from them either. Religion, or piety, contributes to the wholeness of human life. Elsewhere Schleiermacher expresses his longing for harmony among human interests, albeit a harmony without interference or overlap: "If one should imagine both a religious interest and a scientific spirit conjoined in the highest degree and with the finest balance for the purposes of theoretical and practical activity alike, that would be the idea of a 'prince of the church.'"[80] Though humility might keep him from saying so, few persons in his age, or even in the century following, met this description better than Schleiermacher himself.

Schleiermacher insists that religion need never interfere with the advances of modern science. Those who insist that science and religion must be in conflict "confuse all points of view and bring religion into the disrepute of encroaching upon the totality of scientific and empirical judgments."[81] This results in the unfortunate dismissal of religion by those enlightened persons of culture. Yet, Schleiermacher assures these persons they need not fear that embracing religion would necessitate losing the benefits of modern thought or being required to embrace certain outmoded concepts naively identified with religion. He insists, "Religion, however loudly religion demands back all those well abused concepts, leaves you, your physics, and, may it please God, your psychology inviolate."[82]

The Christian religion had for too long, in Schleiermacher's judgment, confused the essence of religion with its dogmas. It seemed evident to Schleiermacher, however, that these doctrines were simply formal expressions of religious feeling—a window, if you will, into the soul and experience of another pious person. These dogmas are "all the result of that contemplation of feeling, of that reflection and comparison . . . [they are] general expressions for definite feeling. They are not necessary for religion

---

78. Ibid., 93.
79. Schleiermacher, *On Religion* (tr. Oman), 190, 39.
80. Schleiermacher, *Brief Outline*, 21.
81. Schleiermacher, *On Religion* (tr. Oman), 88.
82. Ibid., 88.

itself, scarcely even for communicating religion, but reflection requires and creates them."[83]

Theology, then, is nothing else than reflection on religious experience and feeling. The feelings are the norm, the dogmatic statements are meaningless beyond the context of experience. And these concepts and dogmas are surely fallible transmitters of the essence of the pious feeling, far inferior to the experience itself. They are valuable as roadmaps to direct people to the real destiny of religious feeling, but they are not to be confused with the thing itself. Insofar as they are not found to be helpful, however, they may be discarded. Therefore, Schleiermacher writes: "It matters not what conceptions a man adheres to, he can still be pious. His piety, the divine influence in his feeling, may be better than his conception, and his desire to place the essence of piety in conception, only makes him misunderstand himself."[84] Here we see the essence of subjective religion in Schleiermacher. The really trustworthy thing in religion is *Gefühl*—the sense and taste for the infinite found within the individual. All scriptural teaching, all Christian theology, all church dogma must be finally submitted to this inward canon, because this is the infallible guide to religion. It is the rule of authentic faith.

For Schleiermacher, then, the guiding norm for determining the value of religious concepts and dogmatic statements is discovered in the "pious feeling." All doctrines are judged for their respective value as they are viewed through the spectacles of religious emotion. It is here that Schleiermacher significantly breaks with his Reformed tradition, and marks out a profoundly different path from historic orthodoxy, for the result of this shift of emphasis is an unconventional orientation toward objective historic Christian doctrine. As Schleiermacher evaluates the Christian faith by the subjective test of *Gefühl*, he concludes that religion ought to be seen as perfectly *natural* (in contrast to *supernatural* or, as the "cultured despisers" might think, *unnatural*) and should be entirely acceptable to modern sensibilities. There is no need to fall prey to Hume's criticisms about supernatural religion, when religion can be seen as wholly normative to mundane human experience. How, then, does this standpoint affect the traditional doctrines of the Christian faith? Schleiermacher asks, and answers, the obvious questions which arise given his remarkable presuppositions:

"What is a miracle?" he asks. A miracle is a sign which produces a certain state of wonder in the observer. "Every finite thing, however, is a sign of

---

83. Ibid., 87.
84. Ibid., 95.

the infinite," thus, "miracle is simply the religious name for event." Miracle is not a supernatural lightning bolt from the heavens, an otherworldly intrusion into the normative laws of nature and affairs of humans. Instead, the term "miracle" describes a subjective response of awe and wonderment within the individual. But the thing which produces the sense of astonishment is unique only insofar as it evokes such a response, not because of anything inherently preternatural in the event itself. Thus, Schleiermacher determines: "To me all is miracle."[85] How could this scandalize an enlightened modern? Indeed, what cultured despiser of religion could find anything offensive here? For Schleiermacher, a miracle is in the eye of the beholder. It is a way of seeing the world with the "spectacles of faith."

Similar in vein is Schleiermacher's understanding of revelation, inspiration and even of Scripture. None of these need become stumbling blocks to the cultured despisers, for they are fully explicable in terms that would never disrupt the autonomous, rational spirit of Enlightenment. "What is revelation?" Schleiermacher continues, "every original and new communication of the universe to man is a revelation. . . . Every intuition and every original feeling proceeds from revelation."[86] So, revelation is defined not in terms of objectively true knowledge from God, but every intuition and feeling which is experientially new to the knowing subject. And inspiration? Rather than indicating a supernaturally originated, "God-breathed" word of prophecy, "It is simply the general expression for the feeling of true morality and freedom."[87] Therefore, what historic orthodoxy has traditionally defined as the unique and the objective acts and speech of God in history, Schleiermacher characteristically reorients toward believers themselves. Miracle, revelation, and inspiration all speak to subjective *responses* or religious feelings rather than objective activities or things. Therefore, Schleiermacher concludes of Scripture:

> Every sacred writing is in itself a glorious production, a speaking monument from the heroic time of religion, but through servile reverence, it would become merely a mausoleum, a monument that a great spirit once was there, but is now no more. . . . Not every person has religion who believes in a sacred writing, but only the

---

85. Ibid., 88.
86. Ibid., 89.
87. Ibid.

man who has a lively and immediate understanding of it, and who, so far as he himself is concerned, could most easily do without it.[88]

True religion cannot be a mere echo of someone else's truth or a pious gazing upon someone else's experience. If Scripture provides a window into somebody else's religious experience, Schleiermacher would see the nature of traditional orthodoxy as voyeuristic. True religion means moving beyond scrutiny of the experience of the ancients. The point is to experience it for oneself. The spirit of religion, then, does not look backward, or even outward: it looks inward. Faith must be a personal appropriation—a "lively and immediate understanding" of piety—in order to be authentic. Belief must not be servile or blind acceptance of what someone else has once said as an authority, taught Schleiermacher. "You wish always to stand on your own feet and go your own way.... Religion is no slavery, no captivity, least of all for your reason. You must belong to yourselves."[89] Thus, as Pelikan has noted of a trend in nearly all post-Enlightenment religion, the "Dare to know!" of Kant's Enlightenment science has become "Dare to believe!" in Schleiermacher's enlightened faith.[90] The same independent, self-oriented spirit is present in both. The purpose of the Christian church, then, in Schleiermacher's religion, is not to be a museum of spiritual artifacts, but a community which creates anew the spiritual feeling of the "heroic time of religion" for each age, and for each individual. The call is not merely to remember and preserve, but to experience and feel the essence of piety.

Religious faith, for Schleiermacher, has as its object not epic events of supernatural intervention in human history, not portentous miraculous signs which demand affirmation, not sage teachings of inspired prophets and apostles, or special dogmas revealed from above. True religion is the awe produced by the wonders of the natural world, such wonders that cause the human to reflect on the grandeur of human existence and "absolute dependence." Schleiermacher speaks of this religious feeling or pious consciousness also as "self-consciousness." By this he surely does not mean individualistic "consciousness of oneself," for "the self-consciousness of which Schleiermacher speaks is a consciousness of the self as determined by, or acted upon by, what is other than the self.... It is the self in relation which is the object of consciousness."[91] Thus, Schleiermacher's religious

88. Ibid, 91.
89. Ibid.
90. Pelikan, *Christian Doctrine and Modern Culture*, 119.
91. Clements, *Friedrich Schleiermacher*, 37.

consciousness is highly relational—an interdependence found in the world of normal experiences in which we are always in relationship. This is why Schleiermacher could never wholly abandon the Moravian communal ideal of an *ecclesiola*, or even the church community itself. In spite of Schleiermacher's sense of the importance of the individual, and his stress on the subjective feeling as the essence of religion, he never went so far as many of his theoretical progeny in abandoning the church altogether in favor of the religious subject alone.

Schleiermacher's *Christmas Eve*

Further insight into Schleiermacher's view of religious belief and subjectivity can be gained from his little work *A Celebration of Christmas: A Conversation,* or as some have titled it, *Christmas Eve: Dialogue on the Incarnation.* Written in 1805 as a personal Christmas gift to friends who had been encouraging him to write, the sixty-page *Christmas Eve* demonstrates Schleiermacher's skill as an author of fiction as well as his developing theological genius. For, each character in the story (and they range in approach from intellectual skepticism to simple piety) actually represents one aspect of Schleiermacher's own complex and broad thinking.

The setting is a German, middle-class home on Christmas Eve. Family and friends have gathered for an intimate, joyous celebration of the holiday. Gifts are opened and carols are sung, all contributing to the festive mood of the occasion. But the celebration eventually leads to conversation about the nature of the holiday season, while introducing three initial themes to the story. Each theme discloses important aspects of Schleiermacher's view of authentic faith.

The first theme is music. The young daughter of the host and hostess, Sofie, provides much of the music. Music seems to transcend our critical rationalism and evoke the "pious feeling" that is so important to Schleiermacher. The second theme is childhood. Sofie, precocious child that she is, provides a living example of child-like faith and mystical piety. The third and final theme for this section is femininity. Schleiermacher was a great admirer of females (and he frankly confessed that he often wished he had been born a woman due to their natural instincts for feeling, and, therefore, religion). Women, in real contrast to analytical men, had a romantic manner of thinking which had "the capacity to penetrate intuitively to the heart of things."[92] This perspective is demonstrated in the story as the three women all repeat deeply moving and sentimental Christmas reminiscences, each focusing on the theme of mother and child. Thus Schleiermacher creates a scenario which evokes the essence of his religion, as manifested in these three themes of music (as a means of evoking pious sentiment), childlikeness (as a model of simplicity and mystical faith), and womanhood (as a means of prioritizing intuition over reason).

After this, the story takes a dramatic turn to a high-powered intellectual dialogue by the three men on the theological nature of the incarnation. The stark contrast is intentional. In Schleiermacher's shrewd assessment, the women and children in the story got it right, while the men (as they are apt to do) spend their energies on seemingly important (yet truly peripheral and trifling, by Schleiermacher's judgment) matters. In one sense, it shows the ultimate pointlessness of such metaphysical quibbling in relation to the clear piety demonstrated by the previous activity of the women. Yet, in another sense, it conveys that theological and dogmatic formulation properly takes place within the context of the pious experience of the Christian community. All three men, like the other characters in the story, are still speaking for Schleiermacher.

Leonhardt, the lawyer, is a rationalist skeptic. He argues that Christmas, in spite of the absence of real historic foundation, is the epitome of festivals. Its joyous spirit accomplishes the remarkable task of compelling us to believe, if only for a night, what is scientifically and historically unbelievable and absurd. To that, so long as it is confined to one harmless season, it is commendable. Yet, the significance of the actual historic Christ is minimal; the festival is all. The women become upset by this brash display of agnosticism, and another guest, Ernst, is encouraged to refute "the unbelieving rascal."[93]

The essence of Ernst's speech is that what is celebrated by Christmas is, in fact, of real importance. He concedes that the historical evidence for Christ is weak, but the feast produces real joy and the focus of that joy is the coming of a Redeemer in whom we find true meaning in the discovery of the higher life. Eduard, the host, provides the final reply. His response will, he says, rely less on the "mythical" recorders of Christ's life (the synoptic writers) than on the "mystical" evangelist (Saint John, Schleiermacher's own favorite). Eduard then proceeds to explicate a highly mystical

---

92. Gerrish, *A Prince of the Church*, 29.
93. Schleiermacher, *Christmas Eve*, 82.

elucidation of the believer's encounter with the "Word become flesh" concluding that "what we celebrate is nothing other than ourselves as we are collectively, or human nature . . . viewed and known from the perspective of the divine."[94] Therefore, in contrast (or perhaps, in complement?) to Leonhardt's rationalism, Ernst and Eduard reply, not based on historical or scientific grounds, but upon the grounds of the experience of piety. Human religious experience leads us back to the Redeemer.

As Eduard is speaking, Josef, a late guest, arrives and quietly seats himself. When he is compelled to speak as well, the pious man responds with a mild rebuke which brings the entire evening back into focus:

> "By no means," he replied when Eduard addressed him, "You shall certainly be the last. I have not come to deliver a speech, but to enjoy myself with you: and I must quite honestly say that it seems odd, almost folly even, that you should be carrying on with such exercises. . . . Aha! but I already get the drift. Your evil principle is among you again: this Leonhardt, this contriving, reflective, diabolical, super-intellectual man . . . ."[95]

Thus, Leonhardt is the enlightened "cultured despiser" of religion—asking, perhaps, intelligent and necessary questions, but falsely concluding that religious faith cannot co-exist with current science. Then, the pious Josef concludes his speech, getting to what Schleiermacher surely saw as the heart of the whole matter:

> And the poor women must have had to go along with it. Now just think that lovely music they could have sung for you, in which all the piety of your discourse could have dwelt far more profoundly. Or think how charmingly they could have conversed with you, out of hearts full of love and joy. Such would have eased and refreshed you differently and better too, than you could possibly have been affected by these celebratory addresses of yours! For my part, today I am of no use for such things at all. For me, all forms are too rigid, all speech-making too tedious and cold. Itself unbounded by speech, the subject of Christmas claims, indeed creates in me a speechless joy, and I cannot but laugh and exult like a child. Today all men are children to me. . . . Come then, and above all bring the child if she is not yet asleep, and let me see your glories, and let us be glad and sing something religious and joyful.[96]

94. Ibid., 79.
95. Ibid., 85–86.
96. Ibid., 86.

Thus, the story comes full circle back to Schleiermacher's original paradigms for the real essence of religion. The themes of music, childhood, and women are brought back to the reader's attention by the insight of the Pietist Josef. Schleiermacher does not wish the theological conversation to cease. Indeed, he desired to be part of that ongoing conversation. The fact that Schleiermacher wishes the conversation to continue (rather than be stilled by either orthodox or rationalist dogmatism) is indicated by the absence of real "winners" in the dispute. The nature of theology, thought Schleiermacher, was an open-ended dialogue. But should the conversation go on, it must never lose connection to what truly matters. The story of *Christmas Eve* does not disparage theological enquiry or scientific advance in the area of religious studies, not in the least. Theological reflection, and indeed the Christian faith itself, is only valid, says Schleiermacher, if it has as its object piety: the feeling of absolute dependence upon God. For with Schleiermacher, "religion as feeling is emphatically primary, and theology secondary."[97]

Schleiermacher's *Glaubenslehre*

In his later, more sophisticated, opus *The Christian Faith* (often referred to simply as the *Glaubenslehre*, lit., "system of faith") Schleiermacher writes, not to an unbelieving audience, as with his *Speeches*, but as a theologian within and in service to the church. As the title indicates, this work is "The Christian Faith, presented systematically according to the fundamental doctrines of the Evangelical Church"—the church, which is, according to Schleiermacher, "nothing but a communion or association relating to religion or piety." As Schleiermacher had made a practical contribution to the political unification of the Reformed and Lutheran branches of the Protestant tradition in Prussia, he offered this modern dogmatic as a unified theory of faith for the whole Evangelical Church.

In *The Christian Faith*, Schleiermacher defined his all-important notion of the "pious consciousness" more precisely as "the feeling [*Gefühl*] of absolute dependence [*schlechthinningen abhängig*]."[98] He determines "the piety which forms the basis of all ecclesiastical communions is, considered purely in itself, neither a Knowing or a Doing, but a modification of feeling

---

97. Clements, *Friedrich Schleiermacher*, 35.
98. Schleiermacher, *The Christian Faith*, 12, 19, 34, 40, 125.

or of immediate self-consciousness."⁹⁹ This immediate consciousness is what Kant might call "transcendental,"¹⁰⁰ but it goes further than Kant envisioned. For, "in the psychological trinity of knowing, doing, and feeling, it is clear that feeling has a certain priority. . . . Indeed, insofar as the flux of intellectual and volitional experience can be seen to cohere at all, it is by virtue of the unifying of the self in feeling."¹⁰¹ Schleiermacher writes, "We shall endeavor to go into the innermost sanctuary of life . . . . There alone you discover the original relation of intuition and feeling, from which alone this identity and difference is to be understood."¹⁰²

This sense of dependence is reflected directly in Schleiermacher's own personal experience. In spite of the high value placed on community in his thinking, the reality was seldom attained. He was never fully at home in the Romantic circle of Berlin, and he eventually lost that group altogether due to the pointedly religious character of his *Speeches*. The poor reception of Schleiermacher's religious ideas by the Romantic circle is perhaps best demonstrated in the following whimsical piece of poetry by A. W. von Schlegel, elder brother of Friedrich. Playing on the meaning of the name "Schleiermacher" ("veil maker"), Schlegel wrote:

> *Der nackten Wahrheit Schleier machen,*
> *Ist kluger Theologen Amt,*
> *Und Schleiermacher sind bei so bewandten Sachen*
> *Die Meister der Dogmatik ingesamt.*¹⁰³

It would not be long before the circle itself collapsed, succumbing, "to its own boundless and unstructured individualism."¹⁰⁴ The church itself, which Schleiermacher longed to defend and for whom he wrote as a theologian, also condemned and rejected him for what was seen as quasi-pantheism and unorthodox concessions to the Enlightenment. During what some deemed his "morally lax" period in Berlin, he fell in love with another pastor's wife. Due to her unhappy marriage, Schleiermacher tried to convince her to divorce and marry him. But this ended badly and left Schleiermacher

---

99. Ibid., 5.

100. Heron, *A Century of Protestant Theology*, 25.

101. Christian, *Friedrich Schleiermacher*, 55.

102. Schleiermacher, *On Religion* (tr. Oman), 41.

103. "To make veils for the naked truth is the .job of clever theologians: all masters of dogmatics are Schleiermachers ("makers of veils")." Barth, *Theology of Schleiermacher*, 186–87, citing Von Schlegel, *Sämmtliche Werke*, 2:233.

104. Berkhof, *Two Hundred Years of Theology*, 38.

with a stain on his reputation (he later developed more conservative views on divorce and remarriage, but was seen by his religious superiors as profligate). The reality of the depth of longing for human interdependence in Schleiermacher's understanding is illustrated in a letter written to Henriette Herz, his life-long friend and trusted confidant (another married woman, whose friendship with Schleiermacher also raised eyebrows):

> Ah, dear Jette, be generous and write often to me: that alone can keep me alive, for I cannot thrive in solitude. In truth I am the least independent and self-sufficing of mortals: indeed, sometimes I doubt whether I really be an individual. I stretch out all my roots and leaves in search of affection; it is necessary for me to feel myself in immediate contact with it, and when I am unable to drink in full draughts of it, I at once dry up and wither. Such is my nature; there is no remedy for it; and, if there were, I should not wish to employ it.[105]

Schleiermacher was by nature a deeply social creature, whose personal relationships clearly modelled the depth of human interdependence of which he taught, and above all, human dependence upon God. For, it is only in these relationships of absolute dependence that true religion is found. He says, "All is present in vain for those who set themselves alone. In order to receive the life of the World-Spirit and have religion, man must first, in love, and through love, have found humanity."[106] For Schleiermacher, these inter-dependent human relationships are not mere reflections of the divine relationship, they are its vehicle: "To find the most glorious elements of religions, let us enter upon the territory where you are in your peculiar, your most beloved home. Here your inner life had its birth . . . . Humanity itself is for you the true universe."[107]

This sense of utter contingency, for all its subjective implications, is not wholly objectless. In fact, Alexander Schweizer commented that Schleiermacher restored the confidence of the Christian consciousness in its own content."[108] That content, in brief, is *Jesus Christ*. Schleiermacher's remarkably Pietist sensibilities are nowhere more evident than in his clear expression of love of Jesus. D. F. Strauss said Schleiermacher's *The Christian*

---

105. Schleiermacher, *Life of Schleiermacher*, 1:188.
106. Schleiermacher, *On Religion* (tr. Oman), 72.
107. Ibid.
108. Gerrish, *A Prince of the Church*, 44.

Faith has only one dogma: the person of Christ.[109] Schleiermacher's mature theology is foundationally Christocentric—or "Christomorphic," as Richard Niebuhr prefers.[110] In other words, Schleiermacher's "God-consciousness"—his "feeling of absolute dependence"—is undoubtedly focused on the person of Jesus. Schleiermacher puts it this way:

> Christianity is a monotheistic faith, belonging to the theological type of religion, and is essentially distinguished from other such faiths by the fact that in it everything is related to the redemption accomplished by Jesus of Nazareth. . . . [T]here is no other way of obtaining participation in the Christian communion than through faith in Jesus as the Redeemer.[111]

For all the pious language about Christ and the venerable place of Jesus in Schleiermacher's theology, it is clear that Schleiermacher does not conceive of Jesus as the incarnate Son of God, the third Person of the Divine Trinity, or the virgin-born miracle-worker as traditionally understood by the historic creeds and confessions of Christian orthodoxy. These notions are outmoded and simply do not meet Schleiermacher's ultimate test for true religion: "No matter can be thus introduced except in so far as it has a demonstrable and definite connection with the religious affections . . . ."[112] The idea of a Redeemer, says Schleiermacher, is surely not inconsistent with the feeling of absolute dependence, indeed, "all Christian piety rests upon the appearing of the Redeemer."[113] But Christ as Redeemer, says Schleiermacher, does not necessitate such metaphysical notions as his divinity or the incarnation, much less scientific impracticalities as virgin births.

Therefore, while Jesus is clearly the object of faith for Schleiermacher, it is not necessary to affirm the dogma of Jesus as the enfleshed deity of traditional Christian orthodoxy. Instead, Jesus was a human being with perfect "God-consciousness" (a full understanding of the feeling of absolute dependence) who redeems humanity by assuming them into his own experience of absolute dependence with God the Father, "and this," affirms Schleiermacher, "is his redemptive activity."[114] Schleiermacher's Christology is (as he believes the whole church's is) developed "from below." It is the

109. Strauss, *The Christ of Faith and the Jesus of History*, 4.
110. Niebuhr, *Schleiermacher on Christ and Religion*, 212.
111. Schleiermacher, *The Christian Faith*, 52, 68.
112. Ibid., 125.
113. Ibid.
114. Ibid., 425.

church's own reflection upon her experience of Jesus, not the transcendent and unknowable nature of Christ himself, that is the cause of such sublime language.

The insights of the creed of Chalcedon are not set aside, but simply reoriented according to Schleiermacher's subjective test. To speak of Jesus Christ as divine and human is to say that we simultaneously feel toward him "the most unconditional adoration" (God with us) and "brotherly comradeship" (God with us).[115] "Ebionitic Christs fail on the first count, docetic Christs on the second. Schleiermacher believes, however, that the two-natures doctrine is no longer viable in its Chalcedonian form."[116] The intent of the Chalcedonian formula is still discoverable, but the language has been surpassed. For modern thinkers, "sons of Hume and Kant," it "will no longer do to speak of Christ as possessing 'two natures in one person.' 'Nature' means quite simply what a thing is! To speak of a person as possessing two natures is either to describe a pathological condition or to use words without meaning."[117] Necessarily then, the speech of the church about Jesus ought to begin primarily with its experience of him as Redeemer—the one who brings us to full dependence upon God. As with all theological language, this doctrine can be judged for efficacy by means of Schleiermacher's experiential canon.

The orthodox theological language about Jesus, argues Schleiermacher, grew out of the initial experience of the Christian community with Jesus. The faith experience gave rise to the traditional dogma, eventually expressed in the mythical metaphysical terms of Jewish prophetic, and later Greek philosophical, culture. Virgin births, divine humans, miracles were all pre-scientific ways of expressing, the full "God-consciousness" of Jesus. Schleiermacher wished to cut through the aboriginal dogmatic undergrowth and rediscover the original faith experience in Jesus which initially gave rise to the rhetorical dogmatic. This "essence of faith," when discovered, would finally transcend culture and could stand firm even in an age of Enlightenment reason.

The Christian community had for centuries experienced a loving, redemptive relationship with Jesus leading them to a higher "God-consciousness." Often that experience was confused with the propositions of the creeds and theological confessions. But the concept of Christ as both human

---

115. Ibid., 391.

116. Christian, *Friedrich Schleiermacher*, 119.

117. Ibid.

and divine does not demand that the believer cling tenaciously to the naïve, literal meanings of the formal language which dominated the councils of early Christianity. The divinity in Jesus was nothing else than his profound sense and taste for God. It is in this sense that he is both human and divine, for Jesus has been experienced by his disciples as one who was powerfully apperceptive of God. Schleiermacher states, "The Redeemer, then, is like all men in virtue of the identity of human nature, but distinguished from them all by the constant potency of his God-consciousness, which was a veritable existence of God in Him."[118]

The feeling of being utterly dependent upon God was central in Jesus, and Jesus fulfilled that absolute God-consciousness in our behalf as Redeemer. Thus the pious Christian language about Jesus as divine is wholly justifiable because "to ascribe to Christ an absolutely powerful God-consciousness, and to attribute to Him an existence of God in Him, are exactly the same thing."[119] Dogmas, however, about virgins giving birth to divine-human persons, the dead being raised, etc. (insofar as they are taken metaphysically) are only incidental to (and oftentimes even distracting from) the *Gefühl*. Insofar as one thinks that mental assent to such a dogma is equivalent to faith, that person stands in danger of bypassing authentic faith experience. For example, Schleiermacher states, "The ideas of the Resurrection and Ascension of Christ, and the prediction of His Return to Judgment, cannot be laid down as properly constituent parts of the doctrine of his Person."[120] Thus, "all that can be required of any Protestant Christian is that he shall believe them in so far as they seem to him to be adequately attested."[121]

Thus, Schleiermacher's method is consistent throughout: the pious experience of the believing subject (within the Christian community, nonetheless) is the beginning and ending point for all claims about the object of faith—Jesus Christ. The criterion or ground of belief is not objective, scientific knowledge, but subjective human experience—the feeling of absolute dependence. "Henceforth the truth of God and religion would rest on the testimony of the self in the deepest recesses of its own being, and nothing could be affirmed finally as true and meaningful without the confirmation

---

118. Schleiermacher, *The Christian Faith*, 385.
119. Ibid., 387.
120. Ibid., 417
121. Ibid., 420.

of the heart."[122] And it is this emphasis that plants Schleiermacher firmly within the inwardly focused modern age, while simultaneously making him a unique contributor to it.

---

122. Christian, *Friedrich Schleiermacher*, 47.

4

Søren Kierkegaard and the Paradox of Faith

Subjectivity in Christian Existentialism

> *"Mysticism has not the patience to wait for God's revelation."*
>
> –Søren Kierkegaard, *Journals*, 6 September 1839.[1]
> July 11, 1840

THE UNDENIABLY ECCENTRIC DANE Søren Aabye Kierkegaard (1813–55) has been deemed nothing short of a philosophical genius, and his impact on modern as well as post-modern philosophy (though delayed by nearly a century[2]) has been judged nothing less than monumental. Nevertheless, Kierkegaard is not first and foremost a philosopher—he himself rejected that

---

1. Kierkegaard, *Journals of Søren Kierkegaard*, 321.

2. Kierkegaard produced more than twenty-five books in his forty-two years of life, but, because they were written in Danish, they slipped into obscurity. Kierkegaard's impact was delayed until his works began to be translated into German, and then English. In some respects, Kierkegaard's reputation preceded the translation of many of his works. His influence in thinkers such as Sartre, Barth, Brunner, and Bultmann, among others, came to be known among scholars before Kierkegaard himself had been read. This, in addition to the dense and enigmatic nature of his writing, contributed to the varied and often skewed views of Kierkegaard's thought. Kierkegaardian scholarship is still "catching up," as Kierkegaard's works continue to be translated and assessed.

label[3] preferring instead the simple designation of "religious writer"[4]—and indeed in many senses he is more accurately an *anti-philosopher*. Though his influence on the realm of philosophy has been incalculable, perhaps Kierkegaard is better understood as a theologian. His greatest impact as a thinker has clearly been in the area of religious thought. Kierkegaardian scholar Louis Dupré asserts, "Kierkegaard is a theologian and has to be studied as such."[5] Without minimizing his contribution to existentialist philosophy, it is Kierkegaard as a theologian that is the primary interest of this discussion, particularly as he understands the nature of subjectivity in religious faith.

As a theologian as well as cultural critic, Kierkegaard found himself driven by a heartfelt mission of deep pastoral concern—a vocation shaped by his peculiar "genius." His compelling interest revolves around the problem of being a Christian within a Christendom gone cold. Christianity had been dealt a heavy blow by Enlightenment thought, and many forms of Protestant thought had simply buckled under the cultural pressure. In dealing with this problem, Kierkegaard introduced a new perspective in the modern understanding of the justification of religious belief. Certain questions must be raised regarding the understanding of faith in Kierkegaard: Is his existential approach to belief consistent with historic Protestant orthodoxy or is it entirely an innovation? Does the objective content of the Christian faith matter, or is subjective experience sufficient? The answers to these questions cannot be rightly appraised apart from an appreciation of Kierkegaard's passionate struggle to rediscover what he understood to be authentic Christianity in a post-Enlightenment age.

Reared in the pietist sensibilities of the Danish Lutheran Church, Kierkegaard (whose name means "church yard" or "graveyard") fancied himself a reformer of sorts—one who desired a return to the spirit of the Reformation and, more importantly, to the authentic New Testament roots of true Christianity. His own personal pilgrimage became for him a paradigm of the needs of all Danish Christendom—and, he concluded, this was precisely why his critiques were often so violently opposed: "My need of

---

3. Kierkegaard wrote, under pseudonym to be sure, that "I have no intention of competing for any philosophical distinction." *Either/Or*, 2:177.

4. Kierkegaard, *The Point of View for My Work*, 5.

5. Dupré, *Kierkegaard as Theologian*, ix.

Christianity is so great (both on account of my sufferings and my sins and my terrible introversion): that is why I am not understood."[6]

"Halb Gott im Herzen"

Søren Kierkegaard inherited from his father, Michael Pederson Kierkegaard, a pensive intelligence, somber religious sensibilities, and a significant propensity toward melancholy.[7] Michael Kierkegaard's religious piety was shaped by the unfortunate reality that he carried with him an almost emotionally crippling guilt over two instances in his life. The first was a youthful "blasphemy" against God: "[W]hile herding the flocks on the heaths of Jutland, suffering greatly, in hunger and in want, [Michael Kierkegaard] stood upon the hill and cursed God," something he was unable to forget, writes Søren, "even when he was eighty-two years old."[8] The second instance is only inferred, but it can be reasonably reconstructed from various cryptic remarks. It appears that Michael's first wife became sick and died without giving him a child. During her period of illness, or shortly after her death, Michael became involved with Ane Sørendatter Lund, who was living as a servant in the house.[9] Somehow, Kierkegaard's father took the biblical notion that the "sins of the father will be visited upon the sons" as the assurance that his progeny would reap his curse.[10] Young Søren seemed to believe him.

---

6. Kierkegaard, *Journals of Søren Kierkegaard*, 1056.

7. Kierkegaard spoke of his father as an individual from whom "the whole of that melancholy descended in inheritance." Kierkegaard, *Journals of Søren Kierkegaard*, 600.

8. Kierkegaard, *Journals of Søren Kierkegaard*, 556.

9. What is known is that Michael married Ane less than a year after his first wife had died, and the first child, Maren Kirsten, was born just four months and eleven days after the marriage. That Michael Kierkegaard bore a strong sense of guilt about these circumstances is indicated in his apparent belief that his first wife was still his real wife, and he was known to offer money to his pastor to be given to the poor as a sort of penance. Lowrie, *A Short Life of Kierkegaard*, 22–25.

10. This "family mythology" led Søren's father to believe that all seven of his children would die in youth. In fact, this nearly came true, save for Søren and his brother, Peter (who would later be ordained Bishop). They were the only children to live past their father (and Peter was the only one to live to old age), and were surprised at doing so! The depth to which the children took this seriously is manifested in the anecdote that the first editor of Kierkegaard's works, Barfod, recounts of sharing the Jutland story with the aged Bishop Peter Kierkegaard. When inquiring as to whether Peter desired the story to be repeated, Peter exclaimed, "This is our father's story *and ours*." Lowrie, *A Short Life*

In addition to this unfortunate psychological malaise, Søren was physically weak and often sickly, somewhat bent in posture (some scholars say "hunchbacked").[11] Yet, he believed that he was providentially given his genius as a sort of compensation (which, however, would later demand much sacrifice from him). He wrote: "melancholy, soul-sick, profoundly and absolutely a failure in many ways, one thing was given to me: a pre-eminent intelligence, presumably so that I should not be quite defenceless."[12] When he was twenty-six years old, Kierkegaard entered into his journal these words from Goethe's *Faust*: "*Halb Kinderspiele, Halb Gott im Herzen*" ("half child's play, half God in the heart"),[13] remarking that he could not think of a better adage to summarize his childhood. Some scholars seriously question whether "child's play" was ever a significant part of Søren's youth, for he "seemed to leap from infancy to manhood without passing through the happy stage of childhood,"[14] but the notion of "half God in the heart" stands to confirm "the suspicion that . . . the religious education he received from his father, however perverse it may have been, however inappropriate to his childhood, and however deep the scars it left upon him, had nevertheless the effect of planting God indelibly 'in the heart.'"[15]

Kierkegaard's father devoted much time and interest to both the religious piety and education of his brilliant son. Michael Kierkegaard seemed to manifest the worst sensibilities of Moravian piety, which, when coupled with his intrinsic melancholy and guilt, produced a volatile concoction. He passed along his deep anxieties to young Søren, who commented later about his own "crazy upbringing."

> It is terrible to think, even for a single moment, over the dark background which, from the very earliest of time, was part of my life. The dread with which my father filled my soul, his own frightful

---

of Kierkegaard, 71.

11. See, for example, Theodor Haecker's *Kierkegaard the Cripple*. In the introduction to this book, Kierkegaard journal translator, A. Dru suggests that the "thorn in the flesh" and "individual cross" mentioned by Kierkegaard is nothing else than this congenital deformity, v–xi.

12. *Journals of Søren Kierkegaard*, 1335.

13. Ibid., 240. Dru's edition of Kierkegaard's *Journals* mistakenly places this on December 31, 1838 rather than in 1839. For a full description, see Lowrie, *A Short Life of Kierkegaard*, 31–35.

14. Carnell, *The Burden of Søren Kierkegaard*, 15. See *Journals of Søren Kierkegaard*, 860, 921.

15. Lowrie, *A Short Life of Kierkegaard*, 37.

melancholy, and all the things in this connection which I do not even note down. I felt a dread of Christianity and yet felt myself so strongly drawn towards it.[16]

And yet, in the midst of this "crazy" religious upbringing, Kierkegaard would later note, "I owe everything, from the beginning, to my father, when, melancholy as he was, he saw me melancholy, his prayer to me was: Be sure that you really love Jesus Christ."[17] For all the personal turmoil and the vast range of his writings, it seemed that Søren would fulfill his father's prayer. But for a short period as a "prodigal," the pietist love of Jesus and the reality of "*Gott im Herzen*" would remain the invariables of Kierkegaard's life and the underlying impetus of his writing career.

Kierkegaard's rhetorical and inflammatory style (coupled with his habit of writing under different names and perspectives) makes a simple summary of his theological ideas difficult—if not nearly impossible. Nonetheless, with some effort one can come to some moderately clear conclusions about the views of this thinker regarding the character of subjectivity and the nature of religious belief. Since many of Kierkegaard's works were written under various pen names (each representing miscellaneous and, often, disparate personalities and perspectives), it can be somewhat precarious to cite "Kierkegaard" when it is one of his pseudonyms speaking. The question is legitimately raised as to which Kierkegaard is the real one? How does one know what voice truly represents the author's? It is somewhat defensible that the actual ideas of Kierkegaard *qua* Kierkegaard (as opposed to Kierkegaard the creative contriver of manifold dissenting personalities) can be discerned by careful scrutiny of his non-pseudonymous writings and his personal *Journals and Papers*. While in his pseudonymous works it can be argued that Kierkegaard is deliberately posturing and creatively characterizing several stances which are not his own and which are often at variance with one another, most Kierkegaard scholars are assured that the author's thoughts can be accurately discerned in this manner. In the end, C. Stephen Evans argues that, even if one does not accept this approach to discerning the "historic Kierkegaard," one can still offer this framework as an "exploration of an important argument found in Kierkegaard's writings."[18]

Confusion about Kierkegaard's actual authorial intent (if he had one) stems in part from the variety of—often mutually exclusive—viewpoints

---

16. *Journals of Søren Kierkegaard*, 841.
17. Ibid., 773.
18. Evans, *Subjectivity and Religious Belief*, 78, n. 5.

represented in the pseudonymous writings. Evans notes that Kierkegaard's "pronouncements on faith, despair, sin, and the like (particularly in the pseudonymous works) cannot be understood unless one takes care to determine from what standpoint the matter is being viewed."[19]

> In the course of his literature he characterizes a large number of perspectives which we might characterize as polar, or mutually exclusive. Among these would be the poetic/ethical, temporal/eternal, speculative/existential, abstract/concrete, objective/subjective, Christian/worldly, spiritual/unspiritual, truth/untruth.... [T]hough it is accurate to see in his literature a series of standpoints which seem progressively closer to that religious stance, it is nonetheless true that in the final analysis there are only two perspectives, *one* either-or. The religious, the existential, the eternal, the subjective, and the ethical are attempts to describe, in ways which are more or less adequate, one mode of thought which stands in sharp contrast to the poetic, the speculative, the objective, and impersonal, all of which represent life-views regarded by Kierkegaard as decidedly un-Christian.[20]

As Kierkegaard puts it succinctly: "There is an either-or: either God/ or . . . the rest is indifferent."[21] Thus, taking the Kierkegaard of his *Journals* and *Point of View* at his word, he will be read here as a "religious writer" from within the framework of Protestant Lutheran orthodoxy, who is deeply concerned with the matter of being a Christian within modern Christendom.

Kierkegaard and Protestant Orthodoxy

If Evangelical Christian admiration were a test of orthodoxy, then Kierkegaard's orthodoxy would indeed be questionable. He is often portrayed as, at best, seriously misled, and, at worst, diabolical in motive. Kierkegaard has been blamed for almost every modern deviation from historic Christianity imaginable. A favorite "whipping boy" for Protestant Evangelical thinker Francis A. Schaeffer, Kierkegaard is seen as the "father of all modern thinking." Kierkegaard is little more than a thoroughgoing modernist, and as such has perpetuated the modern "line of despair" by insisting on a radical

---

19. Ibid., 77.
20. Ibid.
21. Kierkegaard, *Christian Discourses*, 333.

dichotomy between faith and rationality.²² Orthodoxy, Schaeffer insists, has been seriously threatened by Kierkegaard's denial of an objective, rational criterion for belief:

> As a result of this, from [the time of Kierkegaard], if rationalistic man wants to deal with the really important things of human life (such as purpose, significance, the validity of love), he must discard rational thought about them and make a gigantic, non-rational leap of faith. The rationalistic framework had failed to produce an answer on the basis of reason, and so all hope of a uniform field of knowledge had to be abandoned.²³

Emanuel Hirsch, though a primary translator of Kierkegaard into German, still could not hide his distaste for Kierkegaard's approach. Hirsch paints a flat picture of Kierkegaard as nothing less than a typical nineteenth-century liberal who is "restless in the direction of interiorization."²⁴ Another writer indicates that, in addition to Kierkegaard's radical subjectivization of faith, it is his "separation of Christ's history from all other history" that is the most serious violation of Christian orthodoxy.²⁵ According to this common charge (laid at the feet of Karl Barth a century later), Kierkegaard is accused of denying or stripping the redemptive-historical events of Scripture away from the realm of objective history (and hence, from objective verifiability and historical criticism), thus making them irrelevant as an object of faith. As such, Christianity becomes an a-historical religion, making only claims about the state of the interior self rather than about the nature of the world or God's words and deeds within human history. "With the radical separation of Christ from history, Kierkegaard runs the danger of making Christ a figment of the imagination . . . ."²⁶ He continues by charging that Kierkegaard has effectively sacrificed the "objective Christ for a subjective experience."²⁷

This same criticism is echoed by British theologian Colin Brown, who accuses Kierkegaard of a sort of "pistocentrism" in his apparent unconcern for the object of faith:

---

22. Schaffer, *The God Who Is There, Complete Works*, 1:15, 16.

23. Ibid.

24. Hirsch, *Geschichte der neueren evangelische Theologie*, 5:433–91, as quoted in Berkhof, *Two Hundred Years of Theology*, 81, n. 18.

25. Mayers, *Both/And*, 130.

26. Ibid., 131.

27. Ibid., 132.

> At times [Kierkegaard's] view of God seems to have a good deal in common with the Wizard of Oz. It is not so much his existence that counts but the thought of his existence. In the American fairy story Dorothy, the straw man, the tin man and the cowardly lion take a course of action because they believe in the Wizard of Oz. Their lives are transformed because of their belief in him. But in the end the Wizard turns out to be a fraud. He is not a Wizard at all but an ordinary man. So it often appears with Kierkegaard that it is the thought of God that prompts him to react the way he does, rather than encounter with God himself.[28]

If this reproach is correct, then it may not matter for Kierkegaard whether God is actually out "there" or not as the focus of human faith; what matters is simply the passion or force of the faith experience itself. In this view, then, the validity of faith is determined by the sheer force of the faith response, rather than by whether anything objectively true corresponds to that belief or not. The subjective experience of belief is transformative regardless of its object. This analysis of Kierkegaard is not limited to Evangelical Christians, of course. Wesley K. H. Teo makes the claim in his article "Self-Responsibility in Existentialism and Buddhism" that the object of belief for Kierkegaard is essentially a non-theoretical "fiction," and, thus, in some sense parallel to the non-historically grounded faith of Buddhism.[29] Teo contends that for Kierkegaard "whatever is experienced in the depth of one's being is the truth."[30] C. Stephen Evans responds,

> To the philosopher who insists that only propositions can be true or false, Kierkegaard's problem will not be a genuine problem. But if we take seriously talk about true friendships, true and faithful dogs, and "swords which swing true" then we will not discard at the outset the possibility that some modes of existence may be meaningfully described as true and others as false. Existence for Kierkegaard is equivalent to choosing and acting; he is thus concerned about a kind of truth which is essentially related to ethical decision-making.[31]

---

28. Brown, *Philosophy and the Christian Faith*, 130.

29. Teo, "Self-Responsibility in Existentialism and Buddhism," 80. C. Stephen Evans offers a sound refutation of the opinion in his response. "Kierkegaard on Subjective Truth," 288–99.

30. Teo, "Self-Responsibility in Existentialism and Buddhism," 90.

31. Evans, "Kierkegaard on Subjective Truth," 291.

SØREN KIERKEGAARD AND THE PARADOX OF FAITH

Others, perhaps in less serious criticisms, call into question Kierkegaard's theological or philosophical soundness *in lieu* of his seeming psychological instability. Anglican theologian Stuart Barton Babbage tells the anecdote of Oxford don C. S. Lewis's initial encounter with the ideas of Kierkegaard during the Second World War:

> In my bedroom, soon after [Lewis'] arrival, I proudly showed him some of the works of Søren Kierkegaard. He had never heard of him. I was passing through a stage of youthful and eager enthusiasm for the works of the melancholy Dane, and I brashly proceeded to enlighten him. I expatiated at length on the circumstances under which Kierkegaard had driven Regina Olsen to break their engagement by representing himself to be a seducer and deceiver. Kierkegaard had meditated deeply on the significance of God's command to Abraham to sacrifice his son Isaac: was he, in relation to his own prospective marriage, being called upon to sacrifice the one he loved? Lewis had enough. "Tell me no more," he brusquely interjected, "the man was pathological." And he refused to hear any more.[32]

Apparently, Lewis' opinion never changed. He, like many Christians enamored with rationalism, could never stomach the apparent anti-rationality and eccentricity of the Danish thinker. One writer concedes, "Kierkegaard was a neurotic: of that the story of his life leaves little doubt. His heritage, physique, temperament, upbringing and way of life were all abnormal, and produced a perpetual maladjustment between him and his environment. His *Journals* are happy hunting ground for the psychoanalyst."[33] Yet, E. J. Carnell suggests that it would be careless to

> imply that Kierkegaard's idiosyncrasies disqualified him from engaging in the pursuit of truth. On the contrary, a number of great writers have asserted that neurotic pressures inside an individual create a painful feeling of maladjustment to life: and that his feeling, in turn, may prompt the suffering of the individual to take up the pen and tell what he believes is man's relation to reality, as well as to spell out the responsibilities which accompany that relation. In other words, the slightest spiritual, rational, or emotional impression on the psyche may be used as a clue to the meaning of life in general.[34]

32. Babbage, "To the Royal Air Force," 89–90.
33. Patrick, *Pascal and Kierkegaard*, 2:311.
34. Carnell, *The Burden of Søren Kierkegaard*, 14.

Renowned Kierkegaard translator and biographer Walter Lowrie offers his seasoned perspective on this matter,

> It will not do to dispose of Kierkegaard's psychology by remarking that his own soul, the soul he chiefly studied, was a sick soul. For not only could he reply that all souls are sick, and that the notion that one has a "healthy minded" soul is the most perilous of all sicknesses: but all pathologists will agree with him that the study of abnormal states is essential for the understanding of normal health. If it is true that few men have had so sick a soul to deal with as had Kierkegaard, and that no one of them has ever probed so deeply into his sick soul, with such intellectual competence, we may reasonably expect to learn something from his psychology.[35]

Some may think it careless to be so quickly dismissive of the prospect of Kierkegaard's pathology given the undeniably abnormal nature of his life. Yet, the central concern of most Kierkegaard studies in philosophy and religion (psychology notwithstanding) is not so much his mental state as the intellectual byproduct and influence of his writings. Psychotherapy of the dead is dubious business at best and reconstructing any deceased person's psychological condition is certainly precarious. What one can assess with better assurance, however, is Kierkegaard's writings and the effect of his thought. Whatever anomalies might have existed in the mind of Kierkegaard, they undoubtedly contributed to his uncommon and peculiar genius. Indeed, Kierkegaard himself cites favorably an adage from Seneca (who, in turn, was borrowing from Aristotle): *nullum unquam exstetit magnum ingenium sine aliqua dementia* ("there never was a great genius without some madness").[36] In Kierkegaard the "madness" and "genius" coalesce into a distinctive remedy to what he presumed to be the sick condition of the modern soul.

The other criticisms are more serious, it seems. If Kierkegaard is truly deviating from orthodoxy, then he is simply mistaken about himself. For Kierkegaard's solution is intended to provide a critique from within Protestant orthodoxy rather than from without. If, therefore, he is to be considered an orthodox Protestant thinker (as he perceived himself to be), then his "attack upon Christendom" was a critique from a wounded lover, rather than an assault from an outsider. If this is so, then, what is one to make of the charge that Kierkegaard effectively discards the objective content

---

35. Lowrie, "Introduction by the Translator," xii.
36. Kierkegaard, *Fear and Trembling*, 116.

of faith in favor of passionate, subjective experience alone? Is it possible that Kierkegaard shares with Schleiermacher and Kant not merely a commitment to a subjective approach to religious belief, but also a disregard for the objective, historical tenets of traditional orthodoxy? If Kierkegaard truly does, as many suggest, sacrifice the "objective Christ for a subjective experience," or if he is concerned only with the act or quality of faith rather than with the historic object of faith (that is, Christ), then his orthodoxy (at least by ancient, medieval, or Reformation standards) would indeed be called into question.

In order to better appreciate the accusations against Kierkegaard's orthodoxy, one must begin to understand better to what extent he is working within and from an Enlightenment epistemological framework, and to what degree he is a critic of the same. By some accounts, Kierkegaard has contributed virtually nothing which had not already been said by (and said better, and more clearly by) Kant and Schleiermacher on religion. It is true that Kierkegaard's contrast between abstract (or objective) thought and the subjective thinker is not unlike Kant's distinction between theoretical and practical reason:

> Instead of having the task of understanding the concrete abstractly, as abstract thinking has, the subjective thinker has the opposite task of understanding the abstract concretely. Abstract thinking turns from concrete human beings to humankind in general: the subjective thinker understands the abstract concept to be the concrete human being, to be this individual existing human being.[37]

Thus, abstract or objective thought (like "theoretical reason") is not able to address the individual and ethical aspects of human existence, while the subjective thinker can properly attend to these crucial matters of personal existence. Kierkegaard writes, "Abstraction is disinterested, but to exist is the highest interest for an existing person."[38] In Kierkegaard's assessment, it is impossible to speak legitimately to axiological concerns from the "neutral" standpoint of objectivity, as if one could be dispassionate or unaffected by such matters. It is only when one realizes the importance of the ethical for oneself as an individual that ethics can possibly make sense. "To think about [existential problems] so as to leave out passion is to not think about

---

37. Kierkegaard, *Concluding Unscientific Postscript*, 1:352.
38. Ibid., 1:313.

them at all, is to forget the point, that one indeed is oneself an existing person."[39]

It seems clear that Kierkegaard shares with Kant and Schleiermacher a fundamental distinction between the subjective and the objective in matters of faith. Likewise, these three modern thinkers agree on the limitations of objective, theoretical knowledge in matters of faith, and, therefore, the location of religion in the realm of the subject. "This tying of religion to feelings and morality certainly does suggest a pattern essentially parallel to Kant"[40] as well as Schleiermacher. In all three cases, there is a decided preoccupation with self-awareness as the highest end of humankind.[41] Nevertheless, this chapter will suggest that Kierkegaard's subjectivity is a solution from *within* the orthodox Protestant tradition, rather than a move from, or modification of, it. While Kierkegaard's stance is clearly reflective of similar Enlightenment epistemological concerns as Kant and Schleiermacher, it does not deviate from the primary content of orthodox Protestantism. Kant and Schleiermacher seem to propose a renovation of Christian faith, while Kierkegaard intends a recovery. Though in many respects Kierkegaard is a modern thinker, he still stands solidly within orthodox Christianity—even if his own peculiar psychological makeup and unique context brought him to become a profound critic of "Christendom." Ultimately, Kierkegaard's criticism is not with the objective content of orthodoxy *per se*, but with the inflated assumption that sheer mental assent to orthodoxy was sufficient for authentic faith. While Kant and Schleiermacher seemed to believe that historic Christian faith claims were not up to the high standards of modern, enlightened people, Kierkegaard saw it differently: he feared that modern people were not up to the high standards of the historic Christian faith. Schleiermacher and Kant seemed to focus their interest on the character of faith itself, Kierkegaard seemed more concerned with the character of the faithful.

Thus, Kierkegaard's protest does not seem to be against historic, orthodox "Christianity" (as was Kant's and Schleiermacher's), but against "Christendom" as it had been appropriated by modern people. If Schleiermacher and Kant wished to recover or preserve Christian faith *for* modernity, then Kierkegaard wished to rescue Christian faith *from* modernity. In fact, it seems Kierkegaard's dispute is with modernity itself. He is critical

---

39. Ibid., 1:351.
40. Evans, *Subjectivity and Religious Belief*, 74.
41. Gill, "Kant, Kierkegaard, and Religious Knowledge," 188–204.

of the Enlightenment's stance of arrogance that it can retain *both* a relaxed form of Christianity *and* the sense of moral and intellectual autonomy of the age, without conflict or contradiction. Indeed, it was precisely because of Kierkegaard's commitment to the notion of grace in New Testament (and Lutheran) Christianity, that he stood as a fierce opponent to the presumption that God could be grasped abstractly through Cartesian cogitation—an attitude that had become common in Hegel-influenced modern Protestantism. "What he fought so passionately was the idolatrous identification of objective thought with man's highest end."[42]

Kierkegaard differs from Schleiermacher and Kant particularly in his orthodox view of the effects of original sin. From Augustine to Calvin, it had been understood that human rebellion against God had distinct noetic effects. Humans stood incapable of appropriating redemptive knowledge of God by means of their own reasoning ability or morality, not because reason itself was flawed, but because the reasoner was. Sin produced a pronounced spiritual and noetic blindness in the human race. Enlightenment optimism brushed aside this orthodox notion of the epistemic consequences of sin and proclaimed a doctrine of human self-sufficiency. If anything about the modern spirit was distasteful to Kierkegaard, it was this pretentious attitude of independence before the mysteries of God. "If Kierkegaard is right in thinking that human beings are in the grip of something like original sin . . . then the attempt to justify Christianity before its cultured despisers will likely be a betrayal of Christianity."[43]

In brief, Kierkegaard is not so much juxtaposing faith over against reason as he is contrasting the attitudes of meekness and arrogance before the face of God's self-revelation. Modern Christendom had, by nature of its grandiose confidence in human reason and its sense of autonomy, lost a key component to authentic faith, namely humility. Kierkegaard writes, "Humanly speaking my misfortune has clearly been that I was given a strict Christian upbringing—and that I have to live in so-called Christendom."[44] By "Christendom," Kierkegaard, of course, means a range of influences within the Protestant church, but chief among them is the character of the church in Denmark as it has made concessions to modernity in general, and to the theological effect of Hegelian philosophy in particular.

42. Evans, *Subjectivity and Religious Belief*, 75.

43. Evans, "The Epistemological Significance of Transformative Religious Experiences," 190.

44. *Journals of Søren Kierkegaard*, 892.

Hegelian Idealism and the Eclipse of the Subject

Georg Wilhelm Friedrich Hegel (1770–1831) grew to be deeply unsatisfied with what he saw as the inherent skepticism in Kantian epistemology. He rejected Kant's agnosticism surrounding the knowability of "*das Ding an sich*." Hegel instead postulated that objective reality does indeed correspond to our knowledge and to our experience of it. Against Kant, Hegel argued that our minds do not determine the nature of reality: our minds simply recognize what is objectively true about the world. *Das Ding an sich* is, therefore, ultimately knowable to the human mind. In fact, Hegel postulated an essential unity or oneness between our minds and objective reality. The former is something of a mirror reflection of the latter. Hence, to understand our minds is to understand reality—that is, it is to know universal Mind or *Geist* (or from a religious perspective, "Spirit").

However, if reality is as Hegel describes, then it simultaneously includes many seemingly contradictory concepts or essences. Hegel believes that these are not truly contradictory, while they are, nevertheless, opposites. These opposites (what he calls "thesis" and "antithesis") can be combined into a higher reality—a universal which resolves the contradiction ("synthesis"). Indeed, history is the unfolding of this dialectical process: the *thetical* and *antithetical* perpetually amalgamate into a higher *synthesis*, which itself is another thesis for which there is a corresponding antithesis, etc. In this dialectic, nothing need be rejected as false or useless, since it is all part of a higher synthesis. God, or Absolute Spirit (*Geist*), is seen as the *telos* of this dialectical process—the Absolute mind, the complete and final resolution of all reality and idea. Christianity, according to Hegel, is therefore a kind of evolutionary truth which leads to this end. It is perfectly adaptable to each age, wholly capable of admixing what appear to be conflicting ideas into a purer alloy of superior truth. Hegel is confident that, over time, the human mind is capable of discovering such truth, for the rational intellect has the innate capacity to find perfect resolution within these opposite truths. Henry Allison wrote:

> The tendency towards objective thought finds its culmination in Hegel. In the Hegelian philosophy we are shown the necessity in transcending our finite particularity and viewing things from the standpoint of the Idea. . . . From this standpoint it is incumbent upon the individual to "forget himself" in the sense of his finite

particularity, to become disinterested in his personal existence and absorbed in the Idea.[45]

The primary focus of Hegelianism, then, is this distinct brand of objective rationality and idealism, which significantly downplays the particular existence of the individual person. Hegel wrote, "Among the many consequences that follow from what has been said, it is of importance to emphasize that, that knowledge is only real and can only be set forth fully in the form of science, in the form of system . . . ."[46] Such objective rationality led Hegel to the very necessary conclusion that in order to focus on the Absolute, "the individual must all the more forget himself, as in the fact the very nature of science implies that he should."[47] Science, if it is to remain pure, must be done from this kind of objective stance. It is here where Hegel became fixated with objectivity, reason and the Absolute that Kierkegaard would suggest that he lost touch with reality on the level at which human beings truly function. The subject is swallowed up by the enormity of the object. Hegel, according to Kierkegaard, has sacrificed axiology to epistemology, practical doing to theoretical knowing.

Hegel's pervasive and optimistic view of objective rationality compels him to conclude that reason must never contradict faith. They can always be reconciled. Reason is superior to faith, yet indeed they must both be found synthetically compatible in the end, because rather than being polar opposites, they are two sides of the same coin. Faith, in Hegel's assessment,

> is not opposed to reason: the two have the same content: philosophy is truly theological. Somewhat like the eschatological vision of God in traditional theology, philosophy in Hegel's system gives clear intelligibility and cogent evidence for what faith perceives only in an obscure manner. Hegel is a rationalist insofar as he believes that human reason, even in this present life, can rigorously establish the truth of revealed religion, supplanting faith.[48]

Even the content of faith, for Hegel, seemed perfectly rational. In Jesus Christ, one could embrace the *thesis* of the infinite and the divine along with the *antithesis* of the finite and the human in complete dialectical synthesis. Within the Hegelian dialectic, these two need never be juxtaposed to one

---

45. Allison, "Christianity and Nonsense," 291.
46. Hegel, *Phenomenology of Mind*, 85.
47. Ibid., 130.
48. Dulles, *The Assurance of Things Hoped For*, 79–80.

another. They can make perfect rational sense. It seemed to some that this Hegelian "both/and" offered the Western thinker the best of all theoretical worlds. It implied an optimism that human reason could resolve all human problems and conflicts, so long as humans retained the stance of the objective scientist toward the world-object. Hegel, not surprisingly, understood his own system of philosophy to be the ultimate synthesis and culmination of intellectual history. However, as his system might more appropriately suggest, Hegelianism simply became another thesis in anticipation of an antithesis. Helmut Thielicke suggests that this antithesis takes two forms: the materialist form of Feuerbach and Marx, and the existentialist form of Kierkegaard. Thielicke writes:

> Kierkegaard saw in Hegel's gigantic effort to identify thought and being (i.e. to understand the real as the self-development of the absolute spirit, and the finite spirit as the locus of the self-consciousness of the spirit) a vast deceptive maneuver which it was the task of his thinking to unmask in various ways. Hegel's statements about reality imply no reality for Kierkegaard. They are an empty abstraction, and they construct an absurd reality of thought or phantom of the brain. The difficulty in this gigantic effort is that only God himself, as a transcendent entity distinct from finite reality, can be the subject of pure thought. Only this being is at the sovereign distance at which one can see and survey the whole panorama of being below.[49]

The "aesthetic man" described by Kierkegaard in volume 1 of his *Either/Or* is a caricature of the Hegelian. The aesthetic stance is pure *theoria*: detached spectatorship. It is the consummate stance of objectivity, as the human presumes the position of audience within the "theatre" of the world, passively observing and critiquing the "performance" of history. The aesthete is never actively involved in making actual ethical choices, but merely stands apart, coolly observing and commenting on them in a detached manner. Life for the aesthete is understood in terms of boredom and excitement, never good or evil. Kierkegaard wrote: "Hence in our age as the order of the day we have the disgusting sight of young men who are able to mediate Christianity and paganism, are able to play with the titanic forces of history, and are unable to tell a plain man what he has to do in life, and do not know any better what they themselves have to do."[50]

---

49. Thielicke, *Modern Faith and Thought*, 494.
50. Kierkegaard, *Either/Or*, 2:175.

Hegelianism, in Kierkegaard's assessment, is an elaborate, carefully reasoned philosophical system, but not an adequate way of living. Kierkegaard characterizes the Hegelian as "the philosopher" for whom "world history is concluded, and he mediates" because "he is on the outside, he is not in the game."[51] For the aesthetic man sees no need to be personally or passionately involved in making ethical choices, for he perceives that he can "live off of contemplation."[52] Kierkegaard perceives this to be one of the more serious problems of such abstract theorizing. This is why he became, by means of his own inimitable irony, the Socratic gadfly of nineteenth century Denmark. He says:

> In relation to their systems most systematizers are like a man who builds an enormous castle and lives in a shack nearby: they do not live in their own enormous systematic buildings. But spiritually that is a decisive objection. Spiritually speaking a man's thought must be the building in which he lives—otherwise everything is topsy-turvy.[53]

In opposition to this Hegelian framework, Kierkegaard produced a large body of literature which cleverly and rhetorically posits the antithetical stance in order to shake up the complacent and alert them to the serious condition of Christendom. Most criticisms of Kierkegaard's orthodoxy fail to acknowledge the intentionally dialectical "one-sidedness" in his public writings, especially when compared to the relatively balanced viewpoints expressed in his private journals. However, according to most Kierkegaardian scholars, to fail to appreciate Kierkegaard's rhetorical polarity is to miss his point entirely.

> We thus see that Kierkegaard's protest against objective thought on behalf of existence is not an attack on thought *per se*. It is a protest against the Hegelian notion of speculative thought. It is an assertion that existence involves more than the knowing of particulars in terms of abstract possibilities; existence is the process of actualizing abstract possibilities in the form of concrete particulars. Among the acts which are potentially actualizable are the acts of knowing, but existence is not reducible to those acts. Still,

---

51. Ibid., 175–76.
52. Ibid., 176.
53. *Journals of Søren Kierkegaard*, 583.

existence is far from thoughtless; when a man exists in the fullest sense his life is permeated by reflection.[54]

Kierkegaard's famed focus on subjectivity in religious belief is only part of the picture. While his extreme language can appear to denigrate objective Christian truth, it seems that Kierkegaard is simply employing a rhetorical device to intentionally create a (resolutely non-Hegelian) reaction. In order to deny the legitimacy of the comfortable Hegelian synthesis, Kierkegaard works vigorously to avoid having his statements merely synthesized into the opposing framework. He does not wish to give any ground to the enemy by affirming what they already assume to be true. Therefore, he makes his position as offensive and unaccommodating as possible to force the Hegelians into an either/or decision. By making statements which engaged the individual at the level of both passion and will, Kierkegaard intends to frustrate the autonomous reason of modern Christendom, and thereby make true faith possible.

The Christian faith, in Kierkegaard's assessment, is radically subjective and inward when contrasted to the overly rational and objectified Hegelian system. The content of faith will, to anyone looking for pure rational justification, appear paradoxical and absurd. By granting Hegel no ground, Kierkegaard intends to say that there are no Christian answers to Hegelianism, because they are simply asking the wrong questions. Thus, through the use of "extremist" language and highly subjective rhetoric, Kierkegaard intended to disqualify any religious stance that presumes mere passive objectivity or over-confidence in the human rational ability to understand God. Christianity is not the object of dispassionate science—it belongs only to those who will passionately and existentially commit themselves to it. Kierkegaard writes:

> The thing is to understand myself, to see what God wishes *me* to do; the thing is to find truth which is truth *for me*, to find *the idea for which I can live and die* . . . . What would be the use of discovering so-called objective truth, of working through all the systems of philosophy . . . what good would it do me to be able to explain the meaning of Christianity if it had no deeper significance *for me and for my life* . . . ?[55]

---

54. Evans, *Subjectivity and Religious Belief*, 81.
55. *Journals of Søren Kierkegaard*, 22.

The objective dimension of the Christian faith is not absent for Kierkegaard; it is merely deemed irrelevant if one does not passionately act on its truthfulness. Kierkegaard continues, "I certainly do not deny that I still recognize an *imperative of understanding* and that through it one can work upon men, *but it must be taken up into my life*, and *that* is what I now recognize as the most important thing."[56] In the privacy of his own journals, Kierkegaard acknowledges that while subjectivity has priority in Christian commitment, it is not the whole picture. But Kierkegaard saw little need to state this in his public writings. Given the deep impact Hegelianism was having in the universities and theological seminaries in nineteenth-century Denmark, Kierkegaard simply did not wish to offer any concessions to his opponent.

Publicly, Kierkegaard would never make the concessions seen in his journals. He had a mission. Any visible alignment with the "enemy" would spell doom to this program. Hence, this extreme rhetoric: "God is a subject, and hence only for subjectivity in inwardness."[57] "Faith is a paradox and the individual absolutely cannot make himself intelligible to anyone."[58] And finally, "No knowledge can have as its object this absurdity that the eternal is the historical."[59] Yet while intentionally, rhetorically radical in his public presentation of the Christians message to a reason intoxicated Christendom, Kierkegaard himself never actually abandoned the objective content of Protestant orthodoxy.

Stages On Life's Way

In contrast to the Hegelian dialectic, in which all contraries are finally reconciled in the synthesis of the Absolute, Kierkegaard developed his own mild (and intentionally sardonic) "dialectic." Yet, unlike the pursuit of a rational ideal in Hegel, Kierkegaard's dialectic reaches no synthesis. Contraries remain contraries. There is not the comfort of embracing antithetical realities in a "both/and." Instead, the individual must make a radical choice of "either/or." The goal of the process is not intellectual awareness, but self-actualization through free choice and commitment. It is significant that Kierkegaard sees human agency as the impetus for this process, since

56. Ibid.
57. Kierkegaard, *Concluding Unscientific Postscript*, 200.
58. Kierkegaard, *Fear and Trembling*, 81.
59. Kierkegaard, *Philosophical Fragments*, 62.

he viewed the dialectic of Hegel as coldly deterministic and in violation of the essential free will of the individual.

Kierkegaard's dialectic consists of three levels or stages. The first stage, represented by the young man simply called "The Seducer" or, even more simply, "A" in Volume I of *Either/Or* (pseudonymously published by Kierkegaard under the guise of the editor "Victor Eremita"), is called the *Aesthetic stage*. The aesthetic person is a spectator on life and is devoid of ethical values. Life is categorized as either dull or interesting, never as good or evil. The Seducer, at the height of his rhetoric, declares: "Adam was bored alone; then Adam and Eve were bored together; then Adam and Eve and Cain and Abel were bored *en famille*; then the population of the world increased, and the people were bored *en masse*."[60] An inevitable crisis occurs when the aesthetic man comes to the end of himself in this state and realizes the pointlessness of such an existence. A definitive "either/or" must now be faced by the aesthete. Either the individual remains in the despair of the aesthetic stage or, in a moment of risk, chooses to move on to the next stage toward authentic existence.

The next stage is the *Ethical stage*. Here the individual comes to recognize the validity of universal moral standards. This stage is represented by "the Judge" or "B" in *Either/Or* volume II. While Don Juan might be symbolic of the aesthetic man, Kierkegaard suggests that Socrates exemplifies the ethical man. The ethical man has accepted the limitations that moral responsibility places on his life. Eventually, the dialectic process begins its work on the consciousness of the ethical man. Previously this individual has viewed sin as ignorance or weakness in the will. Now, however, the ethical man realizes his own inability to keep the moral law, which results in despair and guilt. This *Angst* compels the individual to face another inevitable either/or. Here the individual must choose either remain in despair or move to the final stage. Movement here, however, involves a "leap of faith" and a "commitment to the absurd."

Kierkegaard's last stage is the *Religious stage* (divided into religiousness A and religiousness B—that is, respectively, the natural religions and Christianity). Ultimately, this stage results in personal relationship with God. But this involves great risk, for no knowledge of God is possible prior to one's commitment to Him. The choice must be made in the face of the ultimate paradox, the rationally irreconcilable notion that: the Infinite had become finite; the Transcendent had become immanent; Creator

---

60. Kierkegaard, *Either/Or*, 1:282.

had become creature; God had become human in the incarnation of Jesus Christ. It is only by means of this subjective dialectic that one can come to faith in God. Hegel's dialectic (a synthesis of both/and) attempted to eliminate the paradoxical nature of Christian truth—to bring God wholly within the grasp of human reason. This, Kierkegaard insists, simply will not do: "Either/or is the word at which the folding doors fly open and the ideals appear—O blessed Spirit! Either/or is the pass which admits to the absolute—God be praised! Yea, either/or is the key to heaven."[61] On the other hand, "Both/and is the way to hell."[62] Kierkegaard continues, describing the end or goal of his dialectic process:

> As a result of receiving the condition in the moment, his course took the opposite direction, or he was turned around. Let us call this change *conversion*, even though this is a word hitherto unused; but we choose it precisely in order to avoid confusion, for it seems to be created for the very change of which we speak.[63]

Attack upon Christendom

The Most Reverend J. P. Mynster, Bishop of Copenhagen, was a long-time friend of Søren Kierkegaard's father, Michael Pederson Kierkegaard, and had presided over the confirmation of young Søren. Yet, Kierkegaard grew to despise the Bishop and the complacent, culturally accommodated church he stood for. Out of respect, however, he remained silent during the life of the Bishop. In 1849, Kierkegaard wrote in his journals:

> Sometimes I am afraid for the man when I think of Bishop Mynster. He is now 72 and soon he will go to his judgment. And what he has not done to harm Christianity by conjuring up a lying picture—so that he could sit back and rule. His sermons are quite good—but in eternity he will not have to preach—but be judged.[64]

When the Bishop died in January 1854, Kierkegaard launched a full-scale attack. In a funeral oration Professor Hans L. Mortensen (who had been instrumental in introducing Hegelianism into Denmark) eulogized the Bishop as a "witness to the truth." Kierkegaard could stand no more.

61. Kierkegaard, *Attack upon Christendom*, 81–82.
62. Kierkegaard, quoted in Bretall, *A Kierkegaard Anthology*, 19.
63. Kierkegaard, *Philosophical Fragments*, 18.
64. *Journals of Søren Kierkegaard*, 908.

He began publishing a series of papers called *The Instant,* later compiled as the book *Attack upon Christendom*. Kierkegaard attacked the condition of the state church as a serious deviation from biblical Christianity. He proclaimed the necessity of individual choice in faith out of an opposition to the Danish Lutheran Church practice of "christening" all children born in the state. Christianity is not, he insisted, something the state church can dispense at will—it is passionate commitment chosen freely by the individual. Another matter of concern to Kierkegaard was the prosperity of the clergy as state officials. He saw this as quite unlike the picture of New Testament Christianity. Suffering, not prosperity, is the mark of the true Christian, Kierkegaard exclaimed.

> Yes, such is the fact: the official worship of God (with the claim of being the Christianity of the New Testament) is, Christianly, a counterfeit, a forgery. But thou, thou plain Christian, on the average thou has no suspicion, art entirely *bona fide*, confiding in the conviction that everything is all right, that it is the Christianity of the *New* Testament. . . . For really this forgery is the counterfeit which came about in the course of the centuries, whereby little by little Christianity has become exactly the opposite of what it is in the New Testament. So I repeat. This has to be said: by ceasing to take part in the official worship of God as it is now (if in fact thou dost take part in it) thou hast one guilt the less, and that a great one: thou dost not take part in treating God as a fool.[65]

And, "What a fundamental confusion! In the same sense as one speaks of murdering a language, this is murdering Christianity, turning it round about, standing it on its head, or in a polite fashion shuffling it out. Under the color of Christianity the people live as pagans!"[66] And finally,

> If then we really are Christians, if it is quite as it should be "Christendom" and a Christian world—then would I shout, loud enough if possible to be heard in heaven. "Thou infinite One, if in other respects Thou has showed Thyself to be love, this verily was unloving on Thy part, that Thou hast not let men know that the New Testament is no longer a guide for Christians! How cruel, while all has been changed to the very opposite, and yet it is true that we are all Christians, to alarm the weak by the fact that Thy Word has not yet been repealed or altered!"[67]

65. Kierkegaard, *Attack Upon Christendom*, 59–60.
66. Ibid., 132–33.
67. Ibid., 111.

Thus, in the absence of a desire to take seriously the demands of the gospel, Kierkegaard, with characteristically impassioned and incisive rhetoric, offers the following tongue-in-cheek (yet intentionally serious) proposal:

> I might be tempted to make Christendom a proposal different from that of the Bible Society. Let us collect all the New Testaments we have, let us bring them out to an open square or up to the summit of a mountain, and while we all kneel let one man speak to God thus: "Take this book back again: we men, such as we now are, are not fit to go in for this sort of thing, it only makes us unhappy." This is my proposal, that like those inhabitants in Gerasa we beseech Christ to depart from our borders. This would be an honest and human way of talking—rather different from the disgusting, hypocritical priestly fudge about life having no value for us without this priceless blessing which is Christianity.[68]

Due to his "no holds barred" language, it is understandable that the strongest criticism of Kierkegaard's "attack" often comes from apologists of the Christian faith. Kierkegaard has strong words for apologetic attempts to prove Christianity to be rationally justifiable, simply because he believes that the truth of Christianity is not discoverable through autonomous human science, but in the faithful response of the individual and the transformation of authentic faith. Again, it should be remembered that Kierkegaard's words regarding the historicity and objective truthfulness of Christianity must be read in context of his reactionary agenda. Kierkegaard thought that most post-Enlightenment attempts to explain Christianity to the rational human mind had ended in a rape of the very essence of Christian faith. Furthermore, Divinity students can readily memorize facts about sacred history, and even teach them as a clergyman, without ever having been personally transformed by them. Kierkegaard's outrage at these commonplace violations of Christian truth led him to strongly assert the necessity for inwardness and subjectivity in one's Christian commitment.

To criticize Kierkegaard's apologetic (or lack thereof) as subjective, one must always keep in mind that he is not writing, *contra-Gentiles*—he is writing contra-Christendom. Hence, it is difficult to say precisely how Kierkegaard would handle "real apologetics" with actual pagans. That is not his immediate concern. He is surrounded by those who claim to be Christian. So, what one has is a clear example (in the Kierkegaard corpus) of how he would handle polemics within a society which is saturated with

---

68. Ibid., 126.

insincere, self-indulgent, and rationalist Christianity. Thus, it seems that this "attack upon Christendom" is the manifestation of Kierkegaard's serious reflection on a difficult problem: "the problem of becoming a Christian . . . within Christendom."[69]

Colin Brown's criticism that Kierkegaard teaches a "wizard of Oz theology"—that the object of faith is unimportant, only the subjective quality of belief really matters—grows out of reflection on such strong statements as these:

> "History," says faith, "has nothing to do with Christ." With regard to him we have only Sacred History (which is different in kind from general history), Sacred History which tells of his life and career when in debasement and tells also that he affirmed himself to be God. He is the paradox which history never will be able to digest or convert into a general syllogism.[70]

And also:

> But can one, then, learn anything from history about Jesus? No, nothing. Jesus Christ is the object of faith—one either believes in him or is offended by him, for "to know" means precisely that such knowledge does not pertain to him. History can, therefore, to be sure, give one knowledge in abundance; but "knowledge" annihilates Jesus Christ.[71]

Kierkegaard asks in the *Philosophical Fragments*, "Can a historical point of departure be given for an eternal consciousness: how can such a point of departure be of more than historical interest: can an eternal happiness be built on historical knowledge?"[72] Likewise, Kierkegaard writes in the *Concluding Unscientific Postscript*, it is "a dialectical contradiction" to expect that "eternal happiness in time" could result from "something else in time" or from "something historical."[73] The incarnational claims of Christianity stand against all dialectical reasoning, for "the historical under consideration here is not something historical in the ordinary sense but

---

69. Kierkegaard, *The Point of View for My Work*, 95.
70. Kierkegaard, *Preparation for the Christian Life*, 169.
71. Ibid., 175.
72. Kierkegaard, *Philosophical Fragments*, 1.
73. Kierkegaard, *Concluding Unscientific Postscript*, 1:570, 574.

consists of that which can become historical only against its nature, consequently by virtue of the absurd."[74]

Indeed, it is difficult not to simply take Kierkegaard's words at face value. The power of his language would lead many to believe that he leaves Christianity drowning in a sea of subjectivism. Yet, there is a method to Kierkegaard's presumably unorthodox madness. He is not, in fact, denying the historicity of the Christ-event; he is simply declaring the inadequacy of the human science of history to give the complete and necessary picture of Jesus Christ which can lead to personal faith. Note again that Kierkegaard says that "the *historical* under consideration here is not something historical *in the ordinary sense* but consists of that which *can become historical* only *against its nature*, consequently by virtue of the *absurd*" (my italics).[75] Kierkegaard's agenda here is not to assert the *unreality* of the incarnation as an objective historical event, but rather its *implausibility* to the autonomous human mind, thus making it appropriate for the humble stance of faith. He writes:

> The proofs which Scripture presents for Christ's divinity—His miracles, His resurrection from the dead, His Ascension into heaven—are therefore only for faith, that is, they are not "proofs," they have no intention of proving that all this agrees perfectly with reason; on the contrary they would prove that it conflicts with reason and therefore is an object of faith.[76]

Kierkegaard is not concerned with arguing that the incarnation did not really occur, but rather with how we appropriate that fact. That the incarnation did, in fact, occur is a given for Kierkegaard; however, it is our relationship to that fact that is of ultimate concern for him. Is faith merely the acceptance of this dogma because, in Hegelian thinking, it makes perfect rational sense, or is it accepting this truth even though it makes no sense—it is absurd? Affirmation of certain historic details, or confidence in certain ideas arrived at through use of reason, says Kierkegaard, is simply not faith. "For whether now one learns little or much about him, it will not represent what he was in reality. . . . History makes Christ look different from what he looked in truth."[77]

---

74. Ibid., 578.
75. Ibid.
76. Kierkegaard, *Training in Christianity*, 29.
77. Kierkegaard, *Preparation for the Christian Life*, 169.

For example, an "objective" observer witnessing the birth of Christ may be able to report that a male Jewish baby was born in a barn to *Miriam* and *Yoseph ben-Yakor* of Nazareth, but he could not report the incarnation, virgin birth, or any of the redemptively significant dimensions of the birth of this *Y'shua* which are considered to be the essence of orthodox Christianity. Those truths would elude the "objective" observer. Likewise, an eyewitness to the crucifixion of Jesus would see just another Jewish rebel executed by the Romans, but could not "see" atonement, propitiation, justification, or any of the theological significance given by orthodox Christianity to the death of Christ. Kierkegaard wants to assert that there is simply "more than meets the eye" to the historic Christian faith.

The nature of faith demands the inclusion of more than mere scientific facts. Faith's content relies on revelation from God: dependence upon an authority external to oneself rather than reliance on the human faculties of reason or the human *science* of history. Faith is a humble response to God's initiative in self-revealing, and is, by its very nature, contradictory to the confident stance of science. Thus, while faith must be subjectively appropriated in order to be authentic faith for Kierkegaard, the focus of faith is on the person and reliable character of God, not in the reasoning capacities of the self. Interestingly then, the rationalist's faith can, by contrast, become more subjective than the Kierkegaardian existentialist's faith in that confidence is placed on one's own reasoning abilities rather than on the trustworthiness of God. In Kierkegaard's assessment (as with the orthodox medieval Christian thinkers), confidence in God is a surer foundation for faith than trust in either the human heart or mind.

Kierkegaard's Christianity is neither anti-rational nor a-historical. While faith in the incarnation is not grounded in human syllogistic reasoning or the science of history, it is "a genuinely historical belief because the event is believed to be genuinely historical."[78] Kierkegaard writes, "The absolute fact is a historical fact and as such the object of faith."[79] Likewise, though Kierkegaard may not prefer to use this term, faith is reasonable (if not rational) because the self-revealing God who is the object of faith is trustworthy, and stands in a far greater capacity to speak with authority. Nonetheless, Kierkegaard does desire to push Christendom beyond mere reason or history. He is writing within the context of a culture which seriously confuses words about Christianity with the actual experience and ap-

---

78. Evans, *Subjectivity and Religious Belief*, 175.
79. Kierkegaard, *Philosophical Fragments*, 100.

propriation of it. Kierkegaard wishes to move Christendom from scholarly books and doctrines (not necessarily "away from") to personal faith in Jesus Christ—a faith which involves passionate trust, inwardness, and subjective commitment. Faith demands confidence in God, not oneself. If one is compelled to believe simply by nature of the faculties of human reason, then faith, as Hegel wishes, is indistinguishable from reason. Kierkegaard says:

> In every Christian land where Christianity has so permeated all relationships that everyone as a matter of course (i.e. without the decision of inwardness) is in a way a Christian, it is important first and last to pose the problem . . . of becoming a Christian, and that the problem is not to be confused by theological debates.[80]

> [I]n geographical Christendom one may in a way become a Christian, and even a Christian priest, without having the least impression of Christianity in the way of . . . [truly] becoming a Christian.[81]

Attack upon Magister Adler

In light of the "contextually reactionary" nature of Kierkegaard's works, it is difficult to respond to the standard Evangelical critiques against him. Because of his convictions against systematizing and his love for paradox, Kierkegaard intentionally obfuscates as he writes. As Sontag notes, Kierkegaard considered exaggeration "the road to enlightenment."[82] He describes himself as one who "writes in order to be misunderstood" and "is sometimes rather deceitful"—not in the sense that he says one thing and means another, but "in such a way that he carries the thought to extremes, so that, if it is not grasped with the same energy, it appears the next moment to be something different."[83]

Those whose reading of Kierkegaard is limited and cursory, or who have little tolerance for his exaggerated or paradoxical writing style, will find few answers to the questions which have been raised. Since overstatement is his admitted didactic technique, discovering the "real" Kierkegaard beneath the rhetoric of his "attack upon Christendom" is a task only for the

---

80. Kierkegaard, *On Authority and Revelation*, 188.
81. Ibid., 189.
82. Sontag, *A Kierkegaard Handbook*, 156.
83. Kierkegaard, *The Concept of Anxiety*, 17–18; Kierkegaard, *Repetition*, 6–7.

seriously devoted scholar. The work demands careful analysis of the entire Kierkegaardian corpus (including his journals) and thoughtful reconstruction of the intellectual, religious, and cultural climate of Kierkegaard's Copenhagen and Denmark.

Each circumstance in Kierkegaard's life brings a new dimension to his personality—indeed, a new reaction. Kierkegaard is in essence carrying on a Socratic dialogue with himself (for the benefit of his reading audience) by means of his various pseudonyms. This is what so many critics find so troubling about Kierkegaard: there are so many of him! Many critics suffer from underexposure to the multiple Kierkegaardian voices which exist in all of his writings, each one suggesting an alternate viewpoint. Analysis of one of Kierkegaard's lesser-known works can provide a glimpse at one of the "other" Kierkegaards—a Kierkegaard quite unlike the popular misconceptions.

In 1846 Kierkegaard completed a pseudonymous work entitled: *The Religious Confusion of the Present Age. Illustrated by a Magister Adler as a phenomenon, a mimic monograph, by Petrus Minor, Edited by S. Kierkegaard.* This work, later abbreviated as: *On Revelation and Authority: The Book on Adler, or a Cycle of Ethico-Religious Essays*, is seldom acknowledged as a particularly significant work of Kierkegaard. This is unfortunate, for this book contributes an otherwise lost piece of the puzzle in the question of Kierkegaard's objectivity and orthodoxy. Indeed, it is likely that Kierkekaard hints at this fact in the pseudonym he chose: *Petrus Minor*, an allusion, perhaps, to the historic Christian tradition "built upon a rock."

Magister A. P. Adler (1812–69) was a Lutheran priest on the Island of Bornholm who was highly intellectual and a devotee of Hegel. Nevertheless, Adler had intemperate subjective tendencies which disturbed even Kierkegaard. Adler spoke and wrote books based on claims to special revelation. Kierkegaard published *On Religion and Authority* as a response to the highly subjective, spurious revelational claims of Magister Adler. It is in this context that we see Kierkegaard's foundational belief in the objective dimension to Christianity surface. While Kierkegaard is concerned about how Christian truth is appropriated or embraced, he does not deny the objective reality of that Christian. Indeed, Adler's stance forces the reactionary Kierkegaard to defend publicly a position which he, elsewhere, rhetorically denies.

Kierkegaard was concerned that Adler had deviated from the Christian norm—the objective base of the Scriptures—by claiming his own private revelations. This appeared to awaken Kierkegaard from his "individualistic slumbers," so to speak, and prompted a reaction that was quite different in tone from his other attacks. "It is true that Christianity is built upon a revelation, but it is also limited by the definite revelation it has received. It must not be built upon the revelations which John Doe or James Roe may get."[84]

Kierkegaard saw in Magister Adler the results of extreme subjectivity without an objective reference point. He finds it necessary to distinguish between apostolic authority and mere genius. Often, he says, the two are confused. Many people assume that Paul, for instance, is authoritative because he is bright or particularly insightful. This, however, is not the case. Paul is authoritative simply because his message is *from God*—nothing less. Divine inspiration must not be confused with heightened human intelligence, wisdom, or emotion. The greatest genius still does not equal the apostle—for the source of knowledge is infinitely different. Kierkegaard states:

> With geniuses I can hold my own fairly well. God preserve me—if it is in truth the greatest genius, then with aesthetic propriety I gladly express my reverence for the superior mind from whom I am learning; but that I show him religious subjection, that I should submit my judgment to his divine authority—no, that I do not do, neither does any genius require it of me. But when a man coolly wishes to explain away what was intended to be an apostolic existence into being, a genius, without revoking the first claim—then he confounds the situation terribly.[85]

Adler's extremist claim to private revelation jolted Kierkegaard into a concession of the necessity of objective externality to the Christian revelation. Magister Adler, Kierkegaard suggests, "confounds the subjective with the objective, his subjectively altered condition with an external event"[86] when he claims to have received divine revelation. "Subjectively his emotion reached the highest pitch, he chose the highest expression to indicate it, and by a mental deception he used the objective determinant that he had a revelation."[87] Therefore, Kierkegaard states (in a corrective statement

---

84. *On Authority and Revelation*, 92.
85. Ibid., 15.
86. Ibid., 168.
87. Ibid.

that many would wish to address to Kierkegaard himself!) that it must be maintained that:

> Christianity exists before any Christian exists, it must exist in order that one may become a Christian, it contains the determinant by which one may test whether one has become a Christian, it maintains objective subsistence apart from all believers, while at the same time it is the inwardness of the believer.... [E]ven if no one had perceived that God had revealed himself in a human form in Christ, he nevertheless has revealed himself.[88]

In defending the Christian concept of authority as objective truth, Kierkegaard begins to sound very much unlike Schleiermacher, with a disregard for historic orthodox dogmas and a preference for subjective response. A more careful look at the intent of Kierkegaard seems to reveal a conscious orthodoxy beneath the subjective rhetoric. "Authority," Kierkegaard says, "is something which remains unchanged, which one cannot acquire by having understood the doctrine in its fullest sense," it is "a specific quality which comes from another place."[89] Here then, Kierkegaard is compelled to balance his own subjective rhetoric with objectivity in defense of Protestant Christian orthodoxy.

From this particular writing it appears that questions about Kierkegaard's commitment to objective truth are unfounded. His extravagant statements of subjectivity are only part of the whole Kierkegaardian framework. But if one reads him looking for a timeless statement of Christian theology, it is likely that one will come away with little more than disappointment. It was never his intention to write a systematic theology. Kierkegaard is a cultural critic, and he chose to address the specific needs of his culture rather than provide a *Kirchliche Dogmatik*. He is more a pastor than a dogmatician. His theology is worked out in a rough-and-ready interplay with immediate cultural needs. He was radically subjective, and thought it necessary to be so in post-Enlightenment Christendom, but he never departed from objective orthodoxy as the ground for authentic Christian faith. Carnell writes passionately:

> Therefore, let it be asserted for all to hear that Kierkegaard did *not* separate himself from the orthodox claim that the data of Christianity are objective in the sense of existing "out there." What disturbed him, rather, was the way professing Christians

88. Ibid., 168–69.
89. Ibid., 110.

substituted intellectual assent to these data for the decisive, ethical state of *being* Christians . . . . In like manner . . . the dialectic of inwardness is sustained by the fact (objective and historical in the non-Kierkegaardian sense) that the eternal God assumed the form of a finite person, and thus became the God-man at a particular point in time.[90]

Kierkegaard clearly does not deny that "the absolute paradox (the incarnation, that is) . . . existed as an historical fact, and thus [is] objective according to the common sense norm."[91] What he objects to is the inflated sense that such knowledge is attainable to the autonomous human mind. When he speaks of "objective truth" it is a "special usage set forth by Kierkegaard" in which "the objective is the converse of the subjective, and the subjective is character change, spiritual development, personal responsibility, and inner concern."[92] Therefore, "Kierkegaard's protest against objective thought on behalf of existence is not an attack on thought *per se*. It is a protest against the Hegelian notion of speculative thought."[93] For Kierkegaard, existence and faith must involve more than facts gathered by the human intellect. It must involve passionate inwardness, yet an inwardness motivated as a response to something which, while paradoxical, is nevertheless outside of the mind or feelings of the individual: the historic incarnation of the God-man, Jesus Christ.

Kierkegaard's success, if measured by immediate results, was minimal at best. He never saw the reform of Danish Lutheranism that he longed for, and his half-century of relative obscurity after his own death was less than promising. Upon the "rediscovery" of Kierkegaard, most of his readers were products of the tradition he had devoted much of his life opposing. Modernism has made much use of a limited or watered-down Kierkegaard. By contrast, the Evangelical community, with whom Kierkegaard shared much in common, has almost universally rejected him. Furthermore, confusion and lack of consensus regarding his actual teachings make it difficult to declare Kierkegaard a "success" by any standard.

As with Plato and Platonism, it is *Kierkegaardianism* and not *Kierkegaard* that has made the greater impact. The Western world has been mostly influenced by simplistic, one-sided pictures of Kierkegaard. To

---

90. Carnell, *The Burden of Søren Kierkegaard*, 110
91. Ibid., 111.
92. Ibid., 111.
93. Evans, *Subjectivity and Religious Belief*, 81.

reap maximum benefit from Kierkegaard, his writings must be carefully and contextually interpreted. He must be seen, just as he intended, as a corrective to the existing order. In a personal letter, Kierkegaard described his writings as "just a bit of cinnamon." Clearly he intended to "spice up" things with his teachings. He understood that philosophical life cannot be sustained on a constant diet of seasoning. But used as a corrective, the flavor of the existing menu can be dramatically improved. Careful reading of Kierkegaard can be of value precisely where he intended it to be: a passionate, personal corrective to autonomous, reason-drunk modernity and Christendom.

One can legitimately question the effectiveness or value of Søren Kierkegaard's reactionary rhetorical style, on the basis that he was almost universally misunderstood. But he was under firm conviction that this, and this alone, is his special service to God: to risk being misunderstood (as Socrates and even Jesus had been), in order to unmask the error of the "unexamined life" or the dangers of complacent, self-aggrandizing religion. Yet, even in the course of his intentionally overstated subjective view of faith, Kierkegaard does not ultimately neglect the actual object of faith—the historic incarnation—which he understood to be the heart of Christian orthodoxy and the true focus of faith. However, in the face of what he perceived as the greater danger of Hegelian "objectivism," Kierkegaard was willing to risk being misconstrued in the course of his mission. But let Kierkegaard himself have the final word:

> He who would provide the "corrective" must first study in detail the weak points of the existing order—and represent the opposite as one-sidedly as possible; really one-sidedly. This is the very thing that provides the corrective. Herein lies the resignation of the man who must do this. In a sense, the corrective is handed over to the existing order. If the relationship is right, a presumably shrewd fellow can come along and object that the "corrective" is one-sided—and thereby persuades the crowd to believe that there is something to it. Merciful God! Nothing is easier for him who provides the corrective than presenting the other side. But as soon as he does so, he ceases to be the corrective and becomes the existing order.[94]

---

94. Kierkegaard, *On Authority and Revelation*, 110.

5

Subjectivity and Religious Belief in Anglo-American Revivalism

Jonathan Edwards and John Wesley

> "Long my imprisoned spirit lay
> fast bound in sin and nature's night:
> thine eye diffused a quick'ning ray.
> I woke, the dungeon flamed with light:
> My chains fell off, my heart was free:
> I rose, went forth and followed Thee.
> Amazing love! How can it be?
> That Thou, My God, shouldst die for me."
>
> —A hymn by Charles Wesley,
>   "And Can It Be That I Should Gain?"

The "Evangelical Experience"

RELIGIOUS "ORTHODOXIES" OF NEARLY all forms tend to understand themselves as bastions of divine truth, characterized by absolute fidelity to the received tradition and unaffected by human culture or ideas. Nevertheless, as Paul H. Ballard of the University of Wales, Cardiff, indicates, this is rarely the case. "All traditions . . . have a history in which the interplay of past understanding and the demands of the present continually modify the tradition itself, . . . usually unconsciously."[1] This is certainly true of the Anglo-American Evangelical, or revivalist, tradition as well. "Indeed the myth is that this has not happened but that the true Gospel has been handed down untarnished."[2] In Evangelicalism's typical self-evaluation, it is a return to the faith of the past, rather than the emergence of something uniquely modern. Ballard contends that clear analysis of what he calls the "Evangelical experience" makes it evident that "Evangelicalism has reacted to the cultural climate around it and . . . that something of a complete inversion has occurred."[3] While this "inversion" is often noted in modern liberal and existential thought, it is often assumed that Evangelicalism stands apart from this modern impetus. Those in the Evangelical tradition have maintained a reputation for clinging tenaciously to the objective revelation of historic Christian orthodoxy.

Yet, as the Evangelical tradition developed in reaction and response to Enlightenment thought, the objective ground of belief was often eclipsed by an overpowering stress on subjective religious experience. "Immediate experience rather than doctrinal belief"[4] rapidly became the hallmark of Evangelical Christendom. Phillip J. Lee traces this Evangelical trend toward what he calls "Protestant Gnosticism": "Evangelicalism . . . despite all its repetition of the Lord's name, the content of the evangelical Christ remains undisclosed. One is to be converted to Christ, to come to Christ, to love Christ, to bring others to Christ, but the purpose of Christ to the world is a mystery, except perhaps to those who have been born again."[5] The Enlightenment influence upon the subjective character of the Evangelical experience is noted by Richard Brantley:

> Although evangelicalism is "spiritual" and empiricism is "natural," the great principle of empiricism, that one must see for oneself and be in the presence of the thing one knows, applies as well to the evangelical faith. Each of these two methodologies operate along a continuum that joins emotion to intellect; each joins externality to words through "ideas/ideals of sensation," that is, through either

1. Ballard, "Evangelical Experience, 52.
2. Ibid.
3. Ibid.
4. Lee, *Against the Protestant Gnostics*, 109.
5. Ibid., 193.

perception or grace-in-perception or both. While *empiricism* refers to immediate contact with and direct impact from objects and subjects in time and space, *evangelicalism* entertains the notions that religious truth is concerned with experiential presuppositions and that experience need not be nonreligious.[6]

Anglo-American Evangelicalism, of course, has its roots in the continental Protestant Reformation and is typically seen as an unwavering custodian and faithful embodiment of the Reformation truth, or in the cases of those more significantly shaped by Pietism and Puritanism, as diligent executors of the unfinished Reformation agenda. The Protestant tradition has rarely been averse to the possibility of religious experience (except perhaps within certain rigid scholastic versions of Protestant orthodoxy—usually opposed with equal fervor by liberal, existential and Evangelical forms of Protestant thought). Martin Luther's own discovery of personal salvation assurance following his long and agonizing spiritual pilgrimage along with John Calvin's doctrine of the *testimonium internum Spiritus Sancti* are often seen as setting the stage for a later Evangelical understanding of personal religious experience. Yet, for the Reformers, assurance was to be found, not so much in subjective experience, but in the objective person and work of Jesus Christ within redemptive history and in the objective reality of the transformed community of the church. Charles Lloyd Cohen notes:

> For Calvin, assurance is identical to faith, the firm conviction that Christ died for oneself.... One need go no further for assurance than to contemplate the Redeemer, for to believe in Christ is to know that one is saved. In directing the faithful to look to Christ for assurance, Calvin leads them away from self-contemplation, counsel that mitigates against his construing the conversion experience psychologically. Assurance is not sensational perception, so absorption in what one feels and does is irrelevant, even inimical to establishing it: Christ matters, not the fleeting proprioceptions of self.[7]

Though Calvin spoke of the "internal testimony of the Holy Spirit" as a means for assurance to the believer, he is clear that the assurance itself is grounded in the objective Scriptures as revelation of the historical Christ. The Spirit affirms the objective Scriptures as they point to the objective (and historical) Christ. Subjectively inclined readings of Calvin, with the

---

6. Brantley, "The Common Ground of Wesley and Edwards," 271.
7. Cohen, *God's Caress*, 9–10.

impetus found in the Reformational principle of *sola fide* along with a growing concern for personal apprehension of the gospel over against mere creedal *assensus*, provided an unintentional springboard for the shaping of the characteristically subjective "Evangelical experience." The historic bridge between the Reformers and the Evangelicals was the Puritans, who offered a unique combination of Protestant scholastic theology and introspective religious experience. "Puritans learned much from Calvin, but their taste for introspection derived from other sources."[8]

The Puritans and "Heart Religion"

Theodore Beza inherited the mantle of Calvin at Geneva, but he did not merely reiterate Calvin's theology. Beza's version of Calvinism is clearly a scholastic re-working of Reformed themes along Aristotelean lines. This is particularly evident in Beza's soteriology (which essentially became the soteriological framework for much subsequent scholastic Calvinism and Puritan theology). "The path of assurance, which for Calvin ascends from the believer to the Redeemer at God's right hand, for Beza descends back into the self."[9] The scholastic Protestant theologians distinguished three degrees of assent (*assensus*) in matters of faith (*fides*): (1) *firmitas* (which is resolute, unhesitating assent to God, based wholly on authority), (2) *certitudo* (which is faith founded on the basis of accepted testimony, without proof), and, (3) *evidentia* (which is assent based not on authority or testimony, but on reason or experience).[10] Early Scholastic Protestant theologians insisted that "the *assensus theoreticus* of faith is assent with *firmitas* and *certitudo* only. *Evidentia*, by way of contrast, belongs to a science"[11] (*scientia*).

And yet, as the Scholastic tradition calcified into a rigid, external system, and as modern thinking began to impinge upon the authority of the Bible and Christian tradition, *firmitas* and *certitudo* grew to be increasingly unsatisfactory as a basis for full assurance. The cold determinism manifest in many Puritan views of God's election to salvation created a characteristic *angst* among the laity, and created a demand for a personal, internal (and unquestionable) brand of *evidentia*. This becomes a notable element in the later Puritan inversion of religious belief into a largely individualistic and

8. Ibid., 10.
9. Ibid, 11.
10. Muller, *Dictionary of Latin and Greek Theological Terms*, 47.
11. Ibid.

psychological event. God's activity within the individual, much more than God's activity within redemptive history, soon became the center of Puritan preaching and experience:

> Later Puritans refined the paradigm and explored its nuances more deeply, but by the end of the sixteenth century the Spiritual Brotherhood had clothed Reformed soteriology in a distinctive experiential dress. . . . Reformed soteriology did not in itself demand particular emotional modalities yet, unlike John Calvin, the Spiritual Brotherhood spent more time dissecting the marrow of individual piety than in celebrating the Redeemer's sacrifice.[12]

Ballard suggests that while the Puritanism of England was "inspired by the Reformed Churches of Europe," it eventually "took on a flavor of its own."[13] Religious affections, or emotions, became an important sign (sometimes, the only acceptable sign) of the Holy Spirit's active appropriation of the sinner. These affections gave the individual person particular assurance, which was both immediate and personal, that he or she had been included in God's elect people. But the experiences also gave assurance that Christianity was not merely "head knowledge," but had become "heart knowledge," as well. This was an essential Puritan weapon against the onslaught of human-centered rationalism so characteristic of the age. English nonconformist minister John Flavell suggested that "an Honest and well-experienced Heart, is a singular help to a weak Head, such a Heart will serve you instead of a *Commentary* upon a great part of the Scriptures."[14] Harry Stout writes:

> Affections are an "infinite blessing," concluded William Fenner, who devoted an entire book to their study. Without them, "we should be like stocks and like senseless stones," incapable of piety regardless of the mind's enlightenment: "If a mans reason be never so good, he knows hee is bound to repent, and be godly, and obey; yet if he have no affections thereto, he goes like a Chariot without wheeles." Affections are "good chanels for grace to run downe in," and, in the opinion of Sibbes, the focus of the religious life: "Religion is more in the affections of the soul than in the effects and operation." The experience of conversion would be meaningless to

---

12. Cohen, *God's Caress*, 11, 14.
13. Ballard, "Evangelical Experience," 53.
14. Flavel, *A Saint Indeed, or the Great Work of a Christian Explained*, 498.

Puritans bereft of its emotional concomitants . . . . Affections are the mainstay of the life of faith.[15]

One contributing factor to the Puritan stress on the assurance producing potential of such emotional religious experiences was the political struggle faced by the Calvinistic independents in Britain. As a persecuted minority, the Puritans sought certitude that theirs was the true form of Christian faith—a faith worth suffering and dying for. Thus, in order to provide sufficient assurance for both the individual and the community, the pattern of experience needed to become normative and recountable. All who shared this same style of experience, and who could narrate this occurrence to the satisfaction of others within the believing community, found the assurance (both internally from the emotive force of the religious experience, and from the confirmation of the community) that they were in God's favor. Those who experience the Puritan form of conversion "undergo a characteristic series of emotions, an 'affective cycle' that . . . [which] evidences the Spirit's presence, giving proof of election."[16] Ballard states:

> The doctrine of assurance became a central point of debate, with many wanting to go beyond pure Calvinism. Arthur Dent goes so far as to declare, "He who knoweth not in this life that he shall be saved shall never be saved after this life." And Edward Dearing: "If I feel not the Spirit of God to sanctify my heart more and more how can I say I am a child of God?"[17]

The subjective religious experience became an important event for the Puritans by providing both emotional satisfaction and apologetic ammunition. The conversion event was a means of "separating the sheep from the goats" both politically and ecclesiastically. True Christians, as opposed to Papists and Anglican Ritualists, were distinguished by this vivid and recountable experience. Those who lacked this form of "true religion" relied instead upon the externals of liturgy, ritual, vestments and images in order to boost their "heartless religion." Before long, the ability to publicly recount this certain type of conversion experience became the primary criterion for membership within Puritan churches.

Congregationalists and Baptists tended to place deep significance in individual volition for salvation, and thus the oral confession of a personal

---

15. Cohen, *God's Caress*, 119, citing Fenner, *A Treatise of the Affections*, 98.
16. Cohen, *God's Caress*, 76.
17. Ballard, "Evangelical Experience," 54.

"born again" experience (men before the whole congregation; women before the church elders) came to be an unquestioned practice:

> This practice became normal in England. Both Baptists (who have additional reasons for emphasizing this need through the practice of believers' baptism) and Congregationalists expected "any such poor souls to manifest what God has done for them in uniting them to Christ the foundation . . . for the satisfying of those that shall have communion with them in the holy things of God . . . either before the whole Church publicly or else if they are weak and bashful to the Pastor in private with one or two more of the Church.[18]

As the expectation grew that each individual should provide a public "confession, & declaring of God's manner of working upon the soul," the spiritual autobiography of the Puritan conversion experience began to take on a distinctive pattern.[19] Usually the Puritan experience of conversion took the form of a long process of gradual awakening (as allegorically portrayed in John Bunyan's *Pilgrim's Progress*), unlike the instantaneous model which became common to later revivalism and Evangelicalism. Ballard says: "What has begun to be clear by the end of this period is that there is a 'morphology of conversion,' a model as to what part it plays in defining the Christian, but also as to what constitutes proper 'evangelical experience.'"[20] According to Cohen, the pattern included the following details:

> Commencing with the earliest recognitions of sin and the dawning realization of one's innate depravity, the applicant for admission recounted a lifelong struggle against the flesh and detailed the emerging conviction of faith, although entirely unmerited, had been granted by a Gracious God.[21]

The strict Calvinism of the early Puritans insured that the credit for this experience went solely to God. Nevertheless, the converted individual took on a remarkably central place in the Puritan testimony of salvation. In the theology of their Reformational precursors, salvation was understood as focused centrally on the mighty acts of God in redemptive history: in developed Puritan thought salvation is focused centrally on the mighty acts

---

18. Ballard, "Evangelical Experience," 55, citing Bartlett, *Ichonographia, or a Model of the Congregational Way* (1647), 75.
19. Walker, "The Cambridge Platform, 1648," 223.
20. Ballard, "Evangelical Experience," 55.
21. Cohen, *God's Caress*, 157.

of God in the individual's soul. Objective revelation, while still important to the Puritans, now tended to be eclipsed by a growing emphasis upon subjective experience. In terms of personal assurance of salvation, what God the Redeemer has done in history is of secondary importance to what he has done in the heart of the individual:

> The real transformation effected by eighteenth-century Puritan thought was the individualization of the covenant, the appropriation of a corporate Old Testament image to describe what became essentially a private psychological event. . . . Rather than God entering into covenant with His people Israel or with His redeemed Church and the individual participating in covenant insofar as he is related to Israel or Church, under this new form of Calvinism, the individual makes a covenant with God directly; it is a one-on-one relationship.[22]

The individual's personal experience of God became the basis for participation in the covenant of God. Puritan minister Peter Bulkley phrased it this way: "God conveys his salvation by way of covenant, and he doth it to those onely that are in covenant with him. . . . [T]his covenant must every soule enter into, every particular soule must enter into particular covenant with him."[23]

Still, the Puritan emphasis upon the individual did not deny the priority of God's activity in salvation. This "particular covenant" is initiated, enacted and completed by God alone. It is here that classic Puritanism is distinguished from much of Continental Pietism. While much of the Pietist movement tended to be characterized by an Arminian soteriology, the Puritan divines favored the Scholastic Calvinist concept of the *decretum absolutum*. Puritanism has been described as an "experimental (i.e., 'experiential') predestinarianism," a phrase which captures the unique dual emphasis of Puritan soteriology. Alistair McGrath writes:

> It is perfectly legitimate to suggest that perhaps the most important feature of Puritan spirituality—the quest for assurance—results from the tension inherent between the emphasis simultaneously placed upon an emotional searching for communion with God (unquestionably paralleling later Pietism in this respect) and upon divine sovereignty in election.[24]

---

22. Lee, *Against the Protestant Gnostics*, 76–77.
23. Greven, *The Protestant Temperament*, 259.
24. McGrath, *Iustitia Dei*, 299.

Theodore Beza's doctrines of double predestination and limited atonement found their way into English Puritan thought by way of William Perkins' widely read *Armilla aurea* (1590). The inflexible character of this system certainly did not diminish the Puritan anxiety about personal assurance of salvation. The question was inevitably raised: How can the individual know, within a seemingly deterministic system in which the decision for each person's destiny was made by divine fiat in eternity past, if he or she is truly one of God's elect? The rigidity of the federal, or covenantal, system (which was entirely in the control of the sovereign God) seemed to make the personal hope of salvation epistemically inaccessible. The anxiety was perhaps heightened by the frightening complexity of Perkins' "chart of salvation" which, McGrath whimsically comments, "resembling an early map of the London Underground," mapped the course of eternal election beyond history to the eternal decrees of God.[25] Given the overwhelming anxieties regarding personal salvation caused by such emphases, it is little wonder that the subjective Evangelical *experience* became a source of enormous comfort to those who experienced it.

Perkin's theology attempted to balance out the austere predestinarian emphasis of Reformed scholasticism with its *accent* upon the "experimental" or "experiential" aspects of faith. "Although Perkins' theology is essentially Bezan, his piety is overwhelmingly Puritan, demonstrating the intense concern with casuistry and personal election so characteristic of Cambridge Puritanism at the time."[26] In Perkins' theology, the divine covenant is the outward means of election as God's

> contract with men concerning the obtaining life eternall upon a certain condition. This covenant consisteth of two parts: God's promise to man, man's promise to God. God's promise to man is that whereby he bindeth himself to man to be his God, if he perform the condition. Man's promise to God is that whereby he voweth his allegiance unto his Lord and to performe the condition betweene them.[27]

The experience of faith, or vowing allegiance to the Lord, according to Perkins, should be a sufficient source of assurance that one's election is valid. Perkins offered the following syllogism to assert this very point:

---

25. Ibid., 300.
26. Ibid.
27. McGrath, *Iustitia Dei*, 301, citing Perkins, *Works*, 1:32.

Everyone that believes is the childe of God.
But I doe believe.
Therefore I am the childe of God.[28]

For others, however, this comfort was elusive. Second- and third-generation Puritans often found it difficult or impossible to reproduce the exact religious experiences of their parents and grandparents. For these, the Puritan stress on human inability and divine election "tended to induce paralysis rather than renewal."[29] By way of concession to the needs of these sincere, seeking, though "unconverted" New Englanders, a "Half-Way Covenant" was introduced. This enabled unconverted "baptised persons of moral character" to be treated as part of the church (with certain restrictions) and (because of the integral connection of church and state) part of the civil community.[30] Yet the Half-Way Covenant came to be seen by many as a furtive admission of the inherent failure of the Puritan way of salvation.

The notion that the conversion experience belonged to a select few, however, was about to change dramatically. The early Puritan idea that conversion was a painstaking, "extended process of spiritual struggle as the individual waited on God's irresistible grace" would gradually be replaced by a considerably abbreviated style of conversion experience which put "greater emphasis on individual free will and immediate regeneration."[31] With the onset of the "Great Awakening," the Evangelical conversion experience would soon become accessible to all who desired it.

Jonathan Edwards and "Religious Affection"

Although the Northampton revival of the 1730s came as a surprise to Congregationalist minister Jonathan Edwards (1703–58), "that event was neither accidental nor strange; the soil had in many ways been prepared."[32] While Puritanism itself had been "by expressed intention, a vast and extended revival movement," the "Half-Way Covenant" insured that the churches of New England were filled with people who had not personally experienced conversion, as an attempt to accommodate the now spiritually

---

28. McGrath, *Iustitia Dei*, 301, citing Perkins, *Works*, 1:547.
29. McGrath, *Iustitia Dei*, 306.
30. Ibid.
31. Leonard, "Conversion," 317.
32. Ahlstrom, *A Religious History of the American People*, 281.

lax children and grandchildren of the Puritans.[33] The religious fervor of the Puritans had not been immediately passed down to their progeny, and the American colonies were experiencing a lull in religious enthusiasm. In a controversial move of apparent concession to this awkward state of affairs, Edwards' pastoral predecessor and grandfather. Solomon Stoddard (1643–1729) had inaugurated this unique "Half-Way Covenant" in which he begun to baptize the children of the unconverted and admit the unregenerate to the communion table, believing the table could function as a "converting ordinance."[34]

On the other front, Deism, the "spiritual step-child of the Enlightenment," had begun to take its toll on the Puritan consensus in New England. The "Age of Reason" proffered a distinctive threat to religion, but increasingly the danger came from within. Sidney Ahlstrom notes that "the Enlightenment . . . was eating away at federal theology: the national covenant, once a mainstay of Puritan thought, was yielding to moralist individualism."[35] Perry Miller writes that one key reason for this trend is fairly obvious: "The educated classes were tired of the religious squabbling of the seventeenth century, and turned to the more pleasing and not at all contentious generalities of eighteenth-century rationalism."[36]

With this as the backdrop, Jonathan Edwards ministered to the needs of a Northampton congregation which was undoubtedly filled with anxiety about personal salvation both for themselves and for their neighbor. In 1734, he began a sermon series on the thoroughly Reformational theme of "justification by faith," yet with a decidedly modern twist. The revival that ensued became something of a paradigm for later Anglo-American revivals. Edwards' preaching emphasized the general accessibility of the new birth experience to all and the absolute necessity of such conversion for church membership. In regard to his soteriology, Edwards is not merely an old school Puritan—though the influence is still strong, there is also a definitely a modern element to Edwards' preaching. Edwards the philosopher found it necessary to contend with and adapt to the growing Enlightenment influence in the American colonies. Thus, in spite of his traditional Calvinistic orientation, there is something fresh about Edwards'

33. Ibid.

34. Noll, *A History of Christianity in the United States and Canada*, 87. See also Ahlstrom, *A Religious History of the American People*, 159–60.

35. Ahlstrom, *A Religious History of the American People*, 280.

36. Miller, *Errand into the Wilderness*, 156.

appreciation of the human will. The knowing (and feeling) individual took on significantly central role in Edwards' soteriology:

> The resurgence of religious fervor that began in the 1730s can be seen as a watershed, the end of Puritanism, and the dawn of the modern period . . . . Edwards was building a bridge between the classical New England Calvinism and the understanding of humankind that was emerging in the late seventeenth and eighteenth centuries. This included an interest in psychology. We are motivated through our emotions.[37]

Jonathan Edwards' best known sermon, "Sinners in the Hands of an Angry God," provides a fascinating glimpse into this phenomenon. The sermon was preached at Ensfield when the Awakening was already well under way. It was based on the biblical text Deuteronomy 32:35, "Their foot shall slide in due time." Like many of his sermons, this homily "exemplified in a graphic way the wedding of Calvinist soteriology and Locke's psychology of sensation: the sinner's dire need for redemption was first brought home to the senses."[38] Perry Miller's pioneering work on Jonathan Edwards portrayed him

> as an eighteenth-century genius of the Enlightenment in the woods of Western Massachusetts . . . [who] crafted his sermons so that such images as the famous spider hanging over the pit of hell . . . would be impressed into the minds of members of the congregation, in accord with the psychology Locke had set out in the *Essay [concerning Human Understanding]*.[39]

Surprisingly, the sermon does not speak of objective events in redemptive history, the biblical text being used only as a springboard to discuss the more immediate and existential needs of the congregation:

> There are black clouds of God's wrath now hanging directly over your heads, full of the dreadful storm, and big with thunder; and were it not for the restraining hand of God, it would immediately burst forth upon you. . . . The bow of God's wrath is bent, and the arrow made ready on the string, and justice bends the arrow at your heart, and strains the bow, and it is nothing but the mere pleasure of God, that of an angry God, without any promise or obligation at all, that keeps the arrow one moment from being made

---

37. Ballard, "Evangelical Experience," 56.
38. Garrett, "Jonathan Edwards and the Great Awakening," 25.
39. Proudfoot, "From Theology to a Science of Religions," 153.

drunk with your blood. All you that never passed under a great change of heart, by the mighty power of the Spirit of God upon your souls: all you that were never born again, and made new creatures, and raised from being dead in sin, to a state of new, and before altogether unexperienced light and life, are in the hands of an angry God . . . .

The scriptural story is circumvented (or at best used only illustratively) in favor of an emphasis upon the individual sinner's own story:

> The God that holds you over the pit of hell, much as *one* holds a spider, or some loathsome insect over the fire, abhors you, and is dreadfully provoked: his wrath towards you burns like fire . . . and yet it is nothing but his hand that holds you from falling into the fire every moment. . . . O sinner! Consider the fearful danger you are in: it is a great *furnace* of wrath, a wide and bottomless pit, full of the fire of wrath, that you are held over in the hand of that God whose wrath is provoked, and incensed as much against you, as against many of the damned in hell . . . .

The immediacy of individual response called for by Edwards was notably different from the older Puritan notion of passively waiting upon the sovereign God to make his election known (which, in part, contributed to the complacency of the "Half-Way Covenanters"). Instead, the listener was called to respond without delay:

> And now you have an extraordinary opportunity, a day wherein Christ has thrown the door of mercy wide open, and stands in calling and crying with a loud voice to sinners: a day wherein men are flocking to him, and pressing into the kingdom of God. . . . How can you rest one moment in such a condition? Are not your souls as precious as the souls of the people at Suffield, where they are flocking from day to day in Christ?

It is notable that instead of discussing the sinner's disbelief in the objective revelation of God in Christ, Edwards turns the attention inward to the soul of the hearer. He forcefully emphasized the individual sinner's stance before God in the immediate present, thus stressing the need for immediate, personal conversion, and the ability of the individual to willfully choose God:

> The wrath of Almighty God is now undoubtedly hanging over a great part of this congregation: Let every One fly out of Sodom:

"Haste and escape for your lives, look not behind you, escape to the mountain, lest you be consumed."[40]

Witnesses say that Pastor Edwards preached this sermon in subdued, even tones as he read carefully from his prepared script (as was the custom).[41] His manner was almost emotionless. Yet there was clear emotive power in his choice of words. The congregation's response was far from subdued: "The people yelled and shrieked, they rolled in the aisles, they crowded to the pulpit and begged him to stop, they cried for mercy."[42] Occasionally he "was obliged to speak to the people and desire silence, that he might be heard."[43] The contrast between staid preacher and frenzied people must have been dramatic. For some, it gave assurance that this revival was, indeed, of God, and not merely a result of mere emotional manipulation.

The genius of Edwards' preaching, and indeed this representative sermon, lay in his theoretical fusion of "Locke's sensory epistemology to the doctrine of regeneration."[44] Experience, or "sensation," is the only legitimate means of knowledge in Locke's epistemology. Likewise, in Edwards' appropriation of Lockean principles for homiletical use "religious sensation" in the new birth experience became the only legitimate means of supernatural knowledge (information appropriated from biblical revelation at a solely intellectual level would be deemed insufficient apart from the spiritual enlightenment of the regeneration experience). The knower—and in Edwards' case, the unregenerate sinner—was the center of the epistemic universe. What once occurred in past redemptive history is meaningless unless it is appropriated by the individual in both mind and heart. Thus, the focus of Edwards' preaching is placed on the immediacy of the individual's need, the imminence of God's offer of salvation, and the necessity for profound personal religious experience in order to appropriate that salvation and gain assurance.

The striking influence of Locke's epistemology on Edwards' psychology is evident in the conspicuous rhetoric of taste and sensation in the *Religious Affections*:

---

40. Edwards, "Sinners in the Hands of an Angry God," 7–12.

41. Extemporaneous preaching was not yet the common practice of the day, though eventually it would become an Evangelical earmark, and, for some, a sign of authenticity that the preacher was indeed Spirit-driven.

42. Miller, *Errand into the Wilderness*, 155.

43. Garrett, "Jonathan Edwards and the Great Awakening," 25.

44. Stout, "Religion, Communications, and the Career of George Whitefield," 123.

> There is what some metaphysicians call a new simple idea . . . . If grace be, in the sense above described, an entirely new kind of principle; then the exercises of it are also a new kind of exercises . . . then it follows that the mind has an entirely new kind of perception or sensation; and here is, as it were, a new spiritual sense that the mind has, or a principle of a new kind of perception or spiritual sensation, which is in its whole nature different from any former kinds of sensation of the mind, as tasting is diverse from any of the other senses; and something is perceived by the true saint, in the exercise of this new sense of mind, in spiritual and divine things, as entirely diverse from anything that is perceived in them, by natural men, as the sweet taste of honey is diverse from the ideas men get of honey by only looking on it, and feeling it.[45]

Yet, Edwards' appropriation of Lockean principles is not uncritical nor primarily motivated by philosophical concerns.[46] Edwards' principal concern is with theology. In the above passage, "he says that the fact that the mind has an entirely new kind of perception or sensation follows from the fact that grace is an entirely new kind of principle. Edwards does not appeal to empirical evidence or phenomenology, but to theology in order to argue that the new sense must be qualitatively different."[47] The affections of religion are different from the natural empirical experiences of sensation, primarily in that they have an immediate, supernatural origin. Edwards says, "Affections that are truly spiritual and gracious, do arise from those influences and operations of the heart, which are *spiritual, supernatural,* and *divine.*"[48]

The external signs of religious enthusiasm (which were critically tolerated, if not wholly encouraged, by Edwards) would soon gain the censure of the elite Boston clergy and the intellectual faculty of Harvard. Edwards was not unaccustomed to their reproach. In 1731 Edwards had accepted the invitation to deliver the "Great and Thursday Lecture" in Boston, attended largely by Harvard faculty members. To the surprise of many, he used the opportunity to attack the "enlightened" drift of current theology and to

---

45. Edwards, *A Treatise concerning Religious Affections*, 205–6.

46. The degree to which Edwards directly or consciously appropriated the epistemology of John Locke (if at all) is still something of a dispute among Edwards scholars. While Edwards does seem to share a similar notion of experience with Locke, Locke would surely part company with Edwards in his disdain for religious enthusiasm.

47. Proudfoot, "From Theology to a Science of Religions," 155.

48. Edwards, *Religious Affections*, 197 (original emphasis).

denounce their modern "schemes of divinity."⁴⁹ Nevertheless, in spite of this critique, Edwards' own views were not entirely without a distinctive Enlightenment edge of their own.

> [T]he distinctiveness of his utterance lay not only in its assertion that "reasonable" moderations of doctrine were "repugnant to the design and tenor of the gospel," but in two other characteristics: the terms and concepts of the old Puritan covenant theology were notably absent, and (to the discerning) the thought was invaded by concepts of the new learning. Here is Edwards' first public hint of high Dortian doctrines being maintained from a new perspective, one that in a complex way combined philosophical idealism and Lockean psychology . . . something very much like "Calvinism," but in a very new and rational way.⁵⁰

As Ahlstrom observes, "What metaphysical situation could be more exciting: the chief critic of Arminianism forging weapons out of the very Lockean materials which "enlightened" theologians and deists had claimed as their own.⁵¹

Jonathan Edwards was probably the most literate advocate and interpreter of religious experience following the Reformation. When the Great Awakening had died down in Northampton, Edwards began to assess the impact of the revival in a sermon series which was later published as *A Treatise concerning Religious Affections* (Boston, 1746). In this treatise, Edwards concludes that the essence of true religion consisted largely in "holy affections." What he meant by "affections" were the human faculties including, though not limited to, the emotions, but also the moral transformation of life which followed conversion. Traditionally (particularly within scholastic Calvinism) the human soul or mind had been defined largely in terms of intellect or understanding. Edwards proposed that the soul or mind also included the desires or inclinations. Therefore, religious faith should engage the whole person. Edwards wrote:

> God has endued the soul with two principal faculties: The one, that by which it is capable of *perception* and speculation, or by which it discerns and judges of things: which is called the *understanding*. The other, that by which the soul is some way *inclined* with respect to the things it views and considers: or it is the faculty

---

49. Ahlstrom, *A Religious History of the American People*, 300.
50. Ibid., 300, 301.
51. Ibid., 305.

by which the soul beholds things—not as an indifferent unaffected spectator, but—either as liking or disliking, pleased or displeased, approving or rejecting. This faculty is called by various names: it is sometimes called the *inclination*; and, as it respects the actions determined and governed by it, the *will*; and the *mind*, with regard to the exercises of this faculty, is often called the *heart*.[52]

Holy affections are the means whereby individuals appropriate revealed truth to themselves and enter into personal relationship with God. These emotions are the "spring of men's actions" demonstrating "that true religion must consist very much in the affections."[53] These affections ensure that religion is not merely an academic or intellectual phenomenon, which alone accounts for nothing, but also engages the heart. For "he that has doctrinal knowledge and speculation only, without affection, never is *engaged* in the business of religion."[54] But Edwards adds a caution: "A man's having *much affection*, does not prove that he has any true religion: but if he has *no affection*, it proves that he has no true religion."[55]

Edwards does not advocate indiscriminate acceptance of all affections, much less all religious affections. As a pastor, he felt obligated to test such things for authenticity—to test the spirits. Most subsequent revival preachers would not demonstrate Edwards' sobriety and caution about the matter of religious affections. But, then, most subsequent revival preachers were itinerants and not pastors of congregations. Edwards had to deal with the "fallout" of the emotional outbursts connected with religious revival for many years within the same congregation, and this led him to circumspection on the matter. In 1741 Edwards gave the Yale commencement address on the subject "The Distinguishing Marks of a Work of the Spirit of God." He expressed some appreciation for the "tears, trembling, groans, loud outcries, agonies of body, or the failing of bodily strength," exhibited in the throes of the revival experience.[56] He believed that these could be used by God for his ultimate glory. Five years later, however, Edwards published *A Treatise concerning Religious Affections,* in which he offers a more subdued and cautious assessment of the emotionalism of religious revival. "Rather than merely regarding emotional responses per se as neither proving nor disprov-

---

52. Edwards, *A Treatise concerning Religious Affections*, 96.
53. Ibid., 99, 101.
54. Ibid., 101.
55. Ibid., 121.
56. Edwards, *The Great Awakening*, 230–35.

ing the presence of the Spirit, *Religious Affections* excoriates dependence on the unsanctified imagination which leads to emotional excesses."[57]

The authenticity of religious affections is manifested in a visible change in the convert's own moral character. In this regard, Edwards harkens back to Calvin's own notion of assurance.

> The fact that affections are involuntary, that they arrive in a certain order, or that they are pleasing to the godly, is no evidence that they are genuine. . . . Edwards argues that introspection is deeply suspect, and that the only source of evidence for what is going on in one's own mind, as well as in the minds of others, is practice.[58]

Yet, while there may be a danger in the abundance of affections, or even in false or misguided affections, neither is so serious as the complete absence of affections, from which Edwards would conclude the absence of true regeneration. Authentic conversion must, therefore, be experienced by the individual and felt in the heart, but also demonstrated by the moral quality of life.

> Edwards understood conversion as the personal experience of strong feelings of guilt before God. Godly sorrow for sin in abject repentance, release from the bondage of sin, followed by testimony to the fact of the new experience, often with ecstatic signs. Conversion had inscrutable dimensions but also many visible ones. It brought about changes in the dispositions and aspirations of the converted.[59]

By these standards, Edwards developed a growing concern for the presence of "unconverted clergy" in New England's churches and colleges—ministers who only paid lip-service to orthodoxy and for whom theology had become merely an academic exercise, but had never experienced the new birth. Orthodox Christendom was not only in danger from the external influence of the Enlightenment, thought Edwards, but was also threatened from within by those who took comfort in reciting the plethora of confessions produced by the Reformation but had no personal faith in Jesus Christ. The religion of the heart became, for Edwards and others, the true test of Christian orthodoxy. Jaroslav Pelikan comments on this "affectional transposition of doctrine":

57. Eversley, "The Pastor as Revivalist," 115.
58. Proudfoot, "From Theology to a Science of Religions," 154.
59. Eversley, "The Pastor as Revivalist," 120. See also Edwards, "True Repentance Required," 507–19 and Edwards, "The Value of Salvation," 309–37.

> The dichotomy between the authenticity of this private "theology of the heart" and the artificiality of the public and political confessional theology of the churches, between "private" and "public" religion . . . was an epitome of the crisis of orthodoxy. . . . Each in its own way, therefore, the major creeds and confessions of the historic churches all lent themselves to transposition in the light of the theology of the heart: "We believe" had to become "I believe."[60]

Theologian Philip J. Lee sees this revision as resulting "an inversion of Calvinism" which came about "largely through the influence of the eighteenth-century enlightenment."[61] The post-Reformation authors of this shift saw the distinction in terms of a "head/heart" distinction—whether the gospel moved beyond mere creedal formula for the individual believer to become personally appropriated. Lee suggests that the shift is in fact something more dramatic:

> The issue, certainly in North America, is not whether the gospel is perceived by the head or by the heart, but whether the gospel, however perceived, is an objective cosmic reality or a subjective knowledge (emotion) of the individual soul. . . . Very soon after Calvinism was transplanted to New England . . . the importance of *what* is to be known was eclipsed by the importance of *knowing*. . . . With Edwards and the experience of the Great Awakening, the American preoccupation was dramatically shifted from the mighty acts of God to the religious experience of the Christian person.[62]

Edwards' own view of the significance of this shift is intriguing. He believed that the current religious awakenings in the American colonies—manifest in the preponderance of dramatic conversion experiences which were being recounted—were a sure sign of the impending millennial kingdom. A new era—a Golden Age of God's Rule—was now dawning on the New World.

> Edwards conceived of history in terms of a divinely ordained, recurring pattern of revival-declension-revival. Edwards' chief pastoral duty was therefore to conform his ministry to this divine design—to announce his parishioners' apostasy with unflinching resolve and to inspire a continual renewal of their covenant with God. In managing the cycle of revival at Northampton, Edwards

---

60. Pelikan, *Christian Doctrine and Modern Culture*, 122.
61. Lee, *Against the Protestant Gnostics*, 109.
62. Ibid., 103.

incorporated local events—his grandfather's death, his uncle's suicide, the collapse of the meetinghouse gallery—into his sermons as providential warnings of impending judgment. Edwards interpreted these local events as texts, which he skillfully wove together with biblical texts into a narrative of decline and revival under God's providence.[63]

For Edwards, then, the subjective phenomena of the Awakenings had begun to take on almost equal significance to the objective acts of God within past redemptive history. "He viewed the events of the revival in the Connecticut River valley as part of the history of God's great work of redemption, which began with a decision among the persons of the trinity to create the world and will end with the coming of the Kingdom of God."[64] Edwards himself said:

> God has already put his honor on the other continent, that Christ was born there literally . . . so as providence observes a kind of equal distribution of things, 'tis not unlikely that the great *spiritual* birth of Christ, and the most glorious application of redemption is begun in this [continent].[65]

Edwards' carefully reasoned accounts of the New England Awakenings helped contribute to what would become the paradigm—an expected "conversion technique" in subsequent American Evangelicalism. The experiential patterns were described in significant detail and analyzed with great erudition in Edwards' *Faithful Narrative of the Surprising Work of God in the Conversion of Many Hundred Souls in Northampton* and other such works. These writings became transcontinental best-sellers. The widespread popularity of Edwards' works helped solidify the transatlantic Evangelical notion that the subjective conversion experience (and usually of a standard, recognizable pattern) was a necessary phenomenon and the normative technique for salvation. "The 'surprising conversions,' which had begun during the time of . . . Jonathan Edwards, within a short while would become the typical expression of American religion."[66] Sidney Mead wrote of post-Edwards Evangelicalism: "Revivalism in one form or another became *the accepted technique* of practically all the voluntary churches."[67]

63. Stout, "Introduction," xiv.
64. Proudfoot, "From Theology to a Science of Religions," 152.
65. Edwards, *Some Thoughts concerning the Revival*, 354.
66. Lee, *Against the Protestant Gnostics*, 109.
67. Mead, *The Lively Experiment*, 122.

John Wesley and the "Heart Strangely Warmed"

The impact of Edwards' written accounts of the New England Awakening was clearly felt in Britain. Anglican clergyman John Wesley (1703–91) read Edwards' *Faithful Narrative* as he walked from London to Oxford, and felt compelled to proclaim, "Surely this is the Lord's doing, and it is marvelous in our eyes."[68] The character of the conversion accounts discussed by Edwards seemed to parallel Wesley's own experience. Wesley would later revise and edit several works by Edwards, significantly omitting the Calvinistic tendencies, the caution about unrestrained acceptance of all religious affections, and exhibiting, by his selectivity, firm approval "where Edwards posits the experiential context of the soul as a given of the religious life."[69]

John Wesley and his brother Charles had already been functioning as ordained Anglican clergymen, as well as missionaries to the American colonies, before they experienced personal religious awakening of the Evangelical style. Both brothers had agonized for many years over their own lack of personal assurance of salvation, even as they preached and administered the sacraments and rites of their church. Their strong leadership in Oxford's "Holy Club" was characterized by a profoundly ascetic devotionalism and rigorous piety which earned for them the name "Methodist." Yet, in the end, the Wesleys found little spiritual comfort for all this effort. Following a failed missionary endeavor to the Native Americans in the British colony of Georgia, John Wesley reflected on his own spiritual need. He wrote in his journal, "[I]t is now two years and four months since I left my native country, in order to teach the Georgian Indians the nature of Christianity. But what have I learned myself in the meantime? Why, what I the least of all suspected, that I, who went to America to convert others, was never myself converted to God."[70]

Wesley's anxious search for religious certitude was quickened as he closely observed the piety of a band of Moravians on a transatlantic journey. The young Anglican clergyman found himself put to shame by the confident serenity of twenty-six Moravian brethren during a terrible storm at sea. Wesley found he had no assurance in the face of death that he was right with his God. Having returned to London from America, Wesley was introduced to the pietistic society of Peter Boehler. On the evening of 24

---

68. Ahlstrom, *A Religious History of the American People*, 302.
69. Brantley, "The Common Ground of Wesley and Edwards," 274.
70. Outler, *John Wesley*, 48.

May 1738, Wesley sat in on a Moravian meeting at Aldersgate Chapel, London, where one was reading Luther's preface to the *Epistle to the Romans*. Wesley describes the event:

> About a quarter before nine, while he was describing the change which God works in the heart through faith in Christ, I felt my heart strangely warmed. I felt I did trust in Christ, Christ alone for my salvation: and an assurance was given me that He had taken away *my* sins, even *mine*, and saved me from the law of sin and death.[71]

This dramatic encounter transformed Wesley's personal ministry and such experiences became the cardinal theme of his preaching, and not the least something of a paradigm of Evangelicalism itself. True salvation did not rest in the external forms of the church, or affirming the creeds and confessions to be true. Even ordained clergy can be unregenerate, for salvation lay in a subjective, personal encounter with God, rather than in the trappings of ecclesial and priestly religion. An entire theological shift resulted, moving away from Anglo-Catholic ecclesiasticism and sacramentalism toward a more personal and experiential Evangelical faith. Arthur McGiffert says: "This event was epochal in Wesley's life. It meant a transfer of emphasis from baptism to conversion, from the Church . . . to the personal religious experience of the individual Christian."[72]

Wesley's theology became an interesting amalgam of Anglican ecclesiology, Moravian piety, and the "Puritan impulse, reshaped to answer eighteenth-century needs."[73] By this time, however, the nature of the Evangelical experience had moved beyond the Puritan pattern, at least in terms of a new emphasis on immediacy and patterns of recountability of the experience of conversion. "Nothing in seventeenth-century Puritan theory compares to the precision with which John Wesley and his contemporaries ticked off the exact moment of their conversions."[74] The Puritan emphasis on conversion as a long, agonizing process was replaced by "a form of 'painless conversion' and 'instant faith.'"[75]

The role of the individual in the conversion experience was heightened by Wesley's theological commitments to Arminianism and high view of human volition. In a nearly complete break with the Calvinism of Edwards and

---

71. Ibid., 66.
72. McGiffert, *Protestant Thought before Kant*, 163.
73. Ahlstrom, *A Religious History of the American People*, 326.
74. Cohen, *God's Caress*, 99.
75. Ballard, "Evangelical Experience," 57.

the Puritans, "Wesley made a significant shift in Christian understanding," by emphasizing, to a degree previously unseen in orthodox Protestantism, "the human side of faith."[76] Martin Marty notes, "a pendulum was to swing back to the experiential and emotive elements in Protestantism."[77] In Methodism, however, this emphasis became mainstream rather than peripheral.

At the encouragement of Peter Boehler, the newly converted Wesley travelled to Germany in order to visit the Herrnhut community and to confer with Pietist leader Count Nikolaus von Zinzendorf. Count Zinzendorf was unabashed in his espousal of the new subjective view of Christian faith. When questioned about the veracity of the objective truths of the Christian faith, he replied, "Whether the teaching of Jesus is true or not, there is no need to discuss, for it has given me peace and I do not ask for anything else!"[78] In his commentaries on Luther's *Small Catechism* Zinzendorf observes that it is a serious mistake for an individual to "regard what happened on Pentecost . . . as more important than what every child of God always experiences as a secure possession in the bosom of the Holy Spirit."[79] Pentecost (as with much of the scriptural record of redemptive history) was not definitive, but served a paradigm for what can occur in the heart of the individual Christian today if open to the presence of the Spirit of God. Thus, in Zinzendorf's Pietism, the immediate experience of each Christian can be on equal footing with the redemptive events recorded in Scripture.

During Wesley's stay at Herrnhut, the Pietist influence became solidified in his thought. Wesley was a careful and independent theologian, and this led him to find certain points of dissimilarity with the Moravians. However, enormous common ground was found in a distinctive epistemology. "At pietism's heart was an epistemology that differed vastly from orthodoxy's objective and object-centered theology. Now knowledge was to grow out of and be experienced in the hearts of the regenerate."[80] Likewise, in Methodism "the warmed heart was elevated over the informed head."[81]

---

76. Ibid.

77. Marty, *Protestantism*, 46.

78. Pelikan, *Christian Doctrine and Modern Culture*, 170, citing Zinzendorf, *The German Socrates [Der Teutsche Socrates]*, 14.

79. Pelikan, *Christian Doctrine and Modern Culture*, 164, citing Zinzendorf, *Addresses Delivered to the Synod of the [Moravian] Brethren in Zeyst [Die an der Syndrome der Brüder in Zeyst . . . gehaltenen Reden]*, 36.

80. Marty, *Protestantism*, 43.

81. Ibid., 46.

Moravian Pietism confirmed Wesley's own personal experience. Wesley had been a theologically informed clergyman, yet he had not personally experienced regeneration according to Pietist patterns. Pietism was a self-conscious corrective for dead orthodoxy and modern rationalism within the national churches. Wesley, who had at one time only affirmed Christianity with his intellect, was in danger of confusing *historical faith* (intellectual assent to the content of the orthodox creeds) with *personal faith* (a life-challenging experience with Jesus). He noted such concern for a fellow clergyman in a personal letter: "the theory of religion he certainly has. May God give him the living experience of it."[82] Wesley, based on his own experience, found his primary ministry in persuading the "almost Christian" to embrace the true religion of the heart.

To Wesley, genuine faith was not merely an affirmation that something has occurred generally in history, but an indication that something has happened particularly in the individual's heart. As Wesley wrote, real faith is not "a train of ideas in the head; but also a disposition of the heart."[83] For "a man may assent to three-and-twenty creeds . . . and yet have no Christian faith at all."[84] Thus Wesley set the pace for all subsequent Evangelical revivalism, developing a "polemical stance against the kind of Christian commitment which relied on mere 'hearing of the ear,'" and insisting that "direct personal experience of Jesus' saving power was an absolute prerequisite for truly being a Christian."[85]

The subjective conversion experience also had apologetic value for Wesley. External, objective evidence for the Christian faith had been under heavy attack by Enlightenment rationalism. The "internal evidence" of the conversion experience, Wesley thought, offered an always new and immediate confirmation of Christian truth, while "external evidence" had been "weakened by length of time."[86] In some respects this was preferable, because the knowledge of God "passes now, even as it has done from the beginning, directly from God into the believing soul."[87] Pelikan states, "To many defenders as well as to most critics of traditional belief, the search

---

82. Wesley, "To Brian Bury Collins, London, January 3, 1781," *Letters*, 7:47.
83. Wesley, "Salvation by Faith," 9.
84. Wesley, "Plain Account," 189.
85. Bregman, *The Rediscovery of Inner Experience*, 9, 10.
86. Wesley, "Plain Account," 191.
87. Ibid.

for the essence of true religion as an objective 'presence of things outside myself' appeared to have bankrupted itself."[88]

> [M]any defenders of the faith in the eighteenth century saw this as a philosophical confirmation of the belief, already widespread among theologians during that century, that God was opening one door for faith after having closed another. "The moral law within" and the entire range of affections, obligations, and experiences that accompanied it in the inner life could stand even when the supposedly transcendent grounds of faith demonstrated by the "starry heavens above" were being subjected to persistent attack.[89]

Wesley puts it this way:

> I have sometimes been almost inclined to believe that the wisdom of God has, in most later ages, permitted the external evidence of Christianity to be more or less clogged and encumbered for this very end, that men (of reflection especially) might not altogether rest there, but be constrained to look into themselves also and attend to the light shining in their hearts.[90]

However, the apologetic value of the subjective conversion experience was secondary. Wesley simply thought of it as absolutely necessary for personal salvation. Ronald Knox attributes to Wesley the popularity of the notion that the new birth was "always and necessarily an *experience*. . . . In order to be a Christian, as opposed to an almost Christian, you must have *felt*, at sometime or another, that your sins were forgiven . . . . [and have a] *consciousness* of the New Birth . . . ."[91] This is certainly the lesson that subsequent Evangelicals have learned best from him. Wesley clears away the "clutter" of 1800 years of ecclesiastical debate and creedal formulation by insisting that, once and for all, "true Christianity consists in this, that one acknowledge the Lord Jesus as personal Saviour and Lord."[92] Nothing could summarize the subsequent Evangelical-revivalist message more succinctly.

---

88. Pelikan, *Christian Doctrine and Modern Culture*, 121.
89. Ibid., 118.
90. Wesley, "Plain Account," 192.
91. Knox, *Enthusiasm*, 538–39.
92. Pelikan, *Christian Doctrine and Modern Culture*, 122. See Wesley, "Plain Account," 189.

Wesley and Edwards' Epistemic Common Ground

The foundations of the modern Evangelical understanding of religious faith have their origin in Edwards' and Wesley's "shared methodology, harking back to the epistemology of John Locke."[93] In theologizing the empiricism of Locke, they bring an obvious Enlightenment epistemological slant to their orthodoxy. Wesley describes, in his abridgement of Edwards, the character of religious experience as a "stamp and seal" upon the heart—language which is not far removed from Locke's *tabula rasa*:

> Indeed the witness or seal of the Spirit, consists in the effect of the Spirit of God in the heart, in the implantation and exercises of grace there, and so consists in experience: And it is beyond doubt, that this seal of the Spirit is the highest kind of *evidence* in our adoption, that we ever obtain: but in these exercises of grace in practice, God gives witness, and sets to his seal, in the most conspicuous, eminent and evident manner.[94]

Thus, like ideas in Locke's epistemology, faith is not innate, but must be sensed or experienced to be valid. Richard Brantley affirms the shared epistemic common grounds of Wesley and Edwards with the philosophy of Locke:

> Wesley and Edwards, far from just validating spiritual insights by borrowing from sense-language, speak literally to experience in general, including empirical observation, scientific method, and spiritual experience. Their methodology ... links not simply sense to reason and matter to mind but, more importantly, nature to grace .... Wesley and Edwards hold to the moment-by-moment (or at least momentary) efficacy of a consciousness not so much illusory as trustworthy and not so much false as true.[95]

Thus, both revivalists should be considered "philosophically rather than exclusively theologically," and approached "as methodologically alert, even where they thought themselves simply orthodox."[96] Indeed, though their desire was to simply re-establish orthodox Christian faith in an age of

---

93. Brantley, "The Common Ground of Wesley and Edwards," 271.

94. Brantley, "The Common Ground of Wesley and Edwards," 286, quoting from Wesley's abridgement of Edwards, *Religious Affections*.

95. Brantley, "The Common Ground of Wesley and Edwards," 271.

96. Ibid., 271–72.

"heartless religion" and rampant unbelief, both men clearly adopted current philosophical methodology in doing so.

> The twin pioneers of transatlantic revivalism are brothers of both soul and mind in that both men appropriate Lockean empiricism for religious methodology. Indeed, the philosophical as well as religious epistemology of this charismatic diumvirate of the Anglo-American world exemplifies the Anglo-American imagination.[97]

Wesley and Edwards "search for an inclusive, intellectually current way of describing how the mind knows God, and how anyone can verify another's faith. They find it in Lockean doctrine."[98] In this modernizing of Christianity, "Wesley and Edwards lay the intellectual foundation as well as emotional groundwork for religious expression not simply in the Anglo-American Enlightenment, but in the Anglo-American world of the nineteenth century as well."[99]

Both Wesley and Edwards cautiously navigate the rapids of Enlightenment thought and culture by borrowing this experiential epistemology as a means of steering through the precarious waters. Each found it necessary to embrace a subjective justification of religious belief in order to "rescue" their orthodox Christianity from the ravages of Enlightenment science. Certainty of faith was now possible, even in a world made skeptical about the objective content of biblical revelation, by means of personal experience. The subjective epistemological assurance of faith becomes a distinguishing mark of Anglo-American Evangelicalism. While distinctly modern, the Evangelical form of this sentiment is clearly grounded in the works of both Arminian John Wesley and Calvinist Jonathan Edwards, and is echoed clearly in the hymn-writing of Charles Wesley:

> Where the indubitable seal
> That ascertains the kingdom mine?
> The powerful stamp I long to feel.
> The signature of love divine.[100]

---

97. Ibid., 272.
98. Ibid., 301.
99. Ibid., 303.
100. Hymn 280, *A Collection of Hymns, for the Use of the People Called Methodists*.

6

Subjectivity and Religious Belief in Anglo-American Revivalism

George Whitefield and Charles G. Finney

> *"Thus orthodoxy was in a considerable degree methodized, and Methodism in due time became orthodoxed."*
>
> —Samuel Goodrich, 1856[1]

George Whitefield and the "New Birth" Experience

IF THE WESLEY BROTHERS' personal mission to America was a total failure, their impact on American religion was by inverse proportions an overwhelming triumph. John Wesley never personally returned to the American colonies after his failed missionary journey, but his innovations in the Christian religion were keenly felt in the American Awakenings, and in the inevitable shape of modern Evangelicalism. One figure who physically extended the influence of the Wesleys, for all his personal theological differences with them, was the wildly popular Anglican clergyman George Whitefield (1715–70). Whitefield, like Jonathan Edwards, opposed the semi-Pelagian notions which were manifest in Wesley's theology and preaching. Yet to most of their audience, the Calvinism of Whitefield and

---

1. Hatch, *The Democratization of American Christianity*, 193.

the Arminianism of Wesley made little or no practical difference. The revivals resulting from their respective ministries demonstrated a more profound and practical kinship. Revivalism created a kind of Evangelical amalgam which defied denominational barriers, and eventually contributed to the decline of the Calvinist consensus held by the founding Puritan fathers. The modern appreciation of the value of individual human will was far more compelling than the Reformed creeds and confessions. Thus, even classically Reformed and Calvinist denominations would (sometimes grudgingly) give way to the implicit Arminianism which came to be part of the pragmatic revivalist framework. In final analysis, the common ground of Wesley and Whitefield would be more significant to the development of Anglo-American Evangelicalism than the differences ever could be.

> [I]t is an interesting commentary upon the gospel's indifference to philosophy and theology that men representing, however crudely and inconsistently, two radically diverse types of thought should both accomplish so tremendous practical results. . . . [T]he underlying interest of the two types has been essentially the same, and their differences superficial and unimportant . . . in regard to evangelism.[2]

This is testament to the powerfully experiential and pragmatic nature of the revival tradition. Though both Wesleys and Whitefield were ordained churchmen in the Anglican tradition, they both did much to contribute to the strong independent and disestablishment character of Anglo-American Evangelicalism. The immediate needs of the rough-and-ready frontier tradition, coupled with a growing appreciation for the role of human will and religious affections would radically widen the gap between movement and European Christendom. Protestant Evangelicalism would be eventually "methodized."[3]

"On Eagle's Wings"

By the time Anglican deacon Whitefield began his preaching tour of the American colonies, the revival was already well under way. However, it was left to Whitefield's flair for self-promotion, his indifference to denominational lines, and his dramatic homiletical skills to inaugurate what was

---

2. McGiffert, *Protestant Thought before Kant*, 538–39.
3. Hatch, *The Democratization of American Christianity*, 193.

to become known as the first "Great Awakening." The prior revivals of men such as Solomon Stoddard, Jonathan Edwards, William and Gilbert Tennant had their impact, to be sure. Yet, while "sharing a common message, these evangelical revivals remained local private affairs, contained within specific geographic and denominational boundaries."[4] The entire character and scope of the colonial evangelical revivals were transformed by the strident itinerancy of Whitefield. Almost single-handedly, he "connected local awakenings, fashioning them into an inter-colonial movement—crafting a national event before the existence of a nation."[5] A. D. Belden suggests that it is "doubtful if there would have been any Evangelical Revival if Whitefield had been other than he was . . . and if he had not discovered the grace and the audacity to *initiate* out-of-church preaching."[6] Whitefield himself said, "Everyone hath his proper gift. Field preaching is my plan. In this I am carried as if on eagle's wings."[7] Whitefield the churchman blurred the distinction between church and para-church (a confusion which would hereafter plague Evangelicals) by preaching out-of-doors while, nevertheless, wearing the Anglican cassock along with clerical collar and cuffs!

The experience of the "New Birth" was ever at the center of Whitefield's preaching. Whitefield had personally experienced a powerful conversion in the midst of his studies at Pembroke College, Oxford. He had been drawn into the Oxford "Holy Club" at the encouragement of fellow student Charles Wesley. Yet Whitefield's extreme methodistic and ascetic practices eventually endangered his health and brought him to personal despair. It was only as he personally experienced the "New Birth" that he saw the futility of attempting to please God through his own effort, and the need for all to undergo a similar life-altering encounter.

Whitefield wrote that upon conversion "a ray of Divine light—instantaneously darted upon my soul, and from that moment, but not till then, did I know that I must be a new creature."[8] Fueled by this powerful new experience, as well as by the Wesley brothers' descriptions of the great spiritual need of the American colonies, Whitefield inaugurated his preaching ministry. He began the first of seven American revival tours, along with extensive ministry in England, Scotland, and Wales. In Britain

---

4. Lambert, "The Great Awakening as Artifact," *Church History*, 223.
5. Ibid.
6. Belden, "George Whitefield: His Influence on His Time," 2.
7. Philip, *The Life and Times of Reverend George Whitefield*, 385.
8. Whitefield, *Journals*, 47.

as well as America, Whitefield never wavered from the central concern of the necessity of the new birth experience message grounded largely upon his own personal experience. "Whitefield based his qualifications for proclaiming the necessity of the new birth on his acquaintance with 'experimental religion' not his mastery of prescribed theology."[9]

The "British Invasion"

America had never before seen such a popular figure. "Whitefield's triumphant journey up and down the East Coast, preaching to large gatherings wherever he went, was one of the first inter-colonial events. Whitefield was the first 'media star' in American history."[10] The first "British invasion" of American was a religious one. Yet prior to his preaching in the colonies, the people had been well primed for the experience by Whitefield's advance publicity in the popular newspapers. Whitefield judiciously exploited the media preceding his arrival to America by means of press releases and publication of his sermons, letters and journals. This drew large, curious crowds who attended his open-air preaching events in order to witness first hand this self-promoted "celebrity" newly arrived to colonial shores from England. It is estimated that Whitefield preached to more than ten million people in his lifetime.[11] His "print and preach" method was integral to the cross-colonial and cross-denominational spread of revival.

> When Whitefield arrived in the colonies on 30 October 1739, he had already shaped public perception through the press. He had fashioned a message that placed him in the Reformation tradition in opposition to the Church of England whom he depicted as betraying Reformed theology. Whitefield had carefully crafted a view of himself as a special instrument selected by God to proclaim the necessity of the new birth. Writing in promotional language as well as in theological discourse, Whitefield presented himself as a well-publicized success "Recently arrived from England." Just as colonists read about the expanding choice of consumer goods imported from Britain, they read about the one who arrived offering them a new religious experience. And by promoting his revivals in all the colonies, Whitefield prepared the way for a national event

---

9. Lambert, "The Great Awakening as Artifact," 227.
10. Marsden, *Religion and American Culture*, 24.
11. Aldridge, "George Whitefield," 59.

with men and women from disparate regions bound together by shared experiences.[12]

The theatrical manner of Whitefield's preaching was undoubtedly another key factor to his widespread popular appeal. Whitefield had never been much inclined toward the study of theology, yet he did study acting with great interest and with significant impact on his oratorical skills. David Garrick once said that Whitefield could "send an audience into paroxysms by pronouncing, 'Mesopotamia.'"[13] His understanding of human pathos and portrayal of the range of passions made Whitefield a formidable presence in the pulpit, not to mention providing an ideal sermonic vehicle for inducing the emotional conversion experience he sought from audiences. Whitefield would often weep openly as he preached, to great effect. One observer wrote: "Few could withstand the sight. It woke up the affections and touched the hidden springs of the heart as nothing else could ever do; men could not hate one who loved and wept for their souls."[14]

Whitefield's dramatic technique appeared to be the ultimate homiletical embodiment of modern sensibilities. His preaching was something of a fusion of "Locke's sensory epistemology to the doctrine of regeneration"[15] found within Jonathan Edwards' theology. By adding theatrics to the verbal images of his preaching, Whitefield's success as a revivalist was assured. Edwards' scholarly approach to preaching could never match the results of Whitefield's theatrical approach. In the midst of his tremendous success, Whitefield envisioned a "revival-driven, transatlantic para-church committed to the individual experience of the New Birth."[16] The Evangelical experience became the only test of orthodoxy, Harry Stout notes:

> In Whitefield's evangelical para-church, individual experience became the ultimate arbiter of authentic religious faith. Experience—or, in Lockean terminology, "sensation"—came to be the legitimating mark of religion against family, communal covenants, traditional church membership, credal formulations, or sacraments. As sensation represented the only avenue for natural

---

12. Lambert, "The Great Awakening as Artifact," 223, citing Husband, *Remarks on Religion*, 220.

13. Quoted without documentation in Hofstadter, *Anti-Intellectualism in American Life*, 66.

14. Ibid., 61.

15. Stout, "Religion, Communications, and the Career of George Whitefield," 123.

16. Ibid.

knowledge in Lockean epistemology so the supernatural experience of the New Birth became the sole authentic entree to spiritual knowledge in the evangelical revivals.[17]

The message of the need for a new birth experience was, of course, not unique to Whitefield. However, the offer of this experience beyond denominational lines to men and women unassociated with traditional church was clearly the innovation of this Anglican itinerant. Clearly, Whitefield thought, there were many within the traditional churches who were unregenerate, while experience told him that thousands *were* coming to Jesus independent of a church affiliation. Whitefield shared Edwards' concern for those who made intellectual assent to Christ, yet never had a personal experience of Him. Frank Lambert writes:

> Whitefield's message of the necessity of a spiritual new birth echoed the central themes preached by Edwards. . . . More borrowed than created, Whitefield's version of the gospel contained language familiar to Puritan descendants on both sides of the Atlantic. Restricting true conversion to the "indwelling of Christ," Whitefield charged that too many church members were "destitute of a true and living faith in Jesus Christ," possessing only "head-knowledge without that of the heart."[18]

Moreover, "although salvation came only through divine election, the seeker should "never leave off watching, reading, praying, striving, till [he or she] experimentally find[s] Christ Jesus formed within.""[19]

"All Things to All Men"

Whitefield's appeal, much like the "evangelical experience" itself, was trans-denominational. In fact, though Whitefield remained committed to his Anglican heritage for life, he often spoke critically of the established church. And, not surprisingly, he was usually violently opposed by fellow Anglican clergy and embraced warmly by the non-conformists. Denominational and theological differences faded beside the commonality of a shared religious encounter. "Although Whitefield did not invent the concept of the new

17. Ibid.

18. Lambert, "The Great Awakening as Artifact," 225, quoting *The Works of the Reverend George Whitefield*, 4:395; 1:221.

19. Lambert, "The Great Awakening as Artifact," 225, quoting *The Works of the Reverend George Whitefield*, 1:14

birth, he constructed his own meaning of the conversion process. Proclaiming that salvation transcended traditional church boundaries, the revivalist delivered his message to a mass audience."[20] This "catholic" style of evangelism did not please everyone, however. One unfriendly critic wrote that Whitefield was at once

> a staunch Churchman in old England! A thorough Independent in New England! An Anabaptist among Anabaptists! A true-blue Kirkman in Scotland! And a Quaker among Quakers! Becoming all things to all men, that he might not gain some, but make some gain of all![21]

Yet, for those who had personally experienced the new birth, the experience itself was enough. The church boundaries that Whitefield essentially denied in his practice made no practical difference when it came to the new birth. The "ritual confession" of such an experience (often in a revival meeting, rather than a formal church setting) became the ultimate criterion for acceptance of another as a "Christian brother or sister," theology notwithstanding. And the fact of profound religious experience apart from the church and its sacraments could not help but feed the growing sentiment that Christian faith was something other than, and prior to, belonging to a church community.

> Experience. It all came back, in every revival, to this. Seventeenth-century dissenters had spoken often of regeneration and the new birth, but always in the context of local congregations.... When pressed, they denied that true conversion could be experienced by those who were ignorant of the theological terms on which it rested.... In a subtle but profound transformation, Whitefield reversed this emphasis. Instead of theological indoctrination being the foundation of spiritual experience, individual experience became the ground for a shared theology of revival....[22]

"Affecting the Heart"

Even staid Puritan Jonathan Edwards could not ignore the impact of Whitefield's ministry. In spite of their denominational and stylistic differences,

---

20. Lambert, "The Great Awakening as Artifact," 226.
21. Ibid., citing *South Carolina Gazette*, 18 June 1741.
22. Stout, "Religion, Communications, and the Career of George Whitefield," 124.

Edwards welcomed Whitefield to his Northampton pulpit. Edwards found himself deeply affected by Whitefield's preaching, and the Northampton community experienced further revival. Sarah Edwards, wife of Jonathan, wrote of Whitefield in a personal letter, "He makes less of the doctrines than our American preachers generally do and aims more at affecting the heart."[23] Ironically, this characteristic would soon become the identifying trait of American, more than British, Evangelicalism. But, if revivalism engendered an indifference to theology, it became conversely exacting in its expectation of a certain style of new birth experience. Certainty of faith was not, as the Protestant Scholastics implied, connected to precision of doctrine: it was connected to the powerful, subjective and recountable new birth experience. The convert may need not repeat creed or recite catechetical confession, but they must be able to narrate their own personal appropriation of Christ as Savior.

Even the open air preaching style of Whitefield itself (borrowed from the Welsh field preacher Howell Harris) encouraged an individualist and subjective flavor to the revivals. The sermon audience was no longer a tightly-knit church community, but a mass "of disconnected individuals" and "strangers."[24] By means of this approach "Whitefield helped to introduce a new concept of religious experience that grew throughout the nineteenth century into a recognizably 'evangelical' movement."[25]

> The emphasis shifted to a more individualistic and subjective sense piety that found its quintessential expression in the internal, highly personal experience of the "New Birth." Indeed, the individual experience of regeneration, detached from a particular place and time and existing within the self came to be the badge of religiosity and true piety in Whitefield's revivals.... [T]he meaning of "revival" shifted from a mysterious, local, communal event to one that was predictable and highly subjective.[26]

The demand for a personal experience of conversion for all meant that no one could rest on his or her spiritual "laurels." Regeneration was not a birthright, nor did it result from belonging to the "right" denomination or even possessing good theology. Catechesis and sacraments could not save. External forms of religion did not insure the possession of Christ.

23. Stout, *The Divine Dramatist*, 126–27.
24. Ibid., xx.
25. Ibid.
26. Ibid., xx–xxi.

Whitefield was convinced that the lack of "true religion" among the congregations was largely due to the widespread presence of an "unconverted ministry." He became known for his attacks on the faculties of Harvard and Yale for promoting theological "head knowledge" without concern for the heart. How could anyone expect that their ministers be spiritually better off than their professors? And how could the churches be spiritually better off than their pastors? Whitefield concluded:

> [T]he Lord enabled me to open my mouth boldly against unconverted ministers; for, I am persuaded the generality of preachers talk of an unknown and unfelt Christ. The reasons why congregations have been dead is, because they have dead men preaching to them. . . . How can dead men beget living children?[27]

Whitefield had not only learned the method of field preaching from Howell Harris, but he likewise shared his disdain for "unconverted clergymen." When Whitefield first came to preach in Wales, Harris had already travelled over two thousand miles on foot to proclaim revival truths. Whitefield's preaching fanned the flames of revival in Wales, insuring subsequently that the character of Welsh Methodism would be largely Calvinistic, in contrast to Britain and North America. During these years of religious awakening, the conversion of local Welsh clergymen was a commonplace experience.

> In March 1739, Whitefield first visited Wales and met Howell Harris. At that date an awakening was already spreading rapidly in the south and west of Wales, . . . [in] Llangeitho, in Cardiganshire, and the adjacent parishes of *Nantcwnlle* and *Llanddewi Brefi*, [which] were served by Daniel Rowland who was curate . . . . Until his conversion, Rowland was a typical clergyman of the age, serving an "easy-going God." Thereafter, the change in his ministry was immense. "He proclaimed," says his biographer, "eternal perdition to a sinful world." Notwithstanding the message of judgement, his churches were soon crowded and such were the overpowering effects of the Word preached that numbers stricken with conviction of sin lay prostrate on the ground in the churchyard of Llancwnlle.[28]

Just as Whitefield had preached extensively in the American colonies, in "England and Wales . . . there was hardly a single town in north or south,

---

27. Whitefield, *Journals*, 470.
28. Murray, *The Puritan Hope*, 116.

east or west, where he failed to lift up his voice like a silver trumpet with the Gospel message."[29] Thus, Whitefield's contribution to Anglo-American Evangelical religion was unequivocal. He made the "evangelical experience" accessible to large numbers as it had never been before in the English-speaking world. At the popular level of Anglo-American revivalism, Whitefield effectively and irreversibly abbreviated the conversion experience from the long process known in Puritanism to an instant event.

> Whitefield compressed the experience, raising the expectation that men and women could undergo conversion in a finite moment. Indeed, he indicated in his sermons that his auditors and readers could experience the new birth while reflecting on the sermon.... Whitefield called on men and women to "repent therefore and be converted, that your sins may be blotted out. See that you receive the Holy Ghost before you go hence."[30]

Whitefield proclaimed with consistency throughout his entire career the absolute necessity of a new birth experience which was immediate, personal, subjective, and which transcended theological and ecclesiastical barriers. Even in his odd, twenty-year friendship with American deist and skeptic Benjamin Franklin, Whitefield pulled no punches about the *need* for a personal experience of regeneration. In a letter of praise to Franklin for his scientific work with electricity, Whitefield implored, "As you have made a pretty considerable progress in the mysteries of electricity, I would now humbly recommend to your diligent unprejudiced pursuit and study the mystery of the new birth."[31]

It was, to be sure, Whitefield's indefatigable emphasis upon the new birth, and not his Anglicanism or Calvinism, which would have lasting impact on subsequent Evangelical revivalism. "Whitefield's stated theological preferences were, of course, Calvinist and predestinarian. But other revivalists could, and did, build quite different frameworks that enjoyed the same experiential legitimation."[32] If Whitefield as a Calvinist Methodist is deemed as something of an oddity, then Charles Finney's wholly Arminian Presbyterianism would stand as an even starker indication that the old

---

29. Aldridge, "George Whitefield," 58.

30. Lambert, "The Great Awakening as Artifact, 227, including a quotation from Whitefield, "Marks of Having Received the Holy Ghost," 2:193.

31. Stout, *The Divine Dramatist*, 228.

32. Stout, "Religion, Communications, and the Career of George Whitefield," 124.

theological categories had given way to a far more pragmatic, experiential and subjective view of the Christian faith.

Charles Finney's "American Shortcut to Heaven"[33]

"From the time of the Puritans until about the middle of the nineteenth century, American evangelicalism was dominated by a Calvinistic vision of a Christian culture."[34] Charles Grandison Finney (1792–1875) "the Father of Modern Revivalism," maintained this cultural vision long after abandoning a Calvinist soteriology and anthropology. Not unlike Jonathan Edwards, Finney believed that the American revivals demonstrated a new presence of the Spirit of God on the American continent necessary for the inauguration of the millennial kingdom of God. This wave of religious renewal was, like the prophetic ministry of John the Baptist prior to the first advent, an apocalyptic prelude to the second coming of Christ. Finney asserted that "The Christian church was designed to make aggressive movements in every direction . . . to reform individuals, communities, and governments, and never rest until the kingdom . . . shall be given to the people . . . until every form of iniquity shall be driven from the earth."[35] Finney rejected the notion that Christ himself would suddenly return to destroy the wicked and establish his kingdom. While pre-millennial sentiment was on the rise in nineteenth-century Evangelicalism, Finney shared with his predecessor Edwards and other American Puritans a commitment to a post-millennial vision. The "new world" of the Americas was the preamble to *the* new world of Christ's kingdom, and nothing manifested this better than the casting aside of European forms of religion in favor of the "new measures" of frontier-style Evangelical religion. In a debate with a leader of an Adventist, pre-millenarian sect, Finney asked, "Is it not the overthrow of the governments that is intended, instead of the destruction of the people? And is not this to be done, by the influence of the church of God, in enlightening their minds by the Gospel?"[36] The church, with its new-found evangelistic methods, would usher in the kingdom of light by widespread conversion and renewal from within.

---

33. This section heading is borrowed from Carwardine, *Transatlantic Revivalism*, 1.
34. Marsden, *Fundamentalism and American Culture*, 86.
35. Ibid.
36. Finney, *Memoirs*, 371.

Charles Finney, according to Mark Noll, "stands by himself as *the* crucial figure of American evangelicalism since Jonathan Edwards."[37] In his Pulitzer Prize-winning book *Anti-Intellectualism in American Life*, Richard Hofstadter wrote, "although now remembered only by those who have a keen interest in American religion or social history, [Finney] must be reckoned among our great men."[38] There is perhaps no single person who affected the American Evangelical style of conversion more than Charles Finney. "[F]rom 1825 to 1835 [Finney] launched a series of revivals that made him pre-eminent among the evangelical preachers of his time and established him as one of the most compelling figures in the history of American religion."[39] Furthermore, Finney's effect on British revivalism cannot be dismissed. Though Richard Carwardine suggests that Finney is the "high priest of revivalism," with profound influence on both sides of the Atlantic, his effect has been "generally overlooked by British religious historians."[40] British, and especially Welsh, nonconformity proved as fertile a ground for Finney's method of conversion as did the American frontier.[41]

Finney's appeal can only be assessed in terms of the time and spirit of the American frontier, not to mention similar cultural circumstances in Wales. Finney effectively combined the old Puritan demand for a new birth experience as preserved in Whitefield and Edwards, and the Arminian soteriology of the Wesleys, together with his one innovation: "new measures"—revivalistic procedures which were scientifically employed and which guaranteed results. While many traditionalists held disdain for Finney's weak theology and emotionally manipulative methods, it was "Pragmatism" that "won the day. It was statistics—numbers of converts—that counted . . . ." [42] Whitney Cross comments, "But no individual or school of thought could equal experience as Finney's teacher. His doctrine, in fact, grew out of actions which met the pragmatic test; success could only be measured in numbers of converts and in the apparent intensity of their convictions."[43]

---

37. Noll, *A History of Christianity in the United States of America*, 176.
38. Hofstadter, *Anti-Intellectualism in American Life*, 91–92.
39. Ibid.
40. Carwardine, "The Welsh Evangelical Community and 'Finney's Revival,'" 463.
41. Ibid., 465.
42. Hardman, *Charles Grandison Finney*, 25.
43. Cross, *The Burned-Over District*, 8, 9.

The "new measures and liberal Calvinism contributed to a revivalism that stood midway between the emotionalism of American frontier religion and New England traditionalism."[44] Finney's brand of revivalism not only played well in "backwater" villages of Oneida County, New York, and Caernarvonshire, Wales, but in the more "sophisticated" settings of the Oberlin College and New York City.[45] The genius of the "new measures" was that conversion was deemed to be wholly within the grasp of the human agency. If a revival preacher or church community followed prescribed methods, then revival would be assured. Likewise if the targeted sinner responded with the appropriate fashion of emotion, then salvation was guaranteed. There was no need to wait for long periods of time for God to work. All that was necessary was for the individual to respond. "Finney's *Lectures on Revivals of Religion* were wholly devoted to showing what the right means were and how revivals could be produced, so to speak, as they were a series of instructions as to how the heart, the mind, and the will could all be marshaled into the great end of reviving religion."[46]

Few religious ideas could appeal so directly to the modern American sense of voluntarism and autonomy. To produce a revival "at will" now seemed well within the grasp of a people who were conquering and taming the savage new world. Edwards' Calvinistic notion that revival was a "surprising work of God" wholly dependent upon God's sovereignty, was now being viewed as a not-so-surprising, and wholly predictable work of humans. Furthermore, the nineteenth-century's pragmatic and pseudo-scientific preoccupation with technique would almost assure popularity for Finney's "new measures."[47] In Finney's evangelism,

---

44 Carwardine, *Transatlantic Revivalism*, 463–64.

45. Those Welsh revivals which were sparked by Finney's teachings were driven by Welsh preachers (such as Christmas Evans, William Williams (Williams 'o'r Wern), and John Elias, to name a few). Many of these itinerant preachers (some whose likenesses stand in town squares of tiny Welsh villages, and whose names can still be heard on the lips of elderly pious Welshmen) would attain folk-hero status among the Evangelical non-conformist churches of Britain. Wales is dotted with the nonconformist *capeli* (many now abandoned), a testament to the once-pervasive *effect* of these revivalists on the culture of Wales. See Davies, *History of Wales*, 359–60. Finney, at various times in his life, occupied a prominent pulpit in New York City and a professorship and presidency at Oberlin College in Ohio.

46. Hofstadter, *Anti-Intellectualism in American Life*, 109.

47. William James reflected this spirit of pragmatism when he asked, "What, in short, is truth's cash-value in experiential terms?" Accordingly, he acknowledged, "On pragmatic principles, if the hypothesis of God works satisfactorily in the widest sense of the

the revivalistic techniques aimed at getting people saved were increasingly united with the actual experience of salvation. Revivalistic procedures for evangelizing the frontier and the city developed a theological life of their own. Conversion was frequently associated, in the popular mind, with the methods of mass evangelism.[48]

Finney marks a noticeable blurring of theological boundaries between traditional Protestant denominations, beyond even that of Wesley and Whitefield. Though he was ordained a Presbyterian minister, he had nothing but contempt for traditional Calvinist teachings, especially as they manifested themselves in *The Westminster Confession* of the Presbyterians. He charged that the Westminster Divines had established a "paper pope" in the *Confession* and had erringly "elevated their confession and catechism to the Papal throne" and had established it in "place of the Holy Ghost."[49] It would be better, he thought, "to have a living than a dead Pope."[50] Finney hints at the notion of spiritual progress of Christendom when he wrote:

> That the instrument framed by that assembly should in the nineteenth century be recognized as the standard of the church, or any intelligent branch of it, is not only amazing, but I would say that it is highly ridiculous. It is as absurd in theology as it would be in any other science.[51]

William McLoughlin observes, "The first thing that strikes the reader of *Lectures on Revival* is the virulence of Finney's hostility toward traditional Calvinism and all it stood for, . . . to put it . . . succinctly. John Calvin's philosophy was theocentric and organic: Charles Finney's was anthropocentric and individualistic."[52] Princeton theologians B. B. Warfield and Charles Hodge charged Finney with a Kant-like preoccupation with the moral ability of the individual. Hodge criticized Finney's appropriation of Kant's "dictum . . . 'I ought, therefore I can'" as wholly incompatible with the orthodox Calvinist notion of human depravity: "'I ought to be able, but am not.'"[53] Hodge wrote of Finney's theology, "It is altogether a misnomer

---

word, it is true." James, *Pragmatism*, 133, 192.

48. Leonard, "Getting Saved in America," 118.

49. Finney, *Systematic Theology*, xii.

50. Ibid.

51. Ibid.

52. William McLoughlin, "Introduction" in Charles Finney, *Lectures on Revivals of Religion*, ix.

53. Hodge, "Finney's Lectures on Biblical Theology," 244. See also Warfield,

to call such a book 'Lectures on Systematic Theology.' It would give a far more definite idea of its character, to call it 'Lectures on Moral Law and Philosophy.'"[54]

Finney's own sense of call to ministry betrays not only a powerful sense of independence from the traditions of historic Christendom, but a Lockean sense that knowledge (in this case, theological knowledge) should be immediately available to the individual. In preparation for ministry, while "an admitted novice in theology, he still refused to accept instruction or correction when it did not correspond with his own views."[55] Finney wrote, "I had read nothing on the subject [of theology] except my Bible: and what I had there found upon the subject. I had interpreted as I would have understood the same or like passages in a law book—I found myself utterly unable to accept doctrine on the ground of authority. . . . I had nowhere to go but directly to the Bible, and to the philosophy and workings of my own mind . . . ."[56] With this confidence in "the workings of his own mind" Finney came before the ordination board of the Presbyterian Church with some degree of hubris. Noting his lack of theological training, the group of ministers offered to send him to Princeton to study theology. Finney says, "I plainly told them that I would not put myself under such an influence as they had been under; that I was confident that they had been wrongly educated, and they were not ministers that met an ideal of what a minister of Christ should be."[57]

Although Finney was ordained as a Presbyterian minister, in both his theology and practice the "traditional Calvinistic morphology of salvation was modified in more Arminian directions."[58] Indeed, Finney's "modified Calvinism" was in many ways even "more Arminian than John Wesley; Wesley maintained that the human will is incapable of choosing God apart from God's preparatory grace, but Finney rejected this requirement."[59] Finney rejected the traditional Christian notion of original sin as inconsistent with experience, and, therefore, an "anti-Scriptural and nonsensical

---

Perfectionism, 2:173, n. 357, where he cites this statement from Hodge.
54. Hodge, "Finney's Lectures on Biblical Theology," 244.
55. Hofstadter, *Anti-Intellectualism in American Life*, 109.
56. Finney, *Memoirs*, 45–46, 54.
57. Ibid., 42.
58. Leonard, "Getting Saved in America," 118.
59. Noll, *A History of Christianity in the United States and Canada*, 177.

dogma."⁶⁰ It is "a monstrous and blasphemous doctrine" to suggest "original or constitutional sinfulness" for such a doctrine runs contrary to the pragmatic experience of conversion, is "subversive of the gospel, and repulsive to the human intelligence."⁶¹ The experience of conversion was placed fully and entirely within the control of the individual, just as the phenomenon of revival was fully within the control of the clergy and congregation.

> Finney denied that conversion required "a season of protracted conviction," a lengthy process. Rather, he insisted, sinners could rely on their free will to "change the governing preference" of their minds and turn to God by their "own voluntary act." He advised the sinner not to wait on God "to do your duty, but to do it immediately yourself, on pain of eternal death." Indeed, he warned that waiting on the infusion of divine grace could represent a futile form of works which distracted the sinner from the immediacy of salvation.⁶²

Finney argued, contrary to Dortian Calvinist views of limited atonement, that it was already God's will that all should come to the experience of conversion. Thus the only barrier remaining was the individual human will. And the human will had nothing preventing it from responding to God. Finney rejected the notion of "noetic depravity" prevalent in Calvinist theology. "In short, the sinner has full natural ability to perform any of the duties of repentance. And it is a matter of the change of heart . . . which is within our power to do."⁶³ In Finney's sermon "Sinners Bound to Change Their Own Hearts," he says, "The Spirit of God, by truth, influences the sinner to change, and in this sense is the efficient cause of the change. But the sinner actually changes, and is therefore himself, in the most proper sense, the author of the change."⁶⁴ Finney is clear that in conversion "the actual turning . . . is the sinner's own act."⁶⁵

> Where the word of truth can reach the mind and the Spirit of truth can reach the heart, there life can be rendered, as it ought to be,

---

60. Finney, *Systematic Theology*, 179.

61. Ibid., 180, 236.

62. Leonard, 119, citing Finney, "Sinners Bound to Change Their Own Hearts," 29, 37, 38.

63. Stephens, "Changing Conceptions of the Holy Spirit," 220.

64. Finney, "Sinners Bound to Change Their Own Hearts," 21–22; See also Smith, "Theology of Charles Finney," 81.

65. Finney, *Sermons on Various Subjects*, 10.

both rational and moral. Through the mind the heart is finally "something over which we have control: something voluntary; something for which we are to blame, and which we are bound to alter." The choice of what rules life is ours to make, not the Spirit's to give . . . the power to change our heart . . . is well within the individual's control.[66]

Finney adds:

> There is nothing in religion beyond the ordinary powers of nature. . . . . Religion is the work of man. It consists entirely in the right exercise of the powers of nature. It is just that and nothing else. . . . A revival is not a miracle, nor dependent on a miracle, in any sense. It is a purely philosophical result of the right use of constituted means . . . .[67]

Evangelicals found Finney difficult to refute from a purely pragmatic standpoint: his methods produced results! Indeed, one editor of Finney's *Lectures* says that if one is seeking a gospel that "works," "I am happy to state they can find it in this volume."[68] Finney found unprecedented revival success in the famous "Burned-Over District" (an area of New York State which had been so saturated with revivals in the past that it was thought impossible to revive again).

The revival process received significant modification by Finney. Revival, argued Finney, was no longer deemed a miracle or a "surprising work" of God as Edwards and the Calvinists had taught. One need not "wait" for God, within his time, to grant revival to his people. Much as common-sense realism saw the physical world as readily appropriated by the knowing subject, Finney saw spiritual truth as well within the grasp of each individual human. Finney's "new measures" for revival were carefully reasoned and were thought to ensure revival to those who sought it. There was no question in Finney's mind that God wanted revival, and wanted it often. Thus when a congregation or community sponsored a "protracted meeting" the people, if penitent and prayerful enough, were assured that God would work. Just as surely as following certain natural laws of sowing and nurture guaranteed a farmer a crop, following certain spiritual laws would guarantee an outpouring of God's revival blessing. Thus, the

---

66. Stephens, 221, including quotations from Finney, *Sermons on Various Subjects*, 8.
67. Finney, *Lectures on Revival*, 4, 5.
68. Conn, "Foreword," vii.

expected, contrived, "prayed down" or "worked up" revival became commonplace throughout the ministry of Finney.

The Second Great Awakening was a series of revivals which had their beginning in Cane Ridge, Kentucky (1801) and culminated with the ministry of Charles Finney (c.1830–40). This Awakening saw an increased participation and growth of Baptists and Methodists, and the solidification of what were seen as "methodistic" practices in revival. One such practice, used to great effect by Finney, was known as the "mourner's bench" or the "anxious seat." The anxious seat was simply a designated pew of the church set apart from the rest at the front of the sanctuary. It was used to isolate those persons who were seeking God or on the verge of a decision, so that they could be prayed over and addressed directly by the preacher in terms of their specific need of conversion. The anxious seat "institutionalized the invitation and provided the sacramental vehicle for the conversion event."[69] It also had the psychological effect of intensifying the level of social and emotional pressure on each individual "sinner." This method was the predecessor to the "altar call" phenomenon so prevalent in nineteenth and twentieth century Evangelicalism. Richard Carwardine writes:

> [T]he idea behind both devices was identical: to separate the penitents—those actively seeking salvation—from the rest of the congregation so that they could be made more easily and more intensely subject to the psychological and social pressures of the Minister and of the community of the converted. . . . Far more important, however, than the precise pattern of adoption is that by the second decade of the century the call to the altar had become a standard feature of Methodist revivals. Indeed it sometimes happened that mourners would anticipate the minister's call and move to the altar before the instruction was given, so institutionalised had the procedure become.[70]

Prior to his own conversion, Finney had practiced law. Many have suggested that his legal training profoundly shaped his juridical evangelistic style. One writer suggests that Finney's *Lectures* reads less like a theology and more "like a volume of Blackstone's Law."[71] Finney's preaching was preoccupied with an almost legal type of obedience and forensic moral reform, and his style was clearly that of a barrister arguing before a jury. The

---

69. Leonard, "Getting Saved in America," 121.
70. Carwardine, *Transatlantic Revivalism*, 176.
71. As quoted in Horton, *Charles Finney vs. the Westminster Confession*, 13.

now-famous story of his own conversion and call to ministry sets the tone for Finney's notion that salvation is a human effort as well as his courtroom approach to evangelism.

Finney speaks not of God drawing him to salvation (as the old Puritan revivalists might), but of his own pursuit of regeneration. "On a Sabbath evening, just at this time of my history I made up my mind that I would settle the question of my soul's salvation at-once, that if it were possible, I would make my peace with God."[72] Two days later, Finney simply stopped in the street and announced, "I will accept it [the gospel] today, or I will die in attempt."[73] He recalled the biblical passage of Jeremiah 29:12–13, "ye shall seek me and shall find me, when you search for me with all your heart." Nothing could better represent Finney's sense "that salvation was up to him. He was now going to pound at the gate of heaven until he gained admittance."[74] Johnson observes, "In this manner he became convinced that the only inability of man was his voluntary unwillingness to do what he ought to do about his sins."[75]

> On the morning following Finney's conversion, a client came by to confirm Finney's appearance in court as his attorney. In his famous reply, Finney combined the terms of his two professions: "Deacon B—, I have a retainer from the Lord Jesus Christ to plead his cause, and I cannot plead yours." The gospel was a case to be won, and it required that a preacher learn the laws of the court in which he pleads, that he learn to interpret the Bible according to "the close and logical reasonings of judges, as I found them reported in our law works" and that he understand the laws of the mind so that he becomes practiced in persuasive techniques.[76]

Finney thought that the gospel was simply a "republication in another form"[77] of the law of God. "To Charles Finney the Principles of Divine Government were as intelligible as the Science of Law was to William Blackstone, as the system of Nature was to Isaac Newton, or as the Laws of Mind were to John Locke."[78] God's ways were readily accessible to anyone pos-

---

72. Finney, *Memoirs*, 16.
73. Ibid., 18.
74. Weiserberger, *They Gathered at the River*, 91.
75. Johnson, "Charles G. Finney and a Theology of Revivalism," 344.
76. Weddle, "The Law and the Revival," 24.
77. Ibid., 207.
78. Ibid.

sessing simple common sense. So, Finney would address the persons seated on the anxious bench as if they were jurors deliberating a case. He appealed to them as if they had been called to objectively assess the evidence at hand and decide for the truth. Of course, the "juror" was also the "defendant" in this case, whose capital offences were being presented as spiritual evidence of their need for justification. Finney's "theology excised from the spiritual life all uncertainty and mystery, even as civil laws sought to eliminate insecurity in the political life."[79] For Finney, there is nothing in religious experience beyond the ordinary experiences of the human psyche. Religious revival consists entirely in the proper, scientific manipulation of the human nature. Presbyterian Finney surprisingly denies the central Reformation principles of "justification" and "imputed righteousness" as detrimental to the need for moral self-correction:

> The doctrine of an imputed righteousness, or that Christ's obedience to the law was accounted as our obedience, is founded on a most false and nonsensical assumption, for Christ's righteousness could do no more than justify himself. It can never be imputed to us . . . . It was naturally impossible, then, for him to obey on our behalf. Representing the atonement as the ground of the sinner's justification has been a sad occasion of stumbling, to many.[80]

Thus, Finney's understanding of conversion has been characterized as a "system of self-reformation."[81] Warfield decried his theology as "a system of morals" from which "God might be eliminated . . . entirely without essentially changing its character."[82] The anthropocentric tone of Finney's revivals resonated well with the American people who were "ready for a faith of action through self-accomplishment."[83] For Finney to suggest that one's destiny was in one's own hands was simply to tap into the post-Enlightenment spirit which pervaded post-revolution, Jacksonian American culture. One writer wryly observes that "Finney . . . did not study the popular mind; he had it."[84] Finney "reworked Christian orthodoxy to suit the times," and his theology "fitted perfectly the ebullient optimism of the 1830s" as the

---

79. Ibid.
80. Finney, *Systematic Theology*, 46.
81. Smith, "The Theology of Charles Finney," 61–93.
82. Warfield, *Perfectionism*, 2:193.
83. Smith, "The Theology of Charles Finney," 64–65.
84. Weisberger, *They Gathered at the River*, 88.

"Christian counterpart of Jacksonian democracy."[85] Perry Miller comments, "The kind of revival stimulated by Finney in upstate New York . . . was . . . an expression of that kind of energy we call Jacksonian America."[86]

However, Finney not only tapped into the optimism of the American spirit, but he also appealed to the unique insecurities of the "burned-over district" of the American Mid-West. This region was filled with second-generation immigrants, many who had come to share in the prosperity of the newly completed Erie Canal, and the accompanying burgeoning industrial towns. In addition to the legendary after-effects of two previous Evangelical awakenings, these settlers brought with them a variety of peculiar religious sentiments which would spawn many uniquely American religious trends.[87] This rapid industrial change, coupled with the sense of isolation of new settlers, created something of a cultural crisis on this new frontier for which "[e]nthusiastic religion often provided the needed stability."[88] Thus, "by Finney's day, upstate New York had assembled the socioeconomic and religious machinery conducive to the development of an aberrant theology."[89]

The anticipated emotional response to such preaching as Finney's was almost certain. Harold Bloom says in *The American Religion*: "Finney had the insight to know that only a purely personal, violently emotional, totally experiential mode of salvation was appropriate for the Burned-over sinner. What had been spontaneous at Cane Ridge was systematized into a technique by Finney two generations later."[90] D. C. Weddle observes that Finney's systematic, legal approach "took the mystery out of theology,"[91] and "the key to his theology is the unshakeable conviction, gained in the study of law . . . that conversion is a reasoned decision to submit to God's moral government, as an act entirely within the sinner's natural powers."[92]

---

85. McLoughlin, *Modern Revivalism*, 120–21, 100.

86. Miller, *The Life of the Mind in America*, 30.

87. The "burned over district" of western New York State became a kind of "psychic highway" (Cross, *The Burned-Over District*, 3) which drew in various sects: Campbellities, Millerites (later Seventh-Day Adventists), Swedenborgians, Spiritualists, Shakers, Quakers, and others. It was the same fertile religious soil which produced Joseph Smith, founder of the Latter-Day Saint (Mormons).

88. Smith, "Theology of Charles Finney," 66.

89. Ibid.

90. Bloom, *American Religion*, 73.

91. Weddle, *The Law as Gospel*, 5.

92. Ibid., 6.

Finney's appeal was in no sense limited to America, however. Because of the evangelistic work (both in print and presence) of the Wesleys, Edwards, and Whitefield, there was a significant transatlantic bond between British and American Evangelicals. When Finney's *Lectures on Revival* came to Britain, it sold quickly. A colleague of Finney's noted upon his visit to Britain that Finney's *Lectures* were "scattered like leaves of autumn all over the kingdom."[93] This was particularly so in Wales. "[T]he book arguably achieved its most enthusiastic reception in Wales. The rapid sale of the Welsh edition translated by the Swansea Congregationalist, Evan Griffiths, enhanced the reputation of the Welsh as a people who read nothing but theology."[94] Welsh nonconformity, along with the "frontier-like" hardships of daily life, provided similar spiritual soil as found in the American frontier. Wales had always been notably receptive to the Evangelical revivalist style, and the southern industrial region particularly so.

> The practice and character of Welsh evangelical religion shared a number of common features with the evangelicalism of the American frontier. The isolation—through language and geography—of much of the population of rural Wales, and the expanding, unsettled and "disoriented" character of the working, population in the industrial belt offered grounds for comparison with the isolated, moving and restless population of the American West. Since in both regions the Established Church system was either weak or non-existent, the work of evangelizing a "deprived" population was left to the voluntaristic, revivalist Churches.[95]

The nature of Dissent revivalism in Wales paralleled the American distaste for formal religion, and matched its pitch of religious enthusiasm and fervor. The preaching was "extempore, animated, colloquial and colourful" with passionate appeals "to the imaginations and feelings," accompanied by a "great variety of intonation" which was "best exemplified in the *'hwyl'*—the musical semi-chanted, emotional climax to the sermon—which at its most effective could reduce a whole congregation to tears."[96] Finney's techniques came to a Wales already accustomed to emotional revivals, but it provided an experiential theology for both understanding and cre-

---

93. John Keep to Gerrit Smith, 13 November 1839, quoted in Carwardine, "The Welsh Evangelical Community," 464.

94. Carwardine, "The Welsh Evangelical Community," 464.

95. Ibid., 469.

96. Ibid., 467.

ating the revival phenomenon. Indeed, the wave of Evangelical renewals in Wales which followed the publication Finney's *Lectures on Revival* into Welsh were called "Finney's Revivals," even though Finney himself never set foot in Wales. Welsh churches had regularly engaged in heated battles over the relation of traditional Calvinism to the revival phenomenon. As in America, strict Reformed theology was gradually being modified into a more moderate system, though not without strife. In the midst of this division, Finney's *Lectures on Revival* came to Wales. Though not received by all, this work provided a practical means out of the debate. Finney's calculated methods of revival brought much response among the Independent churches, and promoted "a feeling which . . . led them to seek the revival of pure religion in a more suitable manner than they had before."[97] Carwardine believes that the revival techniques of Finney "were well received [in both Wales and America] because they gave positive expression to a growing emphasis on individual responsibility and participation" prevalent in the day, and "because they offered a comprehensible method of perpetuating a revival system regarded as essential to the Churches' livelihood."[98]

Thus, in an amazing adaptation of scientific method by an Evangelical revivalist, Finney's "new measures" had turned the unpredictable revival phenomenon into a scientifically precise technique. "Finney was doing nothing less than shifting the basis of theology from mystery to law."[99] In doing so, Finney completed the shift in understanding from a wholly divine act, as the Puritans understood it, to an experience fully within the grasp of the individual. The place of the autonomous, self-determined individual before God was solidly established by Finney's revival technique. For, not only was the conversion experience subjective and personal for Finney, it was now also wholly reasonable and scientific. In short, it had been placed firmly within the grasp of modern humanity. To the satisfaction of many Evangelicals, Finney had partially reconciled the gap between faith and science that had been introduced by the Enlightenment by making conversion itself a science. Carwardine says that "Finney's *Lectures on Revivals of Religion* . . . propagated the view that revivalism was a science: revivals could be produced by employing prescribed means in obedience to discoverable

---

97. J. Griffiths writing to Charles Finney, 13 July 1840, as quoted in Carwardine, "The Welsh Evangelical Community," 478, 479.

98. Carwardine, "The Welsh Evangelical Community," 480.

99. Weddle, *The Law as Gospel*, 208.

divine laws."¹⁰⁰ Nothing could match the voluntaristic American spirit more fittingly:

> If you want a revival of religion you can have one: if you want regeneration you can have it. Finney had in essence thoroughly domesticated the Holy Spirit, making the Spirit to feel perfectly at home in an environment of religious activism and voluntarism. After all, people who could build a new nation ought easily enough to be able to make new hearts. And as Finney told his listeners in his *Lectures on Revivals*, the important thing is to expect success in these matters, for where the right means are properly employed, effect will follow upon cause with all the predictability in the spiritual world that there is in the natural world. Nature and the supernatural work within the parameters of predictable legal structures, and one needs only to know the laws that govern both.¹⁰¹

Finney advocated a view of religious faith which is a kind of "self-reformation" in which the human subject is at the center. In Warfield's critique, Finney's revivalist technique portrays a person "quite able to save himself and in point of fact does, in every instance of his salvation, save himself."¹⁰² As such, it is a radical move from historic orthodoxy to a very modern form of human religious subjectivism. McLoughlin writes: "The difference between Edwards and Finney is essentially the difference between the medieval and modern temper. One saw God as the center of the universe, the other saw man."¹⁰³

---

100. Carwardine, "The Welsh Evangelical Community," 464.
101. Stephens, "Changing Conceptions of the Holy Spirit," 220.
102. Warfield, *Perfectionism*, 2:178.
103. McLoughlin, *Modern Revivalism*, 11.

Conclusion

IF MODERN PHILOSOPHY IS characterized by any one thing, it is in the value placed on the human subject in the epistemological process. For moderns, the individual human stands at the center of the noetic universe. Primary authority is often deemed to be internal rather than external to the human mind or heart. What the modern Western mind considers most true is that which comes from within the knowing subject. This epistemic shift, or as Immanuel Kant calls it, a "Copernican revolution," moves the focus of knowledge away from the external world (as with the ancient Greek philosophers) and from the objective God or his self-revelation (as with the medieval thinkers) decidedly toward the interior of the individual self. As Kant applied this reversal to religious thought, he saw fit to rescue religion from the ravages of Enlightenment reason by means of a "religion within the bounds of reason alone." Drawing from the recesses of his youthful Pietism, Kant crafted a theoretical framework to ensure that faith would never fall victim to Enlightenment science, locating faith within the subjective realm of practical reason. This subjective fingerprint would mark nearly all subsequent philosophies of religion.

The undisputed father of theological liberalism, Friedrich Schleiermacher, took this cue from Kant and developed it into a full theological system. Schleiermacher firmly established this subjective trend theologically at the onset of nineteenth century by shifting attention away from objective truth claims and dogmatic theology to a subjective theology grounded in the human "feeling of absolute dependence." Like Kant, Schleiermacher appealed to the spirit of his own Pietist upbringing when he suggested that all theological claims should be put to the test of "pious feeling." The result was a radical reformulation of traditional Protestantism along subjective lines. Schleiermacher manages to sustain pious devotion to Christ and love for the church, while at the same time discarding historic orthodox notions which did not commend themselves to modern "cultured despisers of religion." This is both a brilliant response and adaptation of Enlightenment principles.

In another direction, Danish philosophical thinker Søren Kierkegaard both adapts and reacts to Enlightenment thought. Kierkegaard's strange brand of Christian existentialism provides a unique appropriation of the Enlightenment-Pietist subjective justification of faith, while challenging the high view of reason and human autonomy. And yet, unlike Schleiermacher, Kierkegaard seems to sustain a commitment to historic orthodoxy. The surprising common ground between Kant, Schleiermacher, and Kierkegaard is the religious expression of Protestant Pietism with an undeniably modern twist. It appears that the subjectivity of Pietism is not only remarkably suited to Enlightenment epistemology, but it has served as a contributing cause of modernism. Kierkegaard manages to address the modern need for subjectivity in his rhetorical attack upon autonomous human reason, while, at the same time, sustaining a solid commitment to traditional Christian theological principles.

Revivalist Evangelicalism has always been perceived as an anti-intellectual, highly-subjective rejection of modernism. The movement perceives itself as an unchanging bastion of historic orthodoxy against the onslaught of Enlightenment science. Nevertheless, it is the argument of this study that the Evangelical-revivalist movement is not merely a reaction to Enlightenment thought, but is also unmistakably modern in its assumptions regarding the nature of faith. The Pietist impulse, fueled by modern anthropocentrism, and subjectivism in religious belief, was appropriated by the Evangelical revivalists (such as John Wesley, George Whitefield, Jonathan Edwards, and Charles G. Finney), and it enabled them to surpass the scholastic Calvinism of their Protestant traditions as they faced the characteristic concerns and needs of modern humanity. Evangelicalism has been a particularly successful form of modern Christian expression precisely because it shares key assumptions with modernism, not the least of which is the central significance of the knowing individual and the subjective nature of knowledge and religious belief.

CONCLUSION

Religion in the modern era is varied and diverse. And yet one reoccurring theme continues to surface again and again: the subjective nature of faith—the religion of the heart. Whether liberal or existentialist or Evangelical, the differences between these traditions, while often significant, are perhaps less consequential than the core values they all share in common. It is this "affective-experiential" orientation that places each of these solidly within the same intellectual era. As such, each of these theological traditions, however diverse, is a manifestation of the modernist impulse and a shift from the more objectively-oriented ancient and medieval theological traditions. This vast difference is summarized succinctly by C. S. Lewis: "The ancient man approached God . . . as the accused person approaches his judge. For the modern man the roles are reversed. He is the judge: God is in the dock."[1]

---

1. Lewis, *God in the Dock*, 244.

Bibliography

Abelman, Robert, and Kimberly Neuendorf. "Religion in Broadcasting." Washington, DC: Unda-USA, 1982.

Abraham, William J. "The Epistemological Significance of the Inner Witness of the Holy Spirit." *Faith and Philosophy* 7, no. 4 (1990) 434–50.

Ackley, Alfred H. "He Lives!" In *The Covenant Hymnal*, 253. Chicago: Covenant Publications, 1996.

Ahlstrom, Sidney. *A Religious History of the American People*. New Haven: Yale University Press, 1972.

Aldridge, Marion. "George Whitefield: The Necessary Interdependence of Preaching Style and Sermon Content to Effect Revival." *Journal of the Evangelical Theological Society* 23, no. 1 (1980) 55–64.

Allen, Diogenes. *Philosophy for Understanding Theology*. Atlanta: John Knox, 1985.

Allison, Henry E. "Christianity and Nonsense." In *Kierkegaard: A Collection of Critical Essays*, edited by Josiah Thompson, 289–323. New York: Doubleday, 1972.

Babbage, Stuart Barton. "To the Royal Air Force." In *C. S. Lewis: Speaker & Teacher*, edited by Carolyn Keefe, 85–102. Grand Rapids: Zondervan, 1971.

Ballard, Paul H. "Evangelical Experience: Notes on the History of a Tradition." *Journal of Ecumenical Studies* 13, no. 1 (1976) 51–68.

Balmer, Randall. *Blessed Assurance: A History of Evangelicalism in America*. Boston: Beacon, 1999.

Barth, Karl. "Brunners Schleiermacherbuch." *Zwischen den Zeiten* 2, no. 8 (1924) 49–64.

———. *Dogmatics in Outline*. Translated by G. T. Thomson. New York: Harper Torchbooks, 1959.

———. "Nachwort." In Friedrich Schleiermacher, *Schleiermacher-Auswahl*, 290–312. Munich: Siebenstern Taschenbuch, 1968.

———. *Protestant Theology in the Nineteenth Century: Its Background and History*. London: SCM, 1972.

———. "Roman Catholicism: A Question to the Protestant Church." In Karl Barth, *Theology and Church: Shorter Writings 1920–1928*. Translated by Louise Pettibone Smith, 307–33. New York: Harper & Row, 1962.

———. *The Theology of Schleiermacher*. Edited by Dietrich Ritschl. Translated by Geoffrey W. Bromiley. Edinburgh: T. & T. Clark, 1982.
Belden, A. C. "George Whitefield: His Influence on His Time." *The Evangelical Christian*, March 1961, 2–4, 19–20.
Bellah, Robert, et al. *Habits of the Heart: Individualism and Commitment in American Life*. Berkeley: University of California Press, 1985.
Berkhof, Hendrikus. *Two Hundred Years of Theology*. Translated by John Vriend. Grand Rapids: Eerdmans, 1985.
Binstock, Louis. *The Power of Faith*. New York: Prentice-Hall, 1952.
Bloom, Harold. *The American Religion*. New York: Simon and Schuster, 1992.
Blumhofer, Edith L., and Randall Balmer, eds. *Modern Christian Revivals*. Chicago: University of Illinois Press, 1993.
Brantley, Richard E. "The Common Ground of Wesley and Edwards." *Harvard Theological Review* 83, no. 3 (1990) 271–303.
Bregman, Lucy. *The Rediscovery of Inner Experience*. Chicago: Nelson-Hall, 1982.
Bretall, Robert, ed. *A Kierkegaard Anthology*. Princeton: Princeton University Press, 1946.
Brown, Colin. *Christianity and Western Thought*. Vol. 1. *From the Ancient World to the Enlightenment*. Downers Grove, IL: IVP, 1991.
———. *Philosophy and the Christian Faith: A Historical Sketch from the Middle Ages to the Present Day*. Downers Grove, IL: IVP, 1968.
Butler, Jon. *Awash in a Sea of Faith: Christianizing the American People*. Cambridge: Harvard University Press, 1990.
Calvin, John. *Institutes of the Christian Religion*. 2 vols. Translated by Ford Lewis Battle. Edited by John T. McNeill. Library of Christian Classics. Philadelphia: Westminster, 1960.
Carnell, Edward John. *The Burden of Søren Kierkegaard*. Grand Rapids: Eerdmans, 1965.
Carwardine, Richard. *Trans-Atlantic Revivalism: Popular Evangelicalism in Britain and America 1790–1865*. Westport, CT: Greenwood, 1978.
———. "The Welsh Evangelical Community and 'Finney's Revival.'" *Journal of Ecclesiastical History* 29, no. 4 (October 1978) 464–80.
Cassirer, Ernst. *Kant's Life and Thought*. Translated by James Haden. New Haven: Yale University Press, 1981.
Cherry, Conrad. *The Theology of Jonathan Edwards*. New York: Smith, 1974.
Chesterton, G. K. *What I Saw in America*. In *The Collected Works of G. K. Chesterton*, 21:335–63. San Francisco: Ignatius, 1990.
Christian, C. W. *Friedrich Schleiermacher*. Makers of the Modern Theological Mind. Waco, TX: Word, 1979.
Clements, Keith W. *Friedrich Schleiermacher: Pioneer of Modern Theology*. London: Collins, 1987.
Cohen, Charles Lloyd. *God's Caress: The Psychology of Puritan Religious Experience*. New York: Oxford University Press, 1986.
A Collection of Hymns, for the Use of the People Called Methodists. London, 1780.
Conforti, Joseph A. *Jonathan Edwards, Religious Tradition, & American Culture*. Chapel Hill, NC: University of North Carolina Press, 1995.
Conn, Harry. "Foreword." In Charles Grandison Finney, *Finney's Systematic Theology*. Abridged ed. Edited by J. H. Fairchild, vii–viii. Minneapolis: Bethany House, 1976.
Copleston, Frederick. *A History of Philosophy*. Vol. 1, *Greece & Rome*. New York: Doubleday, 1946.

BIBLIOGRAPHY

The Covenant Hymnal. Chicago: Covenant Publications, 1996.
Cragg, Gerald R. *The Church and the Age of Reason, 1648–1789.* New York: Pelican, 1960.
Cross, Whitney R. *The Burned-Over District: The Social and Intellectual History of Enthusiastic Religion in Western New York, 1800–1850.* Ithaca, NY: Cornell University Press, 1950.
Dallimore, Arnold A. *George Whitefield: The Life and Times of the Great Evangelist of the Eighteenth-Century Revivals.* 2 vols. Westchester, IL: Cornerstone, 1970.
Davidson, Edward H. *Jonathan Edwards: The Narrative of a Puritan Mind.* Boston: Harvard University Press, 1969.
Davies, John. *A History of Wales.* London: Penguin, 1993.
Dayton, Donald W., and Robert K. Johnston, eds. *The Variety of American Evangelicalism.* 1991. Reprint. Eugene, OR: Wipf and Stock, 1998.
Descartes, René. *Philosophical Works.* 2 vols. Edited by Elizabeth Haldane. Translated by G. R. T. Ross. Cambridge: Cambridge University Press, 1931.
Dilthey, Wilhelm. *Leben Schleiermachers.* Berlin: Reimer, 1861.
Dogma. Kevin Smith, writer/director. Scott Mosier, producer. A View-Askew Production. Culver City, CA: Columbia/TriStar Pictures, 1999.
Dostoyevsky, Fyodor M. *The Brothers Karamazov.* Translated by Andrew H. McAndrew. New York: Bantam, 1970.
Dru, Alexander. "Introduction." In Theodor Haecker, *Kierkegaard the Cripple.* Translated by C. Van O. Bruyn, v–xi. New York: Philosophical Library, 1950.
Drummond, Lewis. *Charles G. Finney and the Birth of Modern Evangelism.* London: Hodder & Stoughton, 1983.
Dulles, Avery. *The Assurance of Things Hoped For: A Theology of Christian Faith.* New York: Oxford University Press, 1994.
———. *Models of Revelation.* Maryknoll, NY: Orbis, 1994.
Dunstan, J. Leslie, ed. *Protestantism.* New York: Braziller, 1961.
Dupré, Louis. "Toward a Revaluation of Schleiermacher's Philosophy of Religion." *Journal of Religion* 44, no. 2 (1964) 97–112.
Durant, Will. *The Story of Philosophy.* New York: Time, 1926.
Edwards, Jonathan. *The Great Awakening.* The Works of Jonathan Edwards, vol. 4. Edited by C. C. Goen. New Haven: Yale University Press, 1972.
———. "Sinners in the Hands of an Angry God." In *The Works of Jonathan Edwards*, vol. 2, edited by Edward Hickman, 7–12. Edinburgh: Banner of Truth, 1974.
———. *Sermons and Discourses, 1720–1723.* The Works of Jonathan Edwards, vol. 10. Edited by Wilson H. Kimnach. New Haven: Yale University Press, 1992.
———. *A Treatise concerning Religious Affections.* The Works of Jonathan Edwards, vol. 2. Edited by John E. Smith. New Haven: Yale University Press, 1994.
———. "True Repentance Required." In Jonathan Edwards, *Sermons and Discourses, 1720–1723.* The Works of Jonathan Edwards, vol. 10, edited by Wilson H. Kimnach, 507–19. New Haven: Yale University Press, 1992.
———. "The Value of Salvation." In Jonathan Edwards, *Sermons and Discourses, 1720–1723.* The Works of Jonathan Edwards, vol. 10, edited by Wilson H. Kimnach, 309–37. New Haven: Yale University Press, 1992.
Evans, C. Stephen. "The Epistemological Significance of Transformative Religious Experiences: A Kierkegaardian Exploration." *Faith and Philosophy* 8, no. 2 (1991) 180–92.
———. *Faith beyond Reason.* Grand Rapids: Eerdmans, 1998.

BIBLIOGRAPHY

———. "Kierkegaard on Subjective Truth: Is God an Ethical Fiction?" *International Journal for Philosophy of Religion* 7, no. 1 (1976) 288-99.

———. *Subjectivity and Religious Belief*. Grand Rapids: Eerdmans, 1978.

Evans, C. Stephen, and Merold Westphal, eds. *Christian Perspectives on Religious Knowledge*. Grand Rapids: Eerdmans, 1993.

Eversley, Walter V. L. "The Pastor as Revivalist." In *Edwards in Our Time: Jonathan Edwards and the Shaping of American Religion*, edited by Sang Hyun Lee and Allen C. Guelzo, 113-30. Grand Rapids: Eerdmans, 1999.

Farmer, Herbert H. *Religion and Revelation*. New York: Harpers, 1954.

Fee, Joan L. et al. *Young Catholics: A Report to the Knights of Columbus*. Los Angeles: Sadlier, 1981.

Fenner, William. *A Treatise of the Affections: or, The Soule's Pulse*. London, 1642.

Finney, Charles Grandison. *Finney's Systematic Theology*. Edited by Harry Conn. Minneapolis: Bethany House, 1976.

———. *Lectures on Revivals of Religion*. Edited by William G. McLoughlin. Cambridge: Belknap, 1960.

———. *Memoirs of Charles Grandison Finney: The Complete Restored Text*. Edited by Garth Rosell and Richard A. G. Dupuis. Grand Rapids: Zondervan, 1989.

———. *Sermons on Important Subjects*. New York: Taylor & Gould, 1836.

———. *Sermons on Various Subjects*. New York: Taylor, 1835.

———. "Sinners Bound to Change Their Own Hearts." In *Sermons on Important Subjects*, 1-45. New York: Taylor & Gould, 1836.

Fisher, George Park. *History of Christian Doctrine*. International Theological Library. Edinburgh: T. & T. Clark, 1896.

Flavel, John. *Keeping the Heart*. Boston, 1720. *A Saint Indeed, or the Great Work of a Christian Explained*. In *The Works of John Flavel*, 417-509. 1820. Reprint. London: Banner of Truth, 1968.

Friedrich, Carl F., ed. *The Philosophy of Kant*. New York: Modern Library, 1949.

Gardiner, Patrick. *Kierkegaard*. Past Masters. Oxford: Oxford University Press, 1988.

Garrett, Samuel. "Jonathan Edwards and the Great Awakening." In *American Christianity: A Case Approach*, edited by Ronald White, Jr. et al., 19-29. Grand Rapids: Eerdmans, 1986.

Gaustad, Edwin S. *The Great Awakening in New England*. New York: Peter Smith, 1965.

Gay, Peter. *The Enlightenment: An Interpretation*. 2 vols. New York: Knopf, 1969.

Gerrish, B. A. *A Prince of the Church: Schleiermacher and the Beginnings of Modern Theology*. London: SCM, 1984.

Gill, Jerry. "Kant, Kierkegaard, and Religious Knowledge." *Philosophy and Phenomenological Research* 28 (1967) 188-204.

Gilmore, R. Eugene. "A Reappraisal of Liberal Apologetics." *Religion in Life* 32, no. 3 (1963) 369-79.

Gouwens, David J. *Kierkegaard as a Religious Thinker*. Cambridge: Cambridge University Press, 1996.

Greene, Theodore M. "The Historical Context and Religious Significance of Kant's *Religion*." In Immanuel Kant, *Religion within the Limits of Reason Alone*, translated by Theodore M. Greene and Hoyt H. Hudson, vii-lxxviii. New York: Harper Torchbooks, 1960.

Greven, Philip. *The Protestant Temperament: Patterns of Child-Rearing, Religious Experience and the Self in Early America*. New York: Knopf, 1977.

BIBLIOGRAPHY

Gunton, Colin. *Enlightenment & Alienation*. Grand Rapids: Eerdmans, 1985.
Haecker, Theodor. *Kierkegaard the Cripple*. Translated by C. Van O. Bruyn. Introduction by A. Dru. New York: Philosophical Library, 1950.
Hambrick-Stowe, Charles E. *Charles G. Finney and the Spirit of American Evangelicalism*. Grand Rapids: Eerdmans, 1996.
Hampson, Norman. *The Enlightenment: An Evaluation of its Assumptions, Attitudes and Values*. London: Penguin, 1968.
Handy, Robert T. *A Christian America: Protestant Hopes and Historical Realities*. New York: Oxford, 1984.
Hardman, Keith J. *Charles Grandison Finney, 1792-1875: Revivalist and Reformer*. Syracuse, NY: Syracuse University Press, 1987.
Hardman, Keith J. *The Spiritual Awakeners: American Revivalists from Solomon Stoddard to Dwight L. Moody*. Chicago: Moody, 1983.
Hatch, Nathan O. *The Democratization of American Christianity*. New Haven: Yale University Press, 1989.
Hegel, Georg F. W. *Phenomenology of Mind*. Translated by J. B. Ballie. New York: Macmillan, 1931.
Heimert, Alan, and Perry Miller, eds. *The Great Awakening*. Indianapolis: Bobbs-Merrill, 1967.
Heine, Heinrich. *Religion and Philosophy in Germany*. Translated by John Snodgrass. Boston: Beacon, 1959.
Hendrix, Scott H. "Legends about Luther." *Christian History* Issue 34, 11, no. 2 (1992) 48-50.
Herberg, Will. "Judaism and Christianity: Unity and Difference." *Journal of Bible and Religion* 21, no. 2 (1953) 67-78.
―――. *Protestant-Catholic-Jew: An Essay in American Religious Sociology*. Chicago: University of Chicago Press, 1983.
Heron, Alasdair I. C. *A Century of Protestant Theology*. Philadelphia: Westminster, 1980.
Hindmarsh, D. Bruce. "'My chains fell off, my heart was free': Early Methodist Conversion Narrative in England." *Church History* 68, no. 4 (1999) 910-29.
Hirsch, Emanuel. *Geschichte der neueren evangelischen Theologie*. Gütersloh: Bertelsmann, 1954.
Hodge, Charles. "Finney's Lectures on Biblical Theology." *Biblical Repertory and Princeton Review* 19, no. 2 (1847) 237-77.
Hofstadter, Richard. *Anti-Intellectualism in American Life*. Toronto: Vintage, 1966.
Hoge, Dean R. *Converts, Dropouts, Returnees: A Study of Religious Change among Catholics*. Washington, DC: United States Catholic Conference; New York: Pilgrim, 1981.
Holmes, Urban T. *A History of Christian Spirituality*. Minneapolis: Seabury, 1980.
Hook, Sidney, ed. *Religious Experience and Truth*. New York: New York University Press, 1961.
Horton, Michael Scott. *Charles Finney vs. the Westminster Confession*. Escondido, CA: Alliance of Confessing Evangelicals, 1995.
Howard, Irving. "Random Reflections." *Christian Economics* 7, no. 5 (1955) 2.
Hubbard, David Allan. *What We Evangelicals Believe*. Pasadena, CA: Fuller Theological Seminary, 1979.
Huch, R. *Die Romantik*. Tübingen: Wunderlich, 1951.

Hudson, Winthrop. *Religion in America: An Historical Account of the Development of American Religious Life.* 4th ed. London: Collier, 1987.

Hughes, Langston. *The Big Sea: An Autobiography.* New York: Hill & Wang, 1940.

Hunter, James Davison. *American Evangelicalism: Conservative Religion and the Quandary of Modernity.* New Brunswick, NJ: Rutgers University Press, 1983.

Husband, Herman. *Remarks on Religion, with the Author's Experience in Pursuit Thereof.* Philadelphia, 1761.

Hutchinson, Paul. "The President's Religious Faith," *Christian Century*, March 24, 1954, 362–69.

Hütter, Richard. *Suffering Divine Things: Theology as Church Practice.* Translated by Doug Stott. Grand Rapids: Eerdmans, 2000.

James, William. *Pragmatism and Four Essays from* The Meaning of Truth. New York: Meridian, 1955.

———. *The Varieties of Religious Experience.* New York: Modern Library, 1936.

Johnson, J. E. "Charles G. Finney and a Theology of Revivalism." *Church History* 38, no. 3 (1969) 338–58.

Kant, Immanuel. *Critique of Judgment.* Translated by J. H. Bernard. New York: Hafner, 1951.

———. *Critique of Practical Reason.* Translated by T. K. Abbot. Amherst, NY: Prometheus, 1996.

———. *Critique of Pure Reason.* Translated by J. M. D. Meiklejohn. Buffalo, NY: Prometheus, 1990.

———. *Critique of Pure Reason.* Translated by Norman Kemp Smith. New York: St. Martin's, 1965.

———. *Prolegomena to Every Future Metaphysics That May Be Presented as Science.* In *The Philosophy of Kant*, edited by Carl J. Friedrich, 40–115. New York: Modern Library, 1949.

———. *Religion within the Limits of Reason Alone.* Translated by Theodore M. Greene and Hoyt H. Hudson. New York: Harper Torchbooks, 1960.

———. *Was ist Aufklärung?* Stuttgart: Reclam, 1974.

———. "What Is Enlightenment?" In *Foundations of the Metaphysics of Morals* and *What Is Enlightenment?*, translated by Lewis White Beck, 85–92. Indianapolis: Bobbs Merrill, 1959.

———. "What Is Enlightenment?" In *Philosophical Writings.* The German Library, vol. 13, edited by Ernst Behler, 263–69. New York: Continuum, 1986.

Kierkegaard, Søren. *Attack upon Christendom.* Translated by Walter Lowrie. Princeton: Princeton University Press, 1968.

———. *Christian Discourses.* Translated with an introduction by Walter Lowrie. Princeton: Princeton University Press, 1940.

———. *The Concept of Anxiety.* Translated by Reider Thomte. Princeton, NJ: Princeton University Press, 1980.

———. *The Concept of Dread.* Translated with introduction and notes by Walter Lowrie. Princeton: Princeton University Press, 1944.

———. *Concluding Unscientific Postscript.* 2 vols. Edited and translated by Howard V. Hong and Edna H. Hong, with introduction and notes. Princeton: Princeton University Press, 1992.

———. *Either/Or.* 2 vols. Vol. 1 translated by David F. Swenson and Lilian Marvin Swenson with revisions and a foreword by Howard A. Johnson; vol. 2 translated by Walter Lowrie with revisions and a foreword by Howard A. Johnson. Princeton: Princeton University Press, 1959.

———. *Fear and Trembling*. Translated by Walter Lowrie. Princeton: Princeton University Press, 1941.

———. *The Journals of Søren Kierkegaard*. Edited and translated by Alexander Dru. Oxford University Press, 1938.

———. *On Authority and Revelation*. Translated by Walter Lowrie. New York: Harper Torchbooks, 1966.

———. *Philosophical Fragments: Johannes Climacus*. Edited and translated with introduction and notes by Howard V. Hong and Edna H. Hong. Princeton: Princeton University Press, 1985.

———. *The Point of View for My Work as an Author*. Translated by Walter Lowrie. Edited by Benjamin Nelson. New York: Harper Torchbooks, 1956.

———. *Preparation for the Christian Life*. Translated by Walter Lowrie. New York: Harper, 1962.

———. *Repetition*. Translated by Walter Lowrie. 1941. Reprint. New York: Harper Torchbooks, 1964.

———. *Training in Christianity*. Translated by Walter Lowrie. Princeton, NJ: Princeton University Press, 1963.

Knox, Ronald. *Enthusiasm: A Chapter in the History of Religion*. Oxford: Oxford University Press, 1950.

Kroner, Richard. *Speculation and Revelation in Modern Philosophy*. Philadelphia: Westminster, 1961.

———. *The Primacy of Faith*. Translated by J. E. Smith. Chicago: University of Chicago Press, 1956.

Leap of Faith. Produced by Michael Manheim, David V. Picker production. Written by Janus Cercone. Directed by Richard Pearce. Hollywood: Paramount Pictures, 2003.

Lambert, Frank. "The Great Awakening as Artifact: George Whitefield and the Construction of Intercolonial Revival, 1739–1745." *Church History* 60, no. 2 (1991) 223–46.

Lee, Phillip J. *Against the Protestant Gnostics*. New York: Oxford University Press, 1987.

Lee, Sang Hyun, and Allen C. Guelzo, eds. *Edwards in Our Time*. Grand Rapids: Eerdmans, 1999.

Leonard, Bill J. "Conversion." In *Dictionary of Christianity in America*, edited by Daniel G. Reid, 316–17. Downers Grove, IL: IVP, 1990.

———. "Getting Saved in America: Conversion Event in a Pluralistic Culture." *Review and Expositor* 82, no. 1(1985) 111–27.

Lewis, C. S. *God in the Dock: Essays on Theology and Ethics*. Edited by Walter Hooper. Grand Rapids: Eerdmans, 1970.

Lewis, Sinclair. *Elmer Gantry*. New York: Signet, 1927.

Lindbeck, George. *The Nature of Doctrine: Religion and Theology in a Postliberal Age*. Philadelphia: Westminster, 1984.

Locke, John. *An Essay concerning Human Understanding*. New York: Doubleday, 1974.

Lowrie, Walter. *A Short Life of Kierkegaard*. Princeton, NJ: Princeton University Press, 1942.

———. "Introduction by the Translator." In Soren Kierkegaard, *The Concept of Dread*, xi–xiii. Princeton: Princeton University Press, 1944.

———. "Translator's Preface." In Søren Kierkegaard, *The Concept of Dread*, v-x. Princeton: Princeton University Press, 1944.
Mackintosh, Hugh Ross. *Types of Modern Theology: Schleiermacher to Barth*. London: Nisbet, 1937.
Mains, David R. *The Sense of His Presence: Experiencing Spiritual Regenesis*. Waco, TX: Word, 1988.
Marlin, George J., Richard P. Rabatin, and John L. Swan, eds. *More Quotable Chesterton*. San Francisco: Ignatius, 1988.
Marsden, George. *Fundamentalism and American Culture*. New York: Oxford University Press, 1980.
———. *Religion and American Culture*. New York: Harcourt, Brace, Jovanovich, 1990.
———. *Understanding Fundamentalism and Evangelicalism*. Grand Rapids: Eerdmans, 1991.
Marty, Martin. *Protestantism*. London: Holt, Rinehart and Winston, 1972.
May, Henry F. *The Enlightenment in America*. New York: Harper, 1976.
Mayers, Ronald B. *Both/And: A Balanced Apologetic*. Chicago: Moody, 1984.
McGiffert, Arthur C., Jr. *Protestant Thought before Kant*. New York: Scribner's, 1951.
———. "The Theology of Crisis in the Light of Schleiermacher." *Journal of Religion* 10, no. 3 (1930) 362-77.
McGrath, Alister E. "Enlightenment." In *Blackwell Encyclopedia of Modern Christian Thought*, edited by Alister E. McGrath, 150-56. Oxford: Blackwell, 1993.
———. *Iustitia Dei: A History of the Christian Doctrine of Justification*. 2nd ed. Cambridge: Cambridge University Press, 1998.
McLoughlin, William G., ed. *The American Evangelicals, 1800-1900*. New York: Harper Torchbooks, 1968.
———. "Introduction." In Charles Grandison Finney, *Lectures on Revivals of Religion*, edited by William G. McLoughlin, vii-lii. Cambridge: Belknap, 1960.
———. *Modern Revivalism: Charles G. Finney to Billy Graham*. New York: Ronald, 1959.
———. *Revivals, Awakenings, and Reform*. Chicago: University of Chicago, 1978.
Mead, Sidney. *The Lively Experiment: The Shaping of Christianity in America*. New York: Harper & Row, 1963.
Miller, Kevin A., ed. Zinzendorf and the Moravians. *Christian History* Issue 1, no. 1 (1982).
Miller, Perry. *Errand into the Wilderness*. Cambridge, MA: Harvard University Press, 1956.
———. *Jonathan Edwards*. Boston: University of Massachusetts Press, 1981.
———. *The Life of the Mind in America: From the Revolution to the Civil War*. New York: Harcourt, Brace, and World, 1965.
Mitchell, Basil. *The Justification of Religious Belief*. New York: Seabury, 1973.
Muller, Richard A. *Dictionary of Latin & Greek Theological Terms Drawn Principally from Protestant Scholastic Theology*. Grand Rapids: Baker, 1985.
Murray, Iain. *Jonathan Edwards: A New Biography*. Edinburgh: Banner of Truth, 1987.
———. *The Puritan Hope*. Edinburgh: Banner of Truth Trust, 1971.
Niebuhr, H. Richard. *The Meaning of Revelation*. New York: MacMillan, 1941.
———. *The Social Sources of Denominationalism*. New York: Meridian, 1929.
Niebuhr, R. Reinhold. *Experiential Religion*. New York: Harper & Row, 1972.
———. "Religiosity and the Christian Faith." *Christianity and Crisis* 14, no. 24 (1955) 185-86.
———. "Friedrich Schleiermacher." In *Handbook of Christian Theologians*, edited by Dean G. Peerman and Martin E. Marty, 17-35. Nashville: Abingdon, 1965.

———. *Schleiermacher on Christ and Religion: A New Introduction.* New York: Scribner's Sons, 1964.
———. "Schleiermacher on Language and Feeling." *Theology Today* 17 (1960) 150–67.
———. "Schleiermacher: Theology as Human Reflection." *Harvard Theological Review* 55, no. 1 (1962) 20–49.
Noll, Mark A. *A History of Christianity in the United States and Canada.* Grand Rapids: Eerdmans, 1992.
———. "Glimpses of Finney." *The Reformed Journal* 36, no. 5 (1986) 22–24.
———. *Turning Points.* Grand Rapids: Baker, 1997.
Nuttall, Geoffrey F. *The Holy Spirit in Puritan Faith and Experience.* 2nd ed. 1947. Reprint. Chicago: University of Chicago Press, 1992.
Oakeshott, Michael. *Rationalism in Politics and Other Essays.* New York: Basic, 1962.
O'Brian, Susan. "A Transatlantic Community of Saints: The Great Awakening and the First Evangelical Network, 1735–1755." *American Historical Review* 91, no 4 (1986) 811–32.
Olson, Roger E. *The Story of Christian Theology.* Downers Grove, IL: IVP, 1999.
Otto, Rudolf. *The Idea of the Holy.* New York: Oxford University Press, 1923.
———. "Introduction." In Friedrich Schleiermacher, *On Religion: Speeches to Its Cultured Despisers,* translated by John Oman, vii–xx. New York: Harper Torchbooks, 1958.
Outler, Albert C., ed. *John Wesley.* A Library of Protestant Thought. Oxford: Oxford University Press, 1964.
Pascal, Blaise. *Pensees.* Translated with an introduction by A. J. Krailsheimer. Penguin Classics. London: Penguin, 1966.
Patrick, Denzil G. M. *Pascal and Kierkegaard.* London: Lutterworth, 1947.
Paulson, Friedrich. *Immanuel Kant: His Life and Doctrine.* New York: Scribner's, 1902.
Peale, Norman Vincent. *The Power of Positive Thinking.* New York: Prentice-Hall, 1952.
Pelikan, Jaroslav. *Christian Doctrine and Modern Culture (Since 1700).* The Christian Tradition, vol. 5. Chicago: University of Chicago Press, 1989.
Perkins, William. *Works.* 3 vols. Cambridge, 1608–9.
Philip, Robert. *The Life and Times of the Reverend George Whitefield, M.A.* London: Rickerby, 1842.
Phillips, Thomas. *The Welsh Revival: Its Origins and Development.* Edinburgh: Banner of Truth, 1989.
Plantinga, Alvin, and Nicholas Wolterstorff, eds. *Faith and Rationality: Reason and Belief in God.* South Bend, IN: University of Notre Dame Press, 1983.
Plantinga, Alvin. *Warranted Christian Belief.* New York: Oxford University Press, 2000.
Polanyi, Michael. *Personal Knowledge: Towards a Post-Critical Philosophy.* London: Routledge and Kegan Paul, 1962.
Poling, Daniel A. "A Running Start for Every Day." *Parade: The Sunday Picture Magazine. Detroit Free Press,* September 19, 1954, 165.
Pope, Alexander. "An Essay on Man." In *The Complete Poetical Works of Alexander Pope,* edited by Henry Boynton Walcott, 137–55. Boston: Houghton, Mifflin, 1902.
Popkin, Richard H. *The History of Scepticism from Erasmus to Descartes.* Assen: Van Gorcum, 1960.
Postman, Neil. *Amusing Ourselves to Death.* New York: Penguin, 1985.
Proudfoot, Wayne. "From Theology to a Science of Religions: Jonathan Edwards and William James on Religious Affections." *Harvard Theological Review* 82, no. 2 (1986) 149–68.

BIBLIOGRAPHY

———. *Religious Experience*. Berkeley, CA: University of California Press, 1985.
Rack, Henry D. *Reasonable Enthusiast: John Wesley and the Rise of Methodism*. Nashville, TN: Abingdon, 1989.
Raschke, Carl A. *Moral Action, God, and History in the Thought of Immanuel Kant*. Dissertation Series 5. Missoula, MT: American Academy of Religion and Scholar's, 1975.
Radner, Ephraim. "We Believe in One Lord, Jesus Christ." In *The Rule of Faith: Scripture, Canon, and Creed in a Critical Age*, edited by Ephraim Radner and George Sumner, 13-26. Harrisburg, PA: Morehouse, 1998.
Reardon, Bernard M. G. *Kant as Philosophical Theologian*. Totowa, NJ: Barnes & Noble, 1978.
Redeker, Martin. *Schleiermacher: Life and Thought*. Translated by John Wallhausser. Philadelphia: Fortress, 1973.
Reid, Daniel G., ed. *Dictionary of Christianity in America*. Downers Grove, IL: IVP, 1990.
Richardson, Alan. "Instrument of God." *Interpretation* 3, no. 3 (1949) 273-85.
Ritschl, Dietrich. "Editor's Preface." In Karl Barth, *The Theology of Schleiermacher*, translated by Geoffrey W. Bromiley, ix-xii. Grand Rapids: Eerdmans, 1982.
Rink, F. T. *Ansichten aus Immanuel Kant's Leben*. Konigsberg, 1805.
Schaeffer, Francis A. *Complete Works*. 5 vols. Westchester, IL: Crossway, 1982.
Schlegel, A. W. *Sammtliche Werke*. Edited by E. Bocking. Leibzig, 1846/47.
Schleiermacher, Friedrich. *A Brief Outline of the Study of Theology*. Translated by Terrence Tice. Atlanta: John Knox, 1966.
———. *The Christian Faith*. Edited by H. R. Mackintosh. Translated by J. S. Stewart. Edinburgh: T. & T. Clark, 1976.
———. *The Christian Faith in Outline*. Translated by Donald M. Baillie. Edinburgh: Henderson, 1922.
———. *Christmas Eve: Dialogue on the Incarnation*. Translated by Terrence Tice. Richmond, VA: John Knox, 1967.
———. *The Life of Schleiermacher as Unfolded in His Autobiography and Letters*. Translated by Frederica Rowan. London: Smith, Elder, 1860.
———. *On the Glaubenslehre: Two Letters to Dr. Lücke*. Translated by James Duke and Francis Fiorenza. Chico: Scholar's 1981.
———. *On Religion: Addresses in Response to Its Cultured Critics*. Translated by Terrence Tice. Richmond, VA: John Knox, 1969.
———. *On Religion: Speeches to Its Cultured Despisers*. Translated by John Oman. Introduction by Rudolf Otto. New York: Harper Torchbooks, 1958.
———. *On Religion: Speeches to Its Cultured Despisers*. Introduction, translation, and notes by Richard Crouter. Cambridge: Cambridge University Press, 1996.
———. *Soliloquies*. Translated by Horace Leland Freiss. Chicago: Open Court, 1957.
Schneider, Louis, and Sanford M. Dornbusch. *Popular Religion: Inspirational Books in America*. Chicago: University of Chicago Press, 1958.
Scruton, Roger. *Kant*. Past Masters. Oxford: Oxford University Press, 1982.
Simonson, Harold P. *Jonathan Edwards: Theologian of the Heart*. Grand Rapids: Eerdmans, 1974.
Skinner, John E. "Rational Faith in Kant's Philosophy." *Anglican Theological Review* 43, no. 2 (1961) 178-85.
Smith, Jay E. "The Theology of Charles Finney: A System of Self-Reformation." *Trinity Journal* 13, no. 1 (1992) 61-93.

BIBLIOGRAPHY

Smith, Timothy L. *Revivalism and Social Reform: American Protestantism on the Eve of the Civil War*. Nashville: Abingdon, 1957.
Smith, Timothy L., ed. *Whitefield and Wesley on the New Birth*. Grand Rapids: Eerdmans, 1986.
Sontag, Frederick. *A Kierkegaard Handbook*. Atlanta: John Knox, 1979.
Spener, Phillip. *Pia Desideria*. Philadelphia: Fortress, 1964.
Spitz, Lewis. *The Protestant Reformation 1517–1529*. New York: Harper and Row, 1985.
Stephens, Bruce M. "Changing Conceptions of the Holy Spirit in American Protestant Theology from Jonathan Edwards to Charles G. Finney." *Saint Luke's Journal of Theology* 33, no 3 (1990) 209–23.
Stout, Harry S. *The Divine Dramatist: George Whitefield and the Rise of Modern Evangelicalism*. Grand Rapids: Eerdmans, 1991.
Stout, Harry S. "Introduction." In *Edwards in Our Time: Jonathan Edwards and the Shaping of American Religion*, edited by Sang Hyun Lee and Allen C. Guelzo, ix–xvi. Grand Rapids: Eerdmans, 1999.
———. *The New England Soul*. New York: Oxford University Press, 1986.
———. "Religion, Communications, and the Career of George Whitefield." In *Communication and Change in American Religious History*, edited by Leonard Sweet, 108–25. Grand Rapids: Eerdmans, 1993.
Stout, Jeffrey. *The Flight from Authority: Religion, Morality and the Quest for Autonomy*. Notre Dame, IN: University of Notre Dame Press, 1981.
Strathern, Paul. *Kant*. Chicago: See, 1996.
Strauss, David Friedrich. *The Christ of Faith and the Jesus of History: A Critique of Schleiermacher's Life of Jesus*. Translated by Leander E. Keck. Philadelphia: Fortress, 1977.
Sweet, Leonard I., ed. *Communication and Change in American Religious History*. Grand Rapids: Eerdmans, 1993.
———. *The Evangelical Tradition in America*. Macon, GA: Mercer University Press, 1984.
Teo, Wesley K. H. "Self-Responsibility in Existentialism and Buddhism." *International Journal for Philosophy of Religion* 4, no. 2 (1973) 80–91.
Thielicke, Helmut. *Modern Faith and Thought*. Translated by Geoffrey W. Bromiley. Grand Rapids: Eerdmans, 1990.
Thilly, Frank. *History of Philosophy*. New York: Holt, 1914.
Tice, Terrence W. "Introduction." In Friedrich Schleiermacher, *On Religion: Addresses in Response to Its Cultured Critics*. Translated by Terrence N. Tice, 9–30. Richmond, VA: John Knox, 1969.
Tillich, Paul. "Is There a Judeo-Christian Tradition?" *Judaism* 1, no. 2 (1952) 106–9.
———. *Protestant Theology*. 2 vols. Chicago: University of Chicago Press, 1967.
Tocqueville, Alexis de. *Democracy in America*. Translated by George Lawrence. Edited by J. P. Mayer. New York: Doubleday Anchor, 1969.
Troeltsch, Ernst. *The Social Teaching of the Christian Churches*. Translated by Olive Wyon. London: Allen & Unwin, 1931.
Tuttle, Robert G., Jr. *Mysticism in the Wesleyan Tradition*. Grand Rapids: Francis Asbury, 1989.
Vidler, Alec R. *The Church in an Age of Revolution 1789 to Present*. New York: Pelican, 1961.

Walker, William. "The Cambridge Platform, 1648." In *The Creeds and Platforms of Congregationalism*, edited by Williston Walker, 157–237. 1893. Reprint. Boston: Beacon, 1960.

———, et al. *The History of the Christian Church*. 4th ed. New York: Scribner, 1985.

Want, Christopher, and Andrej Klimowski. *Introducing Kant*. New York: Totem, 1997.

Ward, James. *Study of Kant*. Cambridge: Cambridge University Press, 1922.

Warfield, B. B. *Perfectionism*. 2 vols. Edited by Ethelbert D. Warfield. 1931, 1932. Reprint. Grand Rapids: Baker, 1981.

Webster, John B. "Faith." In *Blackwell Encyclopedia of Modern Christian Thought*, edited by Alister E. McGrath, 208–10. Oxford: Blackwell, 1993.

Weddle, David C. *Law as Gospel: Revival and Reform in the Theology of Charles G. Finney*. Metuchen, NJ: Scarecrow, 1985.

Weddle, David C. "The Law and the Revival: A New Divinity for the Settlements." *Church History* 47, no. 2 (1978) 196–214.

Weiseberger, Bernard A. *They Gathered at the River: The Story of the Great Revivalists and Their Impact on Religion in America*. Boston: Little, Brown, 1958.

Welch, Claude. *Protestant Thought in the Nineteenth Century*. 2 vols. New Haven: Yale University Press, 1972.

Wesley, John. *The Letters of the Rev. John Wesley*. 8 vols. Edited by John Telford. London: Epworth, 1931.

———. "A Plain Account of Christian Perfection." In *John Wesley*. Edited by Albert C. Outler, 181–96. A Library of Protestant Thought. New York: Oxford University Press, 1964.

———. "Salvation by Faith." In *The Works of John Wesley*, 3rd ed. vol. 5, Sermons, vol. 1, 6–16. 1872. Reprint. Grand Rapids: Baker, 1979.

White, James. *A Brief History of Christian Worship*. Nashville, TN: Abingdon, 1993.

———. *Protestant Worship*. Louisville, KY: Westminster/John Knox, 1989.

White, Ronald, Jr., ed. *American Christianity*. Grand Rapids: Eerdmans, 1986.

Whitefield, George. *George Whitefield's Journals*. Carlisle, PA: Banner of Truth, 1960.

———. "Marks of Having Received the Holy Ghost." In George Whitefield, *Seventy-Five Sermons on Various Important Subjects*, vol. 2, 183–95. London: Bayne, 1812.

———. *The Works of the Reverend George Whitefield, M.A. Late of Pembroke College, Oxford and Chaplain to the Rt. Hon. The Countess of Huntington, Containing all His Sermons and Tracts Which Have Already Been Published with a Selected Collection of Letters*. 6 vols. Edited by John Gillies. London: Edward and Charles Dilly, 1771.

Wolterstorff, Nicholas. "The Assurance of Faith." *Faith and Philosophy* 7, no. 4 (1990) 396–417.

———. *Reason within the Bounds of Religion*. Grand Rapids: Eerdmans, 1976.

Wood, Allen E. *Kant's Rational Theology*. Ithaca, NY: Cornell University Press, 1978.

Wright, George Frederick. *Charles Grandison Finney*. Boston: Houghton Mifflin, 1891.

Wuthnow, Robert. *The Restructuring of American Religion*. Princeton: Princeton University Press, 1988.

www.ingramcontent.com/pod-product-compliance
Lightning Source LLC
Chambersburg PA
CBHW070256230426
43664CB00014B/2555